The Comprehensive Guide To
Fishing Canada
by Babe Winkelman

Published by
Babe Winkelman Productions
Brainerd, Minnesota

Book Design	Babe Winkelman
Cover Photo	Jeff Howard
Artwork	Duane Ryks
Research	Jeff Howard
Editing	Steve Grooms
Cover Design	Trademark Communications
Typesetting	Rolin Graphics

Published by Babe Winkelman Productions
RT3 Box 267, Brainerd, Minnesota 56401

Printed in The United States of America

Library of Congress Catalogue
Card Number 83-073309

ISBN 0-915405-00-8

Library of Congress Cataloging in
Publication Data

Winkelman, Babe
   The Comprehensive Guide to Fishing Canada

Brainerd, Minn: Babe Winkelman Prod.
230 p.

ISBN 0-915405-00-8

It is with deep love and appreciation that I dedicate this book:
To my mother, for giving me a sense of excitement about living;
to my father, for teaching me ambition, drive and accomplishment;
to my wife Charlie, for being so patient and understanding;
but mostly to my Creator for giving me the right to go fishing.

ACKNOWLEDGMENTS

The thoughts, work, sweat, feelings and dedication of a number of outstanding individuals have helped turn the idea for this book into reality. I'd like to express my sincerest thanks and appreciation to my brother David, my constant fishing companion and pounding pal; Jeff Howard, who has burned the midnight oil with me nights on end and could still see through the camera; Nick Adams for always being there when I needed him...with the right answers; Dave Maiser for his constant guidance and creative eye; Duane Ryks for his excellent drawings and all the days missed fishing while working on layout; Sandy Ryks for being able to put up with Duane throughout production; to Jim Hayes for teaching me the proper way to say "eh!" and to the countless other fantastic anglers I've had the opportunity to spend time fishing with while exploring the mysteries of the Canadian waters.

TABLE OF CONTENTS

Forward

It seems odd that the most extensive fishing water in the Western Hemisphere has received so little attention.

Oh, there are fish stories galore about Canadian fishing trips, about fish on every cast, about lunkers enough to fill a boat.

But the whole story about Canada's fishing, the vast array of angling opportunities from its wilderness lakes to its snow-melt streams to its tundra bays remains untold.

Until now.

The words that follow in these pages represent a grand tour of Canada's vast fishing grounds. It tells of the variety of Canada's fish life and the angling pleasures they provide if you understand HOW to fish their waters.

But doesn't everybody catch fish in Canada?

It's a myth that deserves to die.

Oh, yes, it's still possible to find in Canada waters that ripple with fish eager to inhale anything from a wad of bubble gum to bottle caps. But truly virgin Canadian fishing waters have become rare. Sad, perhaps, but that's progress. Of course, every angler would like to be the first to cast but few of us will have such an opportunity. And someday shortly nobody will.

None of this distracts from the wealth of fishing now available, of course. And Canada's fishing will always be an adventure of solitude and loon calls, of moments and times with good friends that touch the angler's soul.

But fishing also is catching. To take a Canadian fishing adventure is one thing, to bask in the glory of catching those Canadian fish is another.

That is what this book is all about.

And who better to tell the story than Babe Winkelman? He cut his teeth on the tough fishing waters of Minnesota. I first met Babe years ago. He was a construction worker who saw a different blueprint for the rest of his life. He wanted to fish for a living. He confessed that dream to me one day while we shared the pleasures of bass fishing.

Among those who love fishing, who doesn't want to spend his "working" hours in a fishing boat, I replied.

It was, perhaps, an unreachable dream, I suggested.

But I didn't know Babe Winkelman well enough. He honed his angling skills and thirsted for more fishing knowledge. He fine-tuned his speaking skills and sharpened his writing pencil. And he worked hard.

It is easy to say, "I'm going to be a professional fisherman." It is much harder to become one. But Babe did it.

And now this, an enlightening look at fishing in Canada. Again, Babe has done his homework. He's made untold fishing trips across the border, importing his fishing knowledge and applying the same to Canada's waters.

As Babe explains, fishing in Canada is a different world. We may be lulled by its wilderness into thinking there is no challenge to the catching. But, alas, it is a fading truth.

It's better to enjoy with a well-armed angling mind. For a bended rod is what we seek. At home on the lake across the street. Or in the wonderful wilds of Canada.

Ron Schara
Outdoor Writer
Minneapolis Star & Tribune

Introduction

Seldom does one find so accomplished a sportsman with so sincere a desire to educate. Babe Winkelman knows how to fish and he knows how to tell others about it. Drawn from his own first hand experience this book takes us from coast to coast, from species to species with a finesse and comprehensiveness that makes it informative and authoritative.

Babe has married his skills as a fisherman to his role as an educator. Mindful that an increased emphasis on highly technical equipment has left some anglers disdainful of 'Pro Fisherman' and wondering where the fun has gone, he has succeeded in using the resources of modern innovations while maintaining an emphasis on pure enjoyment.

Read along and enjoy a tour of some of Canada's numberless lakes and streams boasting a diversity and challenge not known in fishing anywhere else in the world!

Move from the old country etiquette of Atlantic Salmon streams to the rage of the elusive Muskelunge.

Babe is an outstanding teacher! His language is straightforward and his intentions are refreshingly clear. No presumptuous sea of jargon awaits the reader. Good, clear explanations and easy to follow illustrations are what you'll find. You'll learn about where to fish, how to fish and perhaps a little about why you love to fish.

Babe maintains the mystery and uniqueness of disparate regions, while reinforcing the basic similarities of fishing skills used anywhere. He offers no promises of magic, nor guarantees of any sort of success other than a good time. But that's what its all about!

Canada offers the allure of the frontier and the beauty of the wilderness to any traveller willing to look and see. Distances need not be overwhelming, as Babe demonstrates in his text about waters near the U.S. Border, where the fishing is superb.

Like anything we do, a little planning can go a long way towards a successful fishing trip. Use this book as a guide to new places and new experiences and learn from it how you can improve your fishing skills in the beauty and bounty of Canada.

George Forgie
Professional Fisherman
Noted Outdoorsman
Winnepeg, Canada

Chapter 1
The Mystique of Canada

Canada! The very name is exciting, calling up visions of rugged mountains, vast stretches of uninhabited lands, wolves loping along with migrating caribou and a wealth of perfectly pure rivers and lakes.

If you are an angler, the name means much more. Perhaps the mention of "Canada" calls up visions of iridescent grayling dimpling the surface of a wilderness lake, of northern pike the size of young alligators cruising deep holes in a river or possibly of monster lake trout living in the mysterious depths of a lake in the "land of the midnight sun."

To the first white men that walked her shores, Canada was just part of a rugged new world that got in the way of finding a convenient waterway to the far east. In fact, it was the main responsibility of many of these first explorers to find a waterway through this wilderness to the shores of the Pacific.

During these expeditions, it occurred to some that this new world was a land of extreme beauty, rich in natural resources the old world was in need of. It didn't take long before European countries, such as England and France, took more than just a mild interest in Canada and sent out exploration parties to uncover her wealth.

Exploring became serious business. Men like Pierre Espirit Radisson, sieur des Groseilliers and Henry Hudson came to Canada to start exploring and trading with the native Indians. It was through these early frontiersmen that the first real industry was spawned; Fur Trading.

The fur trading business was to have a great impact on the future of Canada. Even today the spirit of the fur traders can be felt as you walk the same paths they walked and paddle down the same streams they steered their crafts on.

The high demand for fine furs in the European social circles provided work for many who moved to this new land. Small settlements and trading posts such as Quebec, Montreal and Winnipeg sprung up and flourished. The fur trade had begun to boom.

More and more trappers came, forging further into the wilderness by foot or dog sled. But the main mode of transportation was the canoe. An adventurous man could paddle the seemingly endless chain of lakes and rivers for hundreds of miles without leaving the water, except for an occasional portage. These intricate waterways became the arteries of all transportation.

Figure 1. From the native Indians to the modern angler today, Canada has intrigued people with her natural wealth. By letting loose the explorer in you there is no telling what kind of fantastic fishing you'll discover.

13

But, the fur trade was not to go on forever. The demand for furs went down and the intense trapping pressure took it's toll, causing the fur trade to decline.

But by this time, the growing cities that lay south in the United States were crying out for lumber to build more towns, homes and businesses. And, Canada was blessed with what looked like an endless supply of straight, tall red and white pines. The lumber companies took action and sent logging crews to harvest this untapped resource. Thus, the lumber business became a part of Canada's heritage.

Many trappers gave up their traps and canoes for an axe and saw. Lumber camps became the towns of the wilderness. The waterways that had once carried colorful voyagers were now used to float huge rafts of logs down to the lumber mills. Not only were the rivers used for transporting logs and people, but they also provided a source of food for hungry logging crews. Many afternoons were spent by the camp cooks down by the rivers and lakes catching walleye, northern and trout to feed the crews. There always seemed to be an endless supply.

During the late 1800's, another fashion was to influence these wilderness waters. After the Civil War and the industrial boom that followed, business flourished in the United States. People were becoming wealthy and developed great appetites for leisure activities. Sportsmen had been fishing the lakes and streams of the northeastern United States for some time. But with the railroads pushing up into the remote areas of Canada it wasn't long before sporting groups were heading north to take advantage of untouched fishing and virgin wilderness. The day of the sportsman had arrived. Canada has never been the same since.

No single country offers so much to the angler. This is true for several reasons. First, there is the enormous variety of fish species. Second, there is the vast amount of fishable water, much of it so lightly fished (if at all) each year that heavy stringers come easily. Third, there is the fact that, unlike other countries with more or less "virgin" fisheries, Canada offers a wide range of resort, motel, hotel, fishing camp, railway and airline services to make this fishing accessible. Finally, from the point of view of the U.S. angler, Canada is close-to-home, inexpensive, English-speaking and friendly.

What better place to fish?

Those practical reasons, important though they are, miss the point. The United States is a country founded by pioneers, restless folk who kept moving in search of their dreams. For them, the frontier was usually west. That restless pioneer spirit still lives on today. And for the angler of today, the frontiers of fishing lie to the north.

"Up North" is where we all expect to find clean water and giant fish, up north in the pristine beauty of the Canadian wilderness. Up north, in Canada, is where fishing goes beyond being pleasant and becomes exciting. Canada represents the unknown, the new and the challenging for today's anglers who are bored by catching too many too-small fish in heavily exploited local waters.

The spirit of the voyageurs, fur traders and lumber men can still be felt as you wander along portage trails such as this one skirting a water fall on the Albany River.

But, you might be wondering, why bother to write a book about Canadian fishing if the fishing up there is so great. Good question! For one thing, the fishing in quite a few lakes and rivers has gotten a bit more challenging. The most aggressive fish are always the first to go, and in some areas those fish are gone. You'll have to fish a little harder and smarter to get the ones left over.

It is also true that Canadian fishing has never been as easy as a lot of people have been led to believe.

For one thing, Canadian waters often confuse U.S. anglers. You might have heard that smallmouth are found near rocks. Then you arrive in a Canadian wilderness smallie lake...and the whole thing is lined with nothing but rocks! Where are you going to fish? Things can be different in Canada.

Because so many Canadian lakes are relatively infertile, supporting less plant and fish life per acre than U.S. lakes, it can be harder to locate fish. The lake may look beautiful, like something out of a travel brochure, but where are the fish? My fishing has taught me that often they are tightly concentrated in some specific area where they can find food, or perhaps the right water temperature. Even if you catch plenty of fish in your home area, you may get frustrated trying to find fish in Canadian waters.

No matter where you fish — in Canada or anywhere else — you're going to do better and have more fun if you know what you are doing. I think I'm in a position to offer some knowledge and tips that can help you. The last several years of my life have been mainly devoted to fishing education. Whenever possible (and it's never as often as I'd like!) I've fished Canadian waters for a wide variety of species. I've been applying the principles of "structure fishing" developed in the heavily fished lakes of the midwest to Canadian waters. The result has been great fishing and tons of fun.

No doubt, much of the appeal of Canadian fishing has to do with the possibility of getting a hook in a huge fish. Of course, huge fish are caught every year in the lakes and rivers of the United States, but the odds against doing it are often discouraging. In Canada you can fish with that special tingle that comes from expecting the next bite or strike to come from a fish so big it is almost scary.

That tingle is based on more than pipe dreams. Canada genuinely offers more chances for trophy fish than any other water lying so close to U.S. anglers.

Of course, the reason is fishing pressure. There are lakes and rivers, some quite large, that do not see a single angler for years at a time. Many others are fished rarely and casually.

Fisheries biologists and anglers know the lack of fishing pressure favors the production of large fish. In a heavily fished body of water, very few fish will be large adults, while a great many will be "eating size", at best. The opposite is true of a lightly fished body of water, where a good percentage of the fish will be old (big) adults. There are still lunkers in U.S. waters and tiny fish in Canada. It's just that your odds of catching a real "wall-hanger" are far better in Canada.

Kids, novices and experts alike can take advantage of the endless fishing opportunities found here. But planning and a little fishing savvy is still essential to ensure a wonderful fishing trip.

Canada has been blessed with vast amounts of fresh, unpolluted water. This resource, along with possibly the greatest amount of sportfish in the world, make this northern country the "final fishing frontier".

There's a hidden message in what we have just discussed.

To many anglers visiting Canada in the past, and even some fishing it these days, the fishing seems so good that they cannot imagine it ever ending. These people take it for granted that Canada has tremendous numbers of gamefish, many of them trophies. Like the people who used to hunt passenger pigeons, these folks don't worry about the future of the sport they enjoy. This attitude has caused some Canadian lakes that used to be great to be "burned out" by fishing pressure.

The plain truth is that Canadian lakes and rivers are not at all immune to the bad effects of fishing pressure. In fact, they are more vulnerable than U.S. waters because the fertility of many lakes is lower and the cold water temperatures make it difficult for the lakes to replace big fish taken south in coolers. A trophy lake trout taken from a cold Northwestern Territories lake might be 40 or 50 years old. Figure it out. How can one of these clear, icy lakes lose many such big fish without having the fishing quality decline? They can't!

The great fishing in so many Canadian waters, then, is mostly the result of the protection they have enjoyed from pressure, along with the fact that much of Canada has not seen much economic development.

The earliest inhabitants, Indians and Eskimos, did no damage to the abundant fishing resource because their take was limited by both their fishing tackle and their culture. The early European missionaries and fur traders did not have much more impact. They were followed by loggers and miners, and it is probable that efforts to provide food for them did occasionally hurt the fishing in local areas. By and large, most Canadian waters were not affected.

Even today, 90 percent of Canada's population is concentrated in the towns and cities of the far south. The population, in other words, hasn't lived very close to most of the fish. Then there is the problem of getting to those fish. If you study a map of Canada, you'll quickly see that great areas of many provinces have few or no roads. What the map cannot quite convey is how much of Canada will probably never have a road, because the country is too wet to build on. And yet, fairly often, these lands are not suitable for boat traffic.

Thus Canada's fish have historically enjoyed protection from fishing pressure due to the fact they were inaccessible. Of course, many highways, gravel roads and railway lines have finally been built to formerly wilderness waters. Better boats and motors make it possible to reach some areas that once were almost totally inaccessible.

But the big breakthrough came when, after World War II, many airplanes were fitted with pontoons. Suddenly lakes and rivers that had never known recreational angling pressure were "discovered" and popularized. The float planes could go almost everywhere, and did. Soon enterprising Canadian and American businessmen were establishing crude cabins or even full lodges along the shores of the better lakes, bringing in groups of guests each week with airplanes.

That happened just when there was a great rise in the popularity of fishing in the United States. The availability of monofilament line and spinning reels, together with more leisure time, caused a great many U.S. anglers to head north for adventurous fishing. Outdoor magazines printed hundreds of articles that gave the painted Canada as the land where an angler could realize his wildest dreams of success.

Thus much of Canada's finest fishing waters have only known significant fishing pressure for the last 20 or 30 years. In that time, the impact of fishing has begun to be felt.

A few lakes have been badly hurt by careless — although usually legal — pressure. Aggressive fish like smallies and northerns don't stand up to heavy fishing pressure if everything caught is kept. Slow-growing fish like lake trout and trophy brook trout take so long to replace that keeping too many of them will quickly show up in the form of smaller fish populations. Because of greed or ignorance, some waters were hit hard.

At the same time, even today a great many lakes and rivers still have not experienced much pressure. After all, the open water season is quite short in many areas of Canada. And there is so much excellent fishing water that many fishermen can be accommodated with no crowding.

Some lakes have been fished fairly hard without being hurt, either because they were highly productive or because the managers of fishing camps on them were far-sighted enough to enforce catch-and-release policies. In some provinces, bag limits have been reduced and conservation policies promoted.

If this trend continues, the future of Canadian fishing should be secure. I hope so. I've enjoyed my Canadian fishing trips enormously. In this book I will present techniques and knowledge that will definitely improve your chances to catch fish in Canadian waters. I don't mean to preach to anyone, but I sure hope those techniques don't result in fish being killed needlessly.

There's nothing wrong with keeping a few fish for shore lunch or with keeping a trophy fish to mount. But that's a long way from making the point of a trip to "limit out" with fish that will be brought home, perhaps only to be shown off to the neighbors and then given away. That kind of attitude toward Canadian fishing is now clearly outdated.

So let's go fishing in Canada. We'll try hard to apply what we know about fish and their fascinating world to our fishing, but we won't let that get in the way of our enjoying the unique beauty of this great country. Canada still enjoys a wealth of free-running rivers, vast stands of lofty pines, great lakes with water as clear as crystal glass and a landscape that shifts from the big-skyed grandeur of the Arctic to the rugged majesty off mountains.

Oh, Canada!

Great fishing, beautiful surroundings and friendly hosts — that's Canadian fishing. If someone knows of a better place to go fishing, I sure hope they tell me about it!

An evening sunset signals the end of another day of fishing. During moments like this you realize that catching is not the only excitement of fishing. Being out in nature's glory is just as satisfying.

Chapter 2
Formation of the Canadian Fisheries

From the smooth, rolling Torngat Mountains of Newfoundland in the east, to the rugged Canadian Rockies in the west, from the vast islands near the North Pole, to the shores of Lake Erie in the south, Canada offers diversity in geography, topography, and — what concerns us most — "fishography" unmatched anywhere on Earth!

Boarding our private jet on Canada's east coast, we begin a journey across this nation of variety. Look out the window to your right. Please note the terrain. In a few moments it will change. Such is Canada. Each geographical region and terrain provides a different habitat for fish. The more variety of habitats — the more variety of fish! This is why Canada is the angler's best friend.

As we study the eastern coast of Canada from our vantage point in the sky, we see many rivers flowing into the Atlantic. The Atlantic salmon, the most revered fish in the world, spawns in many of these waters.

Below us is the Miramichi River of New Brunswick which attracts salmon fishermen from all over North America. These anglers feverishly desire to join the fraternity of anglers who can lay claim to having caught an Atlantic salmon.

Unfortunately, while many species of Pacific salmon are flourishing in their native north Pacific and the Great Lakes, the Atlantic salmon is losing ground. Once it was abundant in rivers from the Delaware to the Ungava Bay in Quebec. But today dams, pollution, lumbering, poaching, and commercial fishing have nearly made the Atlantic salmon extinct.

These prize fish still exist in the waters of Maine and northeastern Canada, and conservationalists — alarmed at their decline — have taken measures to ensure the future of this great fish. These measures, coupled with the efforts of the sportfishermen and environmentalists who have fought for sound water and lands management, may yet guarantee the continued existence of salmon and salmon fishing. We must not be complacent, however. Because of industrial interests and commercial fishing, the resources of the eastern coastline of Canada will always be pressured. If we wish to preserve the Atlantic salmon we must support fishing societies and conservation groups who strive to protect and further this fish.

Flying north along the east coast, we pass over additional species of gamefish. The shoreline rivers of Quebec and Newfoundland are famous for their Arctic char, an ocean fish closely related to brook and lake trout.

Every September and October those northern regions experience huge runs of these anadromous fish (i.e. fish that live in the ocean but spawn in fresh water). This rugged region of northern Canada also produces other gamefish, but the char is the most popular catch.

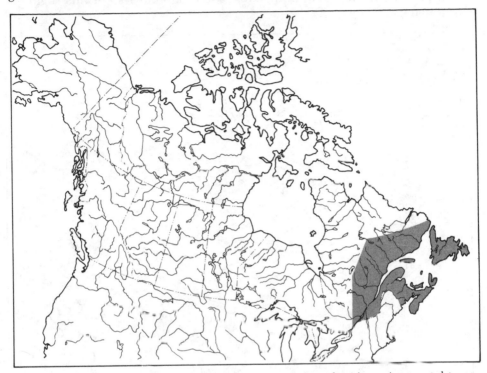

Eastern Coastal — *Even though this area is better known for it's quaint coastal towns and saltwater fishing, it is home to the famous Atlantic salmon and large sea run trouts.*

Leaving the east coast of Canada, with its mile of craggy, rock-studded cliffs, we travel west into central Canada.

Our plane soars over a panorama of perpetual green. Or so it seems, for this is the heavily forested east central Canada. Clear streams that rush through the valleys contain an abundance of brook trout. This beautiful fish is regarded as the "one and only" true sport fish by some locals who love their "speckled trout", as they are commonly called. This eastern portion of Canada is one of the last places on earth where one can catch brook trout weighing five pounds or more. Fly fishermen come here from all over the world to try to catch one of these gorgeous trophies.

Many of the deep, cold, clear lakes of eastern Canada support ounaniche, a landlocked variety of the Atlantic salmon. These freshwater cousins of the sea-faring Atlantic salmon do not get as large as their saltwater relatives. Most ounaniche weigh 2–4 pounds, although some weighing over 40 pounds have been captured on Lake Ontario.

As we dream about landing a 40–pound salmon, our pilot directs us to note the change in topography as we venture west. The land continues to flatten, and the rivers now flow more gently. As they slow, suspended particles in the water fall to form a silty, fertile bottom. That fertility and the higher temperatures create more weed growth. Consequently, northerns, smallmouths, walleyes, and muskies — the popular fish of this region — inhabit these waters.

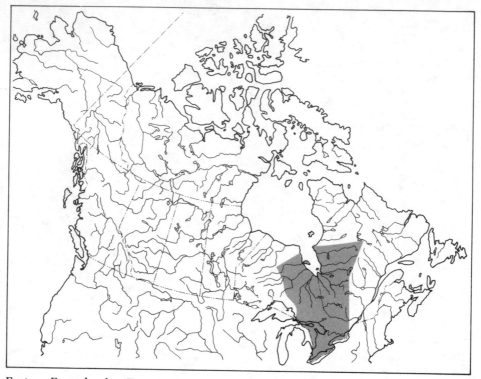

Eastern Forestland *— For many years, sportsmen have come to these great forestlands in pursuit of trophy brook trout, muskies and a variety of other sportfish. Even today it offers some of the best fishing in the world.*

Yet, just as you begin to think this area has everything an angler could hope for, our attention is turned toward the south. There in the distance you see huge, expanses of blue water that seem to stretch on forever. The Great Lakes! The near miraculous "rebirth" of these inland seas are known to many who have experienced the unbelievable fishing found there. Exotic Pacific salmon literally swarm in parts of the five lakes, actually rivaling the great salmon fisheries of the Pacific northwest. Not only do salmon thrive here, but huge brown trout and steelhead are found in great numbers. Plus, walleyes have become so numerous that Lake Erie has been dubbed the "Walleye Capitol of the World". After spending a day there catching dozens of chunky walleyes you would probably agree.

Seeing what has happened to our Great Lakes should not only make us excited, but should give us faith in the future of our sport fishing. Sitting back in your seat you hope that people throughout the world will catch the vision as the people contributing to the Great Lakes have.

24

The further into central Canada we fly, the more fishing variety we find. Fishing variety and quality reach their peak in the area known as the Canadian Shield of central Canada. This rocky area supports more species of fish and has more angling opportunities than perhaps any other area in the world. Lake and brook trout, walleye and northern pike, smallmouths and muskies — are all found here in great numbers. A true angler's paradise!

How did the Canadian Shield become such a hallowed spot for fishermen? Centuries ago most of North America was covered by a succession of continental glaciers. The last glacier covered central Canada as recently as 10,000 years ago. As it inched southward, it plowed large quantities of rock and soil ahead of it. These moving mountains of ice scoured the earth right down to bare bedrock. At times, even the unyielding bedrock was gouged away, leaving huge depressions and grooves. The glaciers eventually melted and retreated, their waters filling the holes and depressions they had carved in the earth, leaving as a legacy an intricate system of lakes and rivers.

Such areas of glacier-scourged bedrock are called shields, and are found throughout the world. None, however, are as large and continuous as the Canadian Shield. This shield includes parts of the Arctic islands, reaches into the northern United States, and covers a substantial area of Canadian wilderness — 1,864,000 square miles of land!

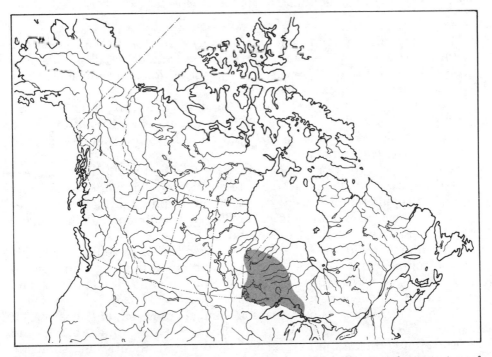

Canadian Shield — *The combination of vast amounts of fresh water, a large variety of sportfish and unbeatable scenery have made the Canadian Shield a "mecca" to fisherman everywhere.*

Parts of the "shield" are visible throughout Central Canada. This scoured bedrock is the initial reason for the outstanding fishing found here.

The exposed rock of the shield is primarily granite, formed some time before the Cambrian age. Molten lava from an ancient crack on the earth welled through the earth's crust to form these precambrian shields, the rock of which is about the oldest in the world.

In contrast to the rock of Canada's Shield, the lakes, rivers, and streams of the shield are all quite young. Although it may be difficult to term a 10,000 year old lake young, most shield lakes have the characteristics of very young (oligotrophic) lakes.

All lakes go through an aging process called euthrophication, and are classified according to age. Along with oligotrophic, or young lakes, there are mesotrophic (middle-aged) lakes and euthrophic (old) lakes. As lakes grow old, their character changes. They fill with sediment and, in time, become swamps and, eventually, dry land.

Canadian Shield lakes are either middle oligotrophic or early mesotrophic. Sometimes they are a combination of the two. Although the main body of a lake may be oligotrophic in nature, some bays and backwaters will have mesotrophic characteristics.

Each lake type has its own character and combination of fish species it can support. Of the three different age types, oligotrophic and mesotrophic provide the best habitat for the majority of gamefish, while euthrophic lakes will harbor some gamefish but will be populated more heavily with rough fish such as carp, sheepshead, and bullheads.

Since oligotrophic and mesotrophic lakes abound in the Canadian Shield, so do about every type of fresh water gamefish found on the North American continent. As we fly further west into the shield, we find increasing numbers of sportfish . . . and sport fishermen!

As we leave the shield area of west central Canada, we remember that this area provides good fishing and a variety of fishing opportunities. From the easily accessible prairie lakes to the areas in remote north and west accessible only by air or foot, the shield waters of west central Canada offer variety and opportunity.

The parklands, forests, and prairies of west central Canada are also well suited for a variety of gamefish. Lake trout, grayling, whitefish, northerns, and walleye are native to the region, but brown, brook and rainbow trout have been stocked as well.

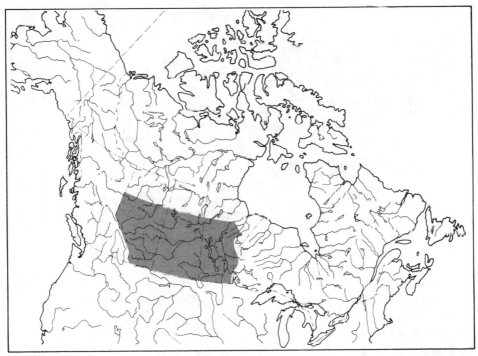

Western Parklands — *From the shield area on the east to the rugged mountains on the west, this area has a variety of lands and fish that can satisfy anyone. Walleye, trout, grayling and northern pike abound here in great numbers.*

As the rugged mountains of western Canada loom ahead, we realize that north of us is the vast expanse of the Northwest Territories. Here is wilderness unmatched. Snowcapped mountains, boundless lakes, tundra, and the rugged arctic coast all await the adventurous fisherman. Fabulous fishing is virtually guaranteed in this territory where the large fish are available in incredible numbers and where 20 hours of daylight is available during the summer. Anglers can happily spend those long days pursuing Arctic char, lake trout, grayling, northern pike, and the rare inconnu!

No place in the world offers better lake trout fishing. The huge, sprawling lakes of this great northland have been a favorite of lake trout enthusiasts for decades.

The rugged coast has superb arctic char fishing, much like that found in the eastern coastal portions of the northern tier of Canada. Trophy hunting fishermen have recently discovered the elusive inconnu, a predatory member of the whitefish family. These huge, silvery fish average 8 to 20 pounds, but may reach 70 pounds. They are unique to this area of North America.

This wilderness of northern Canada stretches to the top of the world and tempts the explorer in all of us.

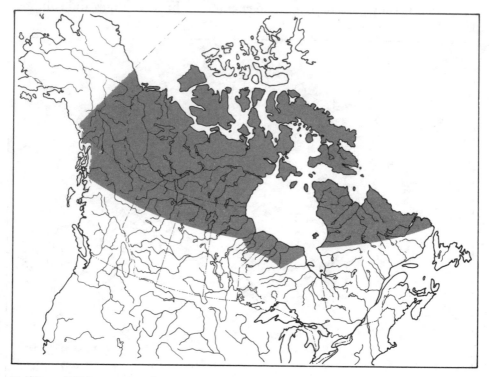

Northern Wilderness — *This rugged, arctic land offers the ultimate in wilderness travel and untouched fishing. Huge arctic char, lake trout and inconnu are just some of the tackle busters found here.*

The sight of awesome peaks and crests of the Canadian Rockies shakes us from our dream of adventure in the Arctic north. These peaks, towering thousands of feet, rise above the prairies of west central Canada. Catastrophic movement within the earth's crust formed these tremendous formations of rock. Among the peaks and valleys of this area are hundreds of sapphire blue alpine lakes that transform a merely gorgeous land into an angler's paradise.

Rushing streams and rivers, as well as some lakes, host the native rainbow and cutthroat trout. The brook and brown trout and the rare golden

Snowcapped peaks, boundless lakes, tundra and rushing arctic rivers await adventurous fishermen who come to the Northern Region of Canada.

trout have also been introduced. These colorful trout are the main angling attraction of this region. In addition to trout, whitefish and grayling await the angler in the alpine lakes.

A visiting walleye fisherman to this area may be surprised to find walleye in large numbers. One reason for their abundance is that the trout-minded local fishermen don't understand or appreciate this newly introduced fish. Consequently, this area has become a new frontier for the walleye hound!

As we sight the rugged, rocklined coast of the Pacific Northwest, we realize our journey is just about complete. The fishing boats and bustling coastal villages remind us that this place is home to the king, coho and other Pacific salmon. Each year, the salmon along with steelhead, Dolly Varden trout and other seafaring salmonids return to the streams and rivers to perpetuate themselves. These "runs" attract the world's greatest fisherman to challenge the great, rushing rivers and take a crack at a 50, 60, even 70 pound king salmon.

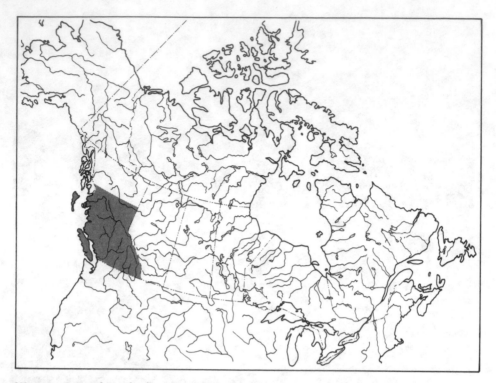

Western Coastal — *The beauty of this rugged land is matched only by the exciting fish found here. Huge silvery Pacific salmon and multicolored rainbow, cutthroat, Dolly Varden, and other trouts offer exciting fishing.*

Beyond the trees below we can see the runway. Our journey finished, the pilot prepares to land on the coast of British Columbia. We've explored the major regions of Canada, the fish and fishing opportunities of each region, and have noted how the geography of each region influences the fishing. We know that whatever we're looking for can be found in Canada. This lovely and varied land has it all — whether it's salmon fishing on a coastal river or lake trout fishing in a remote lake surrounded by stunted spruce trees and moss covered rocks. Canada is an angler's heaven.

Chapter 3
Traveling Canada . . .
It's Easy

If you plan carefully, you can put together a dream fishing trip to Canada. If you fail to plan, the dream can turn into a nightmare, possibly an expensive nightmare.

Part of your planning includes selecting an area to fish. That could be the subject for almost a book itself, but we haven't got that kind of space here. If you go to a big camp that advertises in outdoor magazines, you can be fairly sure of what you are getting into. Many anglers, however, prefer to "pioneer" by going into unknown country. The hazards are higher, but the costs are lower and it is a special thrill to plan your own assault on little-known waters.

Always get as much information as possible before you commit yourself to a trip. What fish are present? What is the forage base? When does the ice usually go out? Are bugs a problem, and if so at what times of year? Has the lake ever been fished commercially? If so, how long ago? Has the lake or river been subjected to heavy fishing pressure from a camp that didn't practice catch and release?

It isn't enough to know that a lake or river has great fishing for, say, walleyes and lake trout. You want to know what time of year is best for each gamefish species. Remember, the ice goes out much later on many Canadian lakes than on U.S. lakes. If you are planning to hit the walleyes when they are shallow and hungry after their spawn, you'll have to time the trip according to the schedule of the water you'll be fishing, not the schedule of lakes at home you usually fish.

Before actually traveling into Canada, you might begin by reminding yourself that you are crossing a border into another country. Yes, it is known as the friendliest border in the world, but don't forget that you are traveling into a country where laws and practices are not quite the same as at home.

Everyone has to enter Canada through some sort of border (or near-border, in the case of some aircraft flights) checkpoint. Usually you can cross after answering a few quick questions, and you usually won't need to leave your vehicle. You will be asked the purpose of your trip and a few questions about what you are carrying with you. The Customs officials might ask more questions, but usually not. Canada's economy benefits enormously from tourism, and everyone wants your trip to be pleasant. For your part, it isn't legal or smart to try to bring in unwanted substances (such as live bait which might introduce alien species in Canadian waters).

Nothing can stir the blood of a fisherman more than setting down on a wilderness lake where fish may have never seen a lure before.

Most customs checkpoints are located at international airports or at the crossing points for major highways. You can get information on the points-of-entry by contacting the province you will be entering.

Before arriving at the point-of-entry, make sure you have a few things with you. First, if you are driving, be sure you have a valid driver's license. A driver's license from another country is good in Canada for three months. You should also have your vehicle registration forms. If the vehicle you are driving is borrowed, you need a letter from the owner stating that you have the vehicle by his or her permission. If you are driving a rented vehicle, be sure to have a copy of the rental contract. You should also have a non-resident insurance card, available from your insurance agent before you leave home.

Visitors crossing the border, either by boat or car, might be asked to prove their citizenship with such documents as a birth certificate, voter's registration certificate or other accepted form. Be sure to bring one such proof with you; it is not necessary to bring a passport.

As a visitor, you are allowed to bring into Canada a reasonable supply of personal items and supplies. You may enter with a two-day supply of food, for example, and a full tank of gas. You should not attempt to enter with more tobacco products or alcohol than you might reasonably consume on your trip. If you are over 19 years old, you may import 40 ounces of liquor or wine or 288 ounces of beer. Canadian beer and ale is so good, by the way, that it doesn't make a lot of sense to haul American beer across the border. Visitors over 16 are allowed up to 200 cigarettes, 50 cigars and two pounds of tobacco.

Those planning on hunting as well as fishing — and some great dual-purpose trips are possible in both spring and fall — are allowed to cross with a hunting rifle or shotgun and up to 200 rounds of ammunition. Fully automatic weapons and guns with barrels under 26 inches in length are prohibited.

If you have any specific questions about what you are allowed to bring into Canada, contact the Customs and Revenue Branch of the province you will be entering (not necessarily the one you will be fishing or hunting in).

At this time it might be appropriate to point out that, each year, a number of Americans get into trouble by not taking Canadian laws and regulations seriously. Canadian officials tend to approach legal matters in a "by-the-book" manner. Tourists from the United States often assume "it won't matter if I am in technical violation of this regulation as long as I obey the spirit." Wrong! Save yourself a great deal of trouble by assuming the laws mean exactly what they say. And don't ask your outfitter or flying service to "shade" the regulations a little, because you could end up costing them their right to do business.

You are welcome to bring your boat or canoe into Canada, either by towing or cartopping it to one of the ports-of-entry. This way you can ensure yourself of having good equipment rather than taking your chances with what can be rented.

But to do so, you must have an entry permit. These allow you to use your boat in Canada for up to 12 months and are available at all points-of-entry. When you leave Canada, you return the permit at the point-of-departure. All boats with motors of ten-horsepower or more must be licensed, with the license number clearly indicated on the bow of the boat. It doesn't matter where the boat is licensed, so long as it is.

It is better to convert your money to Canadian currency before entering Canada. The exchange rate between U.S. and Canadian money changes all the time, and it is a confusing nuisance to everyone if you try to buy bait and gas with U.S. money. You can make the exchange at many locations, including international airports, banks and trust companies. The currency exchanges located at most of the travel centers on the border can also do this for you and they're open every day.

Many outputs camps are accessible by boat and motor, the ideal situation for those who prefer to use their own boat and motor.

Of course, you need a fishing license. Getting a non-resident license is quite easy; they are sold at most points-of-entry, many sporting goods stores, resorts and camps and at the district offices of the Ministry of Natural Resources.

The most popular way of traveling into Canada for a fishing trip is by automobile. Car travel is fast, convenient, relatively inexpensive and — best of all — flexible. There is plenty of good fishing right along Canada's expanding highway system. Cartop boats, canoes and the increasingly popular inflatable boats can be launched just about anywhere. Boat launches for bigger boats have been built at many locations for your convenience.

Because tourist travel is so important to Canada's economy, the government has made that travel easier by fostering a well-kept, convenient highway system with plenty of services available. You can get information on the condition of any road by simply calling the road information centers; the number is available from the tourism branch of the province you'll be visiting. Along many major highways there are clearly marked first aid stations to serve you in case of trouble.

Buying gasoline is no problem. There are many service stations along the way. Most sell premium, unleaded and regular. Many also have diesel fuel, especially along the well traveled roads.

There are alternatives to car travel, attractive alternatives. One of the most pleasant ways to enjoy Canadian fishing is renting a houseboat. This service is particularly common along the border lakes and rivers. The houseboats can hold sizable parties of friends or families and come complete with beds, a kitchen, dining facilities and a bathroom. The owner will give you a few basic instructions on how to operate the boat so you will be free to roam wherever the fishing looks best. It isn't tricky to pilot a houseboat; many firstimers do it each year.

You can, if you please, fish right from the houseboat. But that has limitations (ever try backtrolling a houseboat?), so many anglers trailer their favorite fishing boat to the houseboat rental service, then tow the boat behind the houseboat until they get to a likely looking fishing spot.

Another alternative is railway travel. Many Canadian railway systems link up with U.S. rail lines in border cities. You can get specific details from your travel agent or from Canadian railway companies.

Travel by rail appeals to those of us who have to be careful with our money these days. Many Canadian train routes cross excellent and remote trout streams and pass through miles of virtual wilderness with nearby fishing for popular gamefish. To attract more passengers, the railroad companies have made arrangements to make scheduled stops in small towns or other strategic points near the best fishing. Some will let you load a canoe or (better yet) an inflatable boat on an empty flatbed or boxcar. Then you have a way of moving on the water when you get to where you'll fish.

Or you might prefer to hike. A break-down rod, selection of lures or flies, and the usual backpacker's gear — pack, sleeping bag, clothing, etc. — will put you in business. You can usually count on scrounging up live bait on the site. When you are ready to come back to civilization, you hike back to the railroad and get picked up.

But for a great many fisherman, Canadian fishing is synonymous with fly-in fishing. There is no country in the world where you can enjoy such a wide variety of superb fishing experiences accessible only by airplane. Much Canadian fishing water — in fact, much of the best water — lies far from a driveable road or railway line. To get there, you fly, and flying is part of the fun of it all. You simply can't beat the thrill and romance of landing on a wilderness lake in a Beaver, a wonderfully reliably aircraft that looks like it was designed 40 years ago, which it was. You may not catch fish, but you're assured of a great trip.

You start a fly-in trip by driving or flying to a jumping-off point. In some cases, large fishing camps offer airline service from major cities in the United States, taking care of all travel and living arrangements along the way. That is more expensive, of course, but convenient.

Once you get to the jumping-off point, a float plane will take you to your fishing destination. That might be a sizable, well-established camp with a great many facilities, a totally undeveloped lake campsite or almost anything in between. The "in between" operations, which are common, include semi-permanent tent camps and camps that have log cabins but usually limited facilities (such as no running water). As you see, you have great flexibility. You

Some of the more organized camps like Chummy Plummer's Lodge at Great Slave Lake, have runways that are large enough to accommodate commercial jets. While these are more expensive, they are perfect to those with limited time and want to keep travel at a minimum.

can go directly to a full-fledged camp with guides, or you can pick a lake yourself and pay to be flown into it with camping gear.

Fly-in trips, of course, should be planned with great care. You should select a fly-in service with care. By contacting the tourism department of the province you'll be fishing in, you can get a total listing of fly-in services. If possible, check on them by asking for references, people from your area who have used their service before.

You can also bring private aircraft into Canada. This offers the ultimate in freedom. If you do this, you will be required to file a flight plan that includes a stop at a Canadian airport with a customs office.

So far we've been talking about travel, but much of those comments apply equally well to living accommodations. There are all kinds of accommodations to suit about anyone's needs, but you do need to plan ahead.

Canada has hotels and motels that range from being spartan and inexpensive to some large, luxurious hotels that rank among the world's finest. If you plan to stay in a hotel or motel, be sure to make reservations before arriving, especially in summer. Complete lists of hotels and motels are available from each province's department of tourism.

Those travelling by car (or recreational vehicle) can expect many well-planned campgrounds and wayside rests along the highways. Usually these

There are many flying services available in Canada and most offer several option packages. They can deliver you to a certain camp, or drop you off at a lake of your choosing and pick you up at a predetermined time.

campgrounds are located near tourist attractions, and that includes some popular fishing areas. Many campgrounds are suitable bases for a variety of activities, including fishing as well as hiking, canoeing, or hunting. These campgrounds include places for tenting as well as RV parking, sanitary facilities, picnic tables and shelters. Usually there will be good fishing close at hand, and places where you can launch a boat or canoe.

Perhaps the most popular way to fish Canada is through one of the many fishing camps or lodges. These are designed to let you make the most of your vacation time by providing many services and opportunities in one package. The camps, of course, vary enormously. Some are big, luxurious vacation complexes with stone fireplaces, comfortable bars, large bedrooms and swimming pools. Others, particularly those up in the vicinity of the Arctic Circle where everything has to be flown into camp by float plane, are somewhat rugged but comfortable.

Most camps have the necessary equipment for your fishing. You get boats, motors and guides. Some camps sell a limited assortment of fishing tackle to help out those who come unprepared. Almost all camps have fish cleaning facilities, often providing that service free or for an extra fee to guests. Many camps have freezers, too, so your responsibility for taking care of the fish ends when you land it.

Some camps provide a fairly luxurious base camp, with various fly-in options to take you by float plane to lakes that have received little fishing pressure. Sometimes you'll go in and out of such a spot in one day; other times you'll spend several days in a smaller "outpost" camp.

The least luxurious, but least expensive, camps have no central lodge at all but are like outpost camps. You drive or fly to a pickup point. From there you will be taken by your host, or someone sent by him, to the camp, usually by float plane.

If would be nice to report that all fishing camps are run with perfect attention to every detail, but nobody could seriously expect to believe that. You might find that your rental outboard has fouled plugs or a propeller so worn by contact with rocks that it hardly moves the boat. The boats of some camps leak. Sometimes the guides don't seem to know anything about either cooking shore lunch or fishing. Worse, they sometimes don't speak English. The food served in camp may not please you.

All these things are remarkably rare, in view of the difficulties of running an efficient camp up in the bush country, but they sometimes happen. The best way you can avoid disappointment is by talking to someone — several someones, if possible — who have been there. A reputable camp won't hestitate to supply references. One of the best indications of a well-run camp, by the way, is the presence of a strong conservation program. Camps that don't suggest catch-and-release fishing are usually not as organized and soundly managed as those that clearly indicate a concern for the future of Canada's wonderful fishing.

Fishing camps can vary from quite primitive conditions to elaborate affairs with all the comforts of a posh hotel. Most are simple, yet comfortable, like these at Miminiska Lodge in northern Ontario.

Another, less well-known, way of experiencing Canada's fishing is by tour. These are organized by travel agencies. Almost any kind of tour you might want is possible. Some tours will take you to the Arctic Circle, where you will see walruses and polar bears. Fishing for char among floating icebergs is one of the incredible experiences available through a tour.

You will be able to find whatever type of travel or accommodations you desire. If you plan well, you'll have a good trip. Canadians are among the friendliest of people, and the fishing will make you want to come back every year.

A list of places to write to get fishing information and regulations.

Newfoundland

Tourist Services Division
Newfoundland Dept. of Tourism
St. John's, Newfoundland
AOK3EO

Specific information on the various species of inland fish, location and catch reports are available from:

The Federal Dept. of the Environment
Fisheries and Marine Service
P.O. Box 5667
Pleasantville
St. John's, Newfoundland

Prince Edward's Island

Tourist Information Centre
P.O. Box 940
Charlottetown, Prince Edward Island
C1A 7M5

Fish and Wildlife Division
Environmental Control Commission
P.O. Box 2000
Charlottetown, Prince Edward Island
C1A 7N8

Nova Scotia

The Nova Scotia Department of Tourism
P.O. Box 456
Halifax, Nova Scotia
B3V 2R5

New Brunswick

The Department of Tourism
P.O. Box 1030
Fredericton, New Brunswick
E3B 5C3

The Department of Natural Resources
Fish and Wildlife Branch
Box 6000
Fredericton, New Brunswick
E3B5H1

Quebec

Department of Tourism, Fish and Game
Fish and Game Branch
Place de la Capitale
15th Floor
150 East St. Cyrille Boulevard
Quebec City, Quebec
G1R 4Y3

Ontario

The Ministry of Industry and Tourism
Tourist Services
3rd Floor, Hearst Block, Queen's Park
Toronto, Ontario
M7A 1T3

Sport Fisheries Branch
Ministry of Natural Resources
Queen's Park,
Toronto, Ontario

Manitoba

Department of Tourism, Recreation &
Cultural Affairs
Tourism Branch
200 Vaughan Street
Winnipeg, Manitoba
R3C 0P8

Saskatchewan

Department of Tourism
Government Administration Building
Regina, Saskatchewan
S4S 0B1

Alberta

Alberta Lands and Forests
Fish and Wildlife Division
Natural Resources Building
109th Street and 99th Avenue
Edmonton, Alberta
T5K 2E1

British Columbia

The Department of Recreation and
Conservation
Fish and Wildlife Branch
Parliament Buildings
Victoria, British Columbia
V8V 2Y9

Western Guides and Outfitters
Association
#213 — 1717 Third Avenue
Prince George, British Columbia
V2L 3G7

The Yukon

The Game Branch
Government of the Yukon Territory
Box 2703
Whitehorse, Yukon Territory
Y1A 2C6

The Northwest Territories

TravelArctic
Government, Northwest Territories
Yellowknife, Northwest Territories
XOE 1IO

Chapter 4
Lake Trout: Denizen of the Deep

"Well, we ought to be right about over the top of them now," my boat partner, Chummy Plummer of Great Slave Lake Lodge, said matter of fact-ly. "These big lakers like to orient themselves off some type of structure, like this deep water hump we're sitting on."

With all the faith I could muster, I lowered my Dingo jig into the crystal clear water. This remote lake was only a stone's throw away from the Arctic Circle. When the line ceased to spill off my reel I took up the slack and retrieved the lure straight up from the bottom. After a few turns of the reel handle, something slammed my jig. . . and I mean slammed it like a runaway freight train. I had to remember the story of the man who hooked a truck with his backcast while fishing from a bridge. Now I knew how he felt.

After an initial run that seemed to peel off miles of line, the fish finally stopped. It was a good thing too, because I was beginning to wonder how long my drag could stand the ceaseless friction before it froze up. With a pumping motion, I began to lift the fish up from the deep water, putting as much pressure on him as I dared. After I had regained about 50 feet of line the big laker blasted off in another run that peeled off all of the line I had worked so hard to regain. "He was just resting the whole time I was bring-ing him in," I thought to myself.

"I told you these trout grew big in this lake, and this one is just a baby!" Chummy chortled.

Baby or not, this fish was something else. After he completed his second run I was able to work him in a little closer to the boat, only to have him burst for another run that almost equalled his first run. This was getting to be more like work than fun. I was literally fighting this fish, but after these repeat performances, I began to feel a weakening in the bull-dogging and head shaking my laker was performing. Finally we were able to see the fish down in the green depths. He appeared to be almost four feet long.

It had been almost 20 minutes since the time the huge trout had clamped his jaws on my jig up until the time the fish finally broke the surface of the water. The beauty of lake trout is breathtaking. The back of this one was a dark olive-green, with mottled white markings on his back and sides. As he laid there working his gills and gently finning we took a moment to admire him. But just a moment, because I wanted that fish safely wrapped in the meshes of the biggest landing net we had.

The laker is as wild and unforgiving as the land it is found in. Here the author and friend, Jim Hayes, find out just how determined a big lake trout can be.

With a quick swoop of the net, my companion netted the fish, but he did not hoist it in the boat quite so quickly.

"Now tell me this is a baby," I laughed. "He made you grunt pretty good when you lifted him over the edge of the boat. I figure he'll go over 30 pounds."

"I'll admit to that," Chummy retorted, "but there are bigger ones in here."

For a brief moment I really didn't care if there were bigger ones. After that clash, my arm wasn't ready to go at it again for a bit. It was great to have that weary but satisfied feeling that comes from battling a lunker gamefish. And the lake trout is definitely game through and through.

After that day I have had nothing but respect for this grand fish of the North. The lake trout is actually more than a gamefish. It symbolizes the bleak, remote wilderness country that makes Canada and Canadian fishing so special. Today the Canadian government is taking steps to protect the last strongholds of the lake trout to ensure that future generations can enjoy the tenacity of the laker and the exotic beauty of the lands and waters where they are found.

Unfortunately, lakers have acquired a reputation for being mediocre fighters. They sure don't have that reputation with those lucky enough to encounter them at their best, in Canadian wilderness lakes. Perhaps this bad reputation began back when people fished for lake trout in the Great Lakes, using extremely heavy tackle to get down to the inky depths where they went in summer. Once hooked, these fish were derricked up out of deep water until their swim bladders burst. No wonder they didn't seem to fight well, hauling all that heavy gear.

Other fishermen have only met lakers on Lake Michigan, where they are the least exciting fish to catch. These folks don't realize that a laker growing up in the warm, fertile waters of the Great Lakes is a different fish altogether from the darker, older, tougher fish that swim Canada's lakes and rivers. A 6-pound Canadian lake trout will fight every bit as hard as a 16-pound fish from the Great Lakes, and he'll be far prettier, too.

The lake trout is extremely handsome. The "laker", as it is commonly called, has a body that is typically trout-like, with a soft dorsal fin and a fatty adipose fin located just behind the dorsal fin. The lake trout is not a true trout, but is a member of the char family along with the arctic char and brook trout.

The overall coloration of the laker is usually olive to light silvery green on the back and sides, but gets paler near the belly until it gets milky white or yellowish on the belly. The back and sides are profusely marked with worm-like markings, usually much lighter in color than the background greenish color.

The coloration of the lake trout will vary remarkably from area to area. In some lakes the trout can be green, gray, dark green, brown, almost black or silvery. These color variations may have been caused by environmental qualities of certain areas. But at times you may find trout of different colors in the same body of water.

Regardless of the overall coloration, the lake trout usually exhibits orange or red-orange coloring on the pelvic, pectoral and the caudal fin, accompanied with a bright white border. At times you can see these brilliant white markings before you can actually see the outline of the fish when you bring them up from the deep water. It can be a little spooky to see these white ghostly markings — and no fish - fighting on the end of your line.

Another diagnostic characteristic is the deeply forked tail, or caudal fin. This can be helpful when you want to distinguish between various species of trout or salmon.

A peculiar trait of lake trout is their ability to exhibit different bodily shapes in different environments. Most bodies of water that harbor lake trout will produce the "normal" lake trout. But some produce fish of very different body shape. In some huge bodies of water, like Lake Superior or Great Slave Lake, fish may even vary from section to section. The term given to the fish that exhibit this peculiar trait is "plastic fish".

One example is the siscowet that are found in Lake Superior. "Fat trout" is a good nickname for this close relative of the lake trout, since they have an extremely extended belly which gives them a side profile of a rough oval shape rather than the usual streamlined shape of the lake trout. The siscowet has highly oily flesh that will actually ooze when they are brought up from extreme depths. Many fishery biologists feel that the siscowet may be a separate species, though some also recognize it as a subspecies.

Another variation is the "butterfly" laker, which comes from Great Bear Lake in the Northwest Territories. This variation of the lake trout has a rusty brown coloration and huge pectoral fins that suggest wings when they are spread out.

The lake trout is a true coldwater fish that cannot survive if it cannot find cold water. Virtually all fish have a certain range of water temperatures that suit them. For example, the walleye seeks out water temperatures that range from 55 degrees to 74 degrees F. when it is available; the smallmouth will be most active in water in the 58 degree to 73 degree band. The lake trout, however, will seek out temperatures in the 48 degree to 52 degree F. range, which obviously doesn't allow the lake trout very many options to choose from when it comes to habitat choice. In fact, any water temperature higher than 66 degrees F. can kill any lake trout that spends much time there.

In addition to this critical temperature requirement, the lake trout has rigid dissolved oxygen needs. If a lake is to support a population of lake trout, it must have both accommodating water temperatures and oxygen levels at the same time. These requirements limit a lake trout's presence to waters that are usually oligotrophic in nature. In many Canadian lakes, the lake trout inhabits the deep water niches while walleye, smallmouth bass and northern pike inhabit the warmer shallow water. In the summer months, these deep water requirements limit the lake trout to certain specific locations in a lake, which for us anglers is good news because it aids us considerably when looking for lakers.

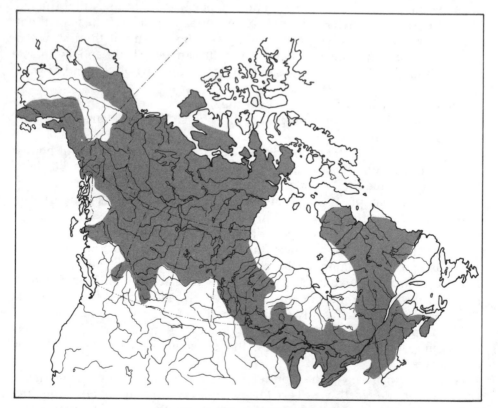

The Home Range of the Lake Trout

In addition to deep water lakers, you may find populations in stream mouths where a river flows into an oligotrophic lake. The lake trout often can find cool streams that provide the necessary water temperature. These rocky streams are usually highly aerated, with plenty of oxygenated water. Such streams are more common in eastern Canada, especially Labrador and Quebec. I've also talked to anglers who have caught lake trout out of rivers in Manitoba until their arms literally ached.

The laker's range covers much of the northern tier of the North American continent. Its range begins in southern Nova Scotia and New Brunswick, then extends northward throughout Quebec and many parts of Labrador, west throughout Ontario (but not generally through the Hudson and James Bay lowlands), and reaches through northern Manitoba and Saskatchewan and the southwestern and northeastern portions of Alberta and northern British Columbia. The laker is common in the Yukon and Northwest Territories and is also established on many of the arctic islands. As you can see, there are plenty of areas to pick from in Canada if you want to plan a lake trout fishing trip.

Like most gamefish, the lake trout will make seasonal movements within the body of water during the year. Usually these movements are related to the predator-prey relationship and the optimum temperature band we previously discussed. You must understand these movements so that you can be fishing for lakers when they are active and more easily found.

When the ice begins to retreat from the edges of the lakes, the lakers prepare to move up from their deep water winter homes and invade the shallows. And by the time the ice begins to break up, the trout will have moved into the shallows, feeding on insects and forage fish and enjoying the warmer water temperatures, even though there may be ice chunks still floating around. During these conditions, you can catch lakers on the surface, often times right up against the bank. This shallow fishing delights many folks because of the lake trout's reputation of being strictly a deep water fish that requires special gear and tackle in order to catch. It is great fun to tie into a spring lake trout, full of vim and vigor in water only 15 feet deep. Most lake trout experts will agree that the summer lake trout they pull up from some deep hole just doesn't exhibit the same pep as the fish taken in the shallow water following iceout.

The key areas to look for when early season trout fishing are those that get the most direct sunlight. During the spring this usually is the northern shores. If you take a temperature reading of the waters on the north side of a northern oligotrophic lake soon after the ice goes out you'll find that the water was already beginning to stratify somewhat. Stratification is the separation of water into layers of varying temperatures.

This is what draws the lakers from their deep water winter haunts. The fish seek water that is 50 degrees F., or a degree or two from it. They will begin to concentrate where it comes in contact with the richest, most oxygenated water. At times this desirable water will lie near some structure like a shallow water reef, sunken rocky island or underwater point. If so, it's all the better because then the fish have something to relate to rather that just open water. Suspended lakers tend to drift and roam a bit, which doesn't help you stay on top of them. When the fish will relate to some type of structure they will concentrate more and usually will stay put.

Another important factor in locating these spring lakers is that they seem to be more attracted to a gradually sloping bottom (such as areas A and B of Figure 1) than to a shallow flat or steep, plunging drop-off. Why? Water does not stratify along a steep drop-off very much, but it will always remain quite cold from top to bottom in spring. The lake trout will not find the warmer water that they are seeking along these areas.

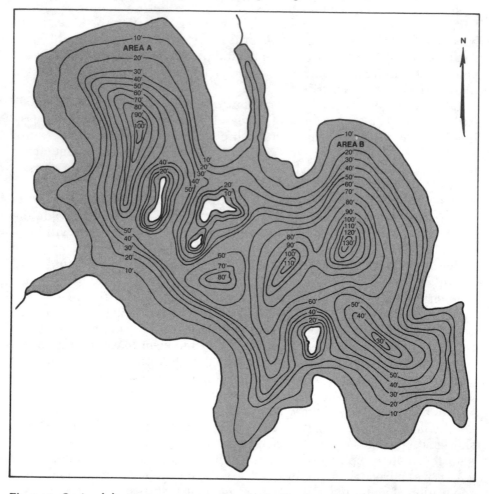

Figure 1. *Spring lake trout are attracted to gradually sloping shorelines, such as areas A and B, rather than sharp, plunging areas. The reason why? During the spring, water will stratify along the gradual tapering areas before the deep water areas. Stratification results in layers of warmer water that will attract active trout.*

48

The shallow bays on the other hand, offer warmer temperatures, but are usually isolated from the deep water areas. The trout, especially lunkers, will not travel very far from deep water. If they can find the preferred temperature adjacent to deep water, you can bet that this is where they'll be. Again, the best areas for early season lake trout will be where the bottom gradually rises out of the depths until the water is shallow enough for the fish to find a layer of water to their liking.

As spring wears on, the trout will begin to suspend in the 10 to 30 foot range. Then in the mornings and evenings they will come up to feed on or near the surface. Previously the fish were suspending off more sloping shoreline structure, but now the fish will use more cliff-like structures. Or they may hang around steep rock or rubble points that drop from the shore into very deep water.

During the early season, it is common to find trout changing the depth at which they suspend during the same day. I have found the fish in water from 10 to 100 feet deep. They are notorious for extreme vertical movements.

Wind is another key to early season lake trout location. If a steady wind has prevailed for a period of at least two days, it tends to pile up the warmer water on one side of the lake. If this has been the case, the lake trout will follow the wind so they can keep with the warmer water. This wind-blown water is not only warmer, but it attracts baitfish that are feeding on the microscopic organisms that pile up in front of the wind.

These two key location factors are very important, but there are other prime areas where you can find fish in the early season. But the ingredients are always the same: 1) water with the temperature near 60 degrees F. 2) a shallow area, about 15 feet, that is close to deep water where the lakers have been during the winter. This opens up areas like long underwater points, shoals, humps and reefs also.

With the coming of summer, the days lengthen in this land of the midnight sun. With daylight lasting as long as 20 hours up in the far north, it doesn't take long for the water in the shallows to get too warm for the lake trout. Oligotrophic lakes stratify, separating into three distinct layers, with the top layer being the warmest, the bottom layer the coldest, and a band of rapid temperature change in between. This middle layer of water is called the thermocline.

Of course, Canada is a mighty big country, and the differences in climate between various regions are remarkable. In some of the finest lake trout lakes of the far North, surface water temperatures rarely or never rise above the preferred level of these fish. Some of the best lakes are those where even midsummer will find lakers in water 20 feet deep or shallower, where the fish can be caught with light tackle all summer. Since such lakes are so easy to fish, I'll talk mostly here about lakes that do warm up enough to drive the fish deep in summer. And that applies to a great many lakes that attract fishermen from the United States.

During the summer, the lakers will almost always be found below the thermocline, because that is where the water ranging from 48 to 52 degrees F. can be found (see Figure 2). In the shallower, more fertile lakes, there is usually very little dissolved oxygen found in the water below the thermocline. This is not true, however, in oligotrophic lakes. The water found below the thermocline is so huge in volume and so devoid of plant life that the oxygen is never depleted. Below the thermocline the trout can find the preferred water temperature and plenty of highly oxygenated water.

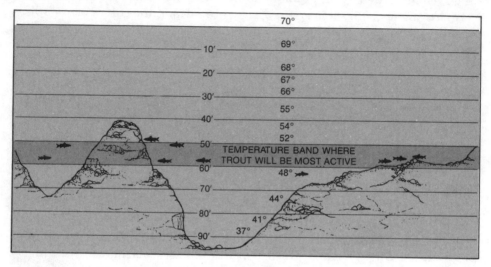

Figure 2. *This drawing illustrates how summer lakers will normally suspend below the thermocline where that magic 48-52° water is found. In shallow, fertile lakes there is very little dissolved oxygen found below the thermocline. But, in deep oligotrophic lakes where there is huge expanses of water, the oxygen will never be depleted under normal conditions.*

Lakers use deep water during the summer because this is where their preferred forage food, the ciscoes and other small members of the whitefish family, are found. These small, high-protein fish have much the same requirements as the lake trout: cold water and water with a high amount of dissolved oxygen.

How deep will a lake trout move in the summer? This, of course, varies with the particular lake that you are dealing with and the conditions that exist there. Lakers have been caught in water as deep as 600 feet in some of the Great Lakes. Of course this is an extreme, but it shows what kind of fish we are dealing with here. The lake trout will go to great lengths to find the water that suits them, especially in the summer. But, as we mentioned earlier, the needs of the lake trout force them into a very small portion of the body of water that you are fishing.

Find the depth where the preferred temperature band lies and you will find the lakers. Sounds simple? It is, but you must remember that the layer of water with that perfect water temperature covers the whole lake, and that will be one big area to find fish in! But, don't give up in despair. There are certain other helpful clues that will help you narrow down the areas within the preferred temperature band where the lake trout will congregate.

In oligotrophic trout lakes certain structures on the lake bottom will attract the fish. A small part of the preferred temperature band will hold a vast majority of the fish. These "high percentage" areas usually exist where the preferred water temperature meet a fish-attracting structure on the bottom, such as deep water flats, humps, slots, holes or points. The best of these will have rock and boulders on them. Summer lakers will almost always seek out a very hard, rocky bottom, usually with rock from small boulders down to small rock rubble.

Some lakes have several of these structures, while others may have only one or two. If you happen to find a lake with only one such structure, you won't have to look too far to find the fish. Large lakes with all of these fishy structures will force you to work many areas. But you may find fish on all of them.

Perhaps the most productive of these structures is the deep water hump. These humps (see Figure 3) are quite different from the sunken island that most anglers are familiar with. A deep water hump in an

Figure 3. Deep water humps are a favorite place for summer lake trout, especially if the structures top out in the comfort zone. If they don't, the trout will hang on the sides where the water temperature is to their liking.

oligotrophic lake can be large or small, can be flat and rounded, have steep mountainous edges, or exhibit a number of other shapes. But they all attract lake trout.

Humps that top out at the same depth as the lakers' preferred temperature range receive the most use. Early in the summer the trout will use shallower humps. But if these humps top off at water that will eventually warm past their preferred temperature, they will abandon them as the summer progresses and move to deeper humps. The bigger humps attract more fish than the smaller ones.

Lake trout will be attracted to various parts of the humps and don't seem to prefer one area over another. Often the trout suspend slightly above the crest of the hump.

At times when the trout are using the humps and feeding at a particular level, say 60 feet, they will move off the hump and suspend at that same depth. Then in the mornings and evenings they will move back to the 60-foot level on the hump and begin to feed. Usually this movement is triggered by a school of ciscoes that move onto the hump to forage.

However, those fish that sit at the base of the hump usually are "belly to the bottom" and will not move for any kind of presentation or technique. This doesn't mean that these fish are uncatchable, but you will find that lake trout that are active and ready to feed are those that are suspended three to seven feet above the bottom. These are fish you want to invest your time in.

Another productive structure that you will find in many of these oligotrophic trout lakes is the flat (see Figure 4). A flat is any area with a level bottom of uniform depth, bounded on both sides by gradually tapering shallow water. These shallow borders are usually shorelines points or islands. Lake trout definitely prefer some flats over others. For example, trout will choose flats with a hard bottom rather than a silty bottom. Hard bottom areas have rock, gravel or boulder-strewn bottoms. The depth of a flat can be important. Again, the trout will prefer flats with depths that fall within their preferred temperature range. Most of the time, however, you will find that the most productive summertime flats have a maximum depth of 50 to 80 feet.

On some lakes the lake trout will spend the entire summer in one flat. If their temperature, oxygen and food needs are all supplied by one flat, the trout don't have to move. As long as the fish can find what they want, they will stay put.

If you happen to locate trout holding in one area in a flat, the chances are that you will find the fish there every time you return, providing there are baitfish on the flat. It is hard to understand why the trout prefer one area over another in a flat, although these preferred areas may be the points where schools of ciscoes move onto the flat to forage. A change from a silt bottom to a gravel bottom or an inflowing spring bringing in highly oxygenated water may also cause the lakers to prefer one part of the flat over another. But if you find the fish in one particular area of the flat, by all means note the location and fish the same place next time.

Figure 4. Flats will also hold summer trout, especially if they have a hard bottom and enough depth for the trout to find comfortable water.

Deep holes are another prime lake trout structure during the summer and many fish are taken from these every year (see Figure 5). A deep hole is any hole that drops off considerably deeper than the adjoining bottom. Holes, depending on the lake, can have bottom depths of as much as 200 feet or more. You will rarely have to deal with a hole that deep, though. Holes can range from long narrow trough-like structures to extensive bowl-shaped depressions that constitute a large part of the main body of the lake.

Holes can be found just about anywhere. They can be found between two islands, at the end of a bay, in the main body of the lake or almost anywhere else. A nice thing about holes is that they are fairly easy to find. All you need to do is watch your depth finder, if you have one. If you don't have one, you can often times find these areas of deep water by noting the change in water color. Deeper water is usually a much darker blue or bluish green. Some anglers become quite adept at this and can find the holes in no time.

To find fish in a deep hole you should note at what depth the lip, or rim, of the hole begins. This rim can be the primary holding area for trout, especially early in the summer. If the rim of the hole is at the same depth as the magical 48 to 52 degree band of water, you may have the hot spot of all hot spots.

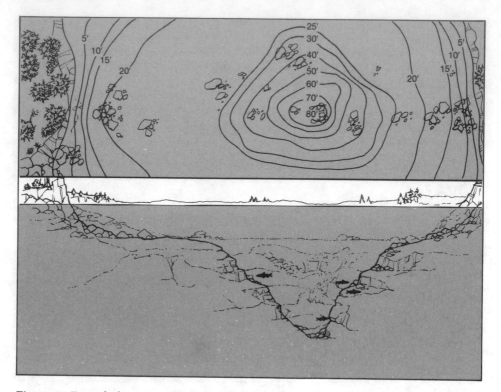

Figure 5. Deep holes can vary from long trough-like structures to huge, bowl-shaped areas. Regardless of the shape, these are prime laker spots.

As the season progresses the fish will settle down deeper in the hole as the thermocline sets up and the preferred temperature band settles deeper and deeper. By summer's end the trout might be right in the bottom of the hole.

While the lip of a deep hole will be the primary holding area for the lakers, the fish will also position themselves along the sides of the hole, especially near any breaklines along the side. They will also suspend out in the middle of the hole or lay belly to the bottom down in the depths. But, first find the temperature of 48 to 52 degree F. water and work from there. That will tell you where to look in the hole for the trout.

One of the harder summer lake trout structures to find is a slot. Slots are narrow, canyon-like holes that extend into shallower water (see Figure 6). These structures usually are found at the back ends of holes or flats where the bottom begins to taper up towards the shoreline. Like many of the other structures, slots can be found in many places in a lake. However, I have found that slots occur most often where two points of land come closely together with steep banks that plunge down at a steep angle into the deep water. This should tell you to begin your search for slots in the back end of bays, in narrows that connect two larger bodies of water or where a small hole is located between two islands.

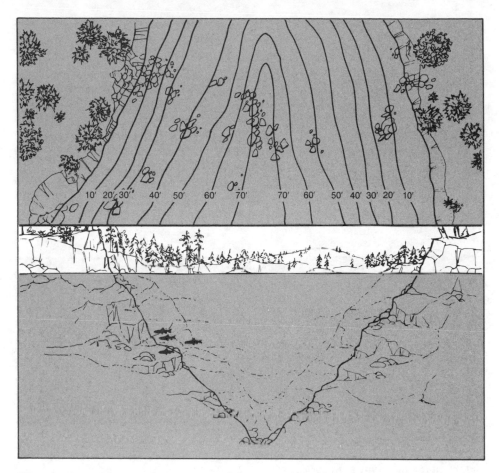

Figure 6. *Long, narrow slots are one of the more difficult structures to find. However, they are one of the most productive trout hangouts during the early part of summer before the water warms too much.*

Lake trout seem to be attracted to slots all summer, especially in the early days before warm water forces them into deeper water. Trout might position themselves just about anywhere in the slot, but prefer to lie along the steep sides. From past encounters with slot lakers, we've found that they will find a ledge, lip, or a breakline on the sides where they can lay. At times they will suspend out over the middle of a slot, but they will stick to the edges if they can.

Points are perhaps the most common and easy to find lake trout structure in Canadian lakes (see Figure 7). The fact that they are so common can pose a problem, though; unless you know what points have the qualities that make for good laker fishing, finding fish can be hard. In order to even have the potential to be productive, a point must intercept or run into a hole or flat that has the proper depth, oxygen, temperature and available baitfish.

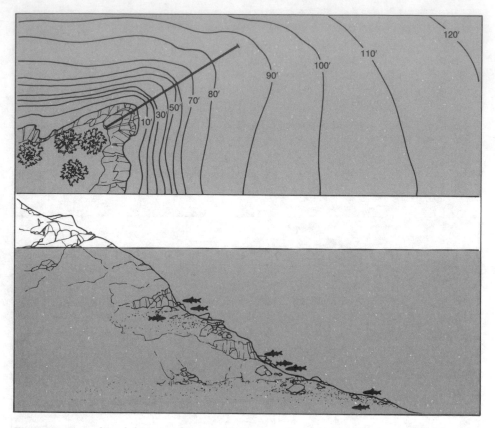

Figure 7. *Canadian lakes can be so full of points that it can be frustrating finding the ones holding fish. The "hot" ones usually jut out from shore far enough to intercept deep water and then rapidly drop off.*

The type of point that you are looking for is one that juts out from the shoreline and rapidly plunges into a deep hole or flat. If the point is long, tapering and flat-bottomed, it will probably be worthless and should be left alone. If a point is covered with boulders, rock, rubble, stair-like ledges or other irregularities, it will be a good place to drop a line. These craggy bottoms almost always make a point even more attractive to lakers.

Lake trout will use points throughout the summer. In the early part of the summer, you will find the lakers sitting up high on the point in shallow water. As the summer progresses, they will move down deeper in order to remain in the comfort zone. In fact, during the peak of summer, the trout may be situated right at the base or deep water end of the point. This area tends to attract trout during the summer.

What probably attracts the trout to the tips of these points is the change in the bottom content. Usually there is a change from rock rubble to sand or clay here. Sometimes this is all it takes to attract a school of lakers. But depending on the season and water temperature, the trout can be found anywhere along the point.

Summer lake trout can be a challenge at times. Any lake trout expert will tell you that.

There is a tool, however, that will help you find summer lake trout, and that is a depth finder. Sonar units such as the Lowrance 2360 or their X-15 graph will prove invaluable in helping you find holes, humps, points and other lake trout haunts. The X-15 can take a certain depth level and "blow it up" so you can specifically study that one section in detail, locating baitfish, structure and even lakers.

Under most conditions, you should be able to knit together the key summer locational factors — preferred water temperature, structures, depth and the presence of prey — and put yourself on top of those big summer lakers.

Granted, these waters are sometimes huge, sometimes sprawling out for thousands of acres, and they seem awesome when it comes to finding a few fish in them. But with the patterns for summer lakers that we've discussed, even a novice fisherman can find fish in a surprisingly short period of time.

Finding the lakers is more than half of the battle. So on your next trip up to the far north, stop and try a little summer laker fishing. But, if you don't want to get addicted to a super type of fresh water fishing, don't try it. Because, once you get a taste of the brutish battle these deep water denizens put up, you will never get enough. You'll be, as we say in the fishing world, hooked.

A reliable, high quality graph recorder is perhaps the most valuable tool for lake trout fishing. Notice how this Eagle unit has recorded several lake trout along underwater rock piles and even tracks the downrigger weights.

Summer tends to be very short in this far northern region, some lakes are ice free for less than four months out of the year, some much less than that. In August, an air conditioner month in the States, lake trout lakes might see heavy snowstorms. Soon the warm summer breeze will turn into an angry northerly wind that will quickly cool the surface water. This brings on what we call the fall turnover. The cold air will cause the surface water to become even colder than the deeper water.

This colder, heavier surface water will then sink and mix with the warmer, lighter water below. This mixing process, the fall turnover, causes the water to mix together, top to bottom, until there is a uniform temperature throughout the lake.

After the fall turnover and all the water is of the same temperature, the lakers could be just about anywhere. But soon the fish return to the shallows to begin their fall spawning ritual.

In some parts of Canada, the fishing season will close to allow the lake trout to spawn. Regulations like this are important. Lake trout grow so slowly that it is quite easy to over-harvest them.

Like most members of the salmonid family, the lake trout is a fall spawner. As the waters in the shallows begin to reach 48 to 57 degrees F. the trout will begin to move in from their deep summer haunts to do their part in regeneration. The spawning cycle usually takes place from early September through late November. The timing will vary as you travel from the north to the south.

Lake trout will seek out areas with gravel or rubble bottoms on which to spawn, usually on a bar, underwater point, reef, or shoal (see Figure 8).

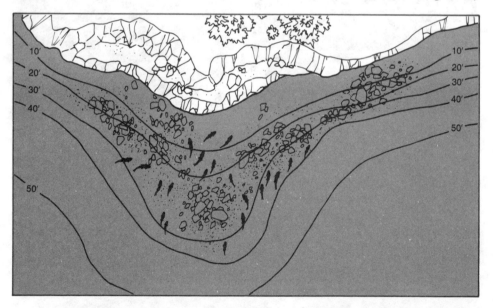

Figure 8. *Like most members of the salmonid family, lake trout are fall spawners. They will spawn on gravel or rubble bottomed areas that may be as shallow as two or three feet. However, most spawning will take place in areas deeper than this.*

On most inland lakes, this takes place in water less than 40 feet deep, but at times trout have been seen spawning on gravel shoreline areas only one foot deep. On the other hand, in some of the great lakes, the lake trout may never come into shallow water but may spawn in water 80 to 100 feet deep. Trout will also spawn on mid-lake rock and gravel reefs that top from two to ten feet. Not all spawning takes place on shoreline related structures.

The spawn is the biggest single moment in the trouts' year, one they prepare for long in advance. So while the best fishing on actual spawning grounds tends to be in September, where legal, the fish are homing in on those spawning areas in August throughout much of Canada. Water temperatures may keep the trout in deep water through much of August, but week by week the lakers will drift nearer the reefs or points where they will spawn when fall brings surface water temperatures down. Experienced fishermen know that August lake trout won't usually be far from suitable spawning sites.

This fall movement into the shallows inspires a new group of fishermen to return to have another whirl at the lake trout before everything locks up in ice. Many anglers are still under the impression that it is only worthwhile to fish for lakers when they come in shallow. Thus, you see many fishermen who only fish the trout in the spring or fall. No doubt fall is a great time to fish lakers, but no one should be afraid to try for them in the summer too.

Fall lake trout congregate around the spawning areas. These areas might be the same ones that the trout were found on in spring. Areas with a firm bottom in about 10 to 30 feet of water that lie near deep summer structures will usually hold trout. Remember that temperature zone that the trout always seek out. When this zone merges with a shallow point, hump or other structure, it may be "trout heaven".

With the coming of winter, water temperatures remain pretty much constant throughout the lake. Under these conditions, the trout will move just about anywhere. Since lake trout remain active during the frigid winter months, hardy ice fishermen take some nice catches all winter. Many parties of ice fishermen snowmobile or snowshoe back into these lakes to try their hand at winter lake trout.

In general, lake trout have an undeserved reputation of being hard to find, difficult to hook and easy to land. Not true! Every year, thousands of anglers head north to Canada to fish for walleyes, northern pike, and smallmouth bass, passing by countless deep lakes that support excellent lake trout populations. It is too bad these anglers don't stop to take advantage of this excellent sport fishery. They don't know what they are missing.

It is still true: the lake trout is a misunderstood fish. When hooked on modern spinning or casting gear, they will put any other fish to shame. And you don't need to have any specialized rods, reels or line to catch them. In fact, you can be more effective by using the modern light gear since it is so much easier to use.

This is especially true when you're dealing with shallow water lake trout in the spring and fall. When the fish have moved up into water 30 feet or less, the best tactics are not much different than those you would use for walleyes, bass or northerns. More lakers are taken in spring by plain, old fashioned shallow water trolling than by any other method. The basic technique used is to troll along the shallow water points, reefs and sunken islands at the depth that has temperatures attractive to lake trout.

This is much easier if you have a depth finder and a temperature probe of some sort, such as Lowrance Fish-N-Temp. All you need to do is simply lower the probe until you find the band of water with a reading of 48 to 52 degrees F. and stick to that depth, using your depth finder. Concentrate your efforts on the places where optimum temperature band comes in contact with the trout-attracting structures we've talked about (see Figure 9).

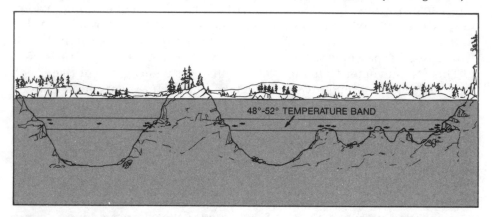

48°-52° TEMPERATURE BAND

Figure 9. *The key to finding lake trout in these huge expanses of water is to determine the depth of the comfort zone and key in on any spots where this band of water comes in contact with some sort of structure. These structures may be points, reefs, humps, or even the shoreline itself. But find these fish magnets and you should find trout.*

Many lures will work well for spring lake trout fishing. However there are times when one type will outproduce others. One of the lures that consistently works great is a spinner-minnow combination. Little Joe, Red Devil and Prescott spinners all fit the bill. Simply combine one of these with a three to four-inch fathead or shiner minnow and you've got one of the best spring laker baits that there is. I've also found that the new weight-forward spinners, such as Tom's spinner, that were made famous by Lake Erie walleye guides work extremely well for shallow water lakers.

When you hook your minnow on to the spinner, it's important to pass the hook through the minnow's mouth and out the gill, then hook it under the dorsal fin. This gives the minnow a lifelike action, yet puts the hook in a position to catch those short strikers. When I've used other methods, like hooking the minnow through the lips, I lost many fish right after the strike, and after the bait was retrieved I could see where the end of the minnow was scraped and skinned short of the point of the hook. After some experimentation, I found that using the hooking method described above vastly increased the number of hooked trout.

When you use a spinner-minnow combination you may find it necessary to add some weight to the bait to get it down to within a foot or so from the bottom where the fish are. How much weight you use will depend upon how fast you troll, how deep the water is and what size line you are using. Eight- or ten-pound test line works very well for this type of fishing. With line of this size, I like to troll at a moderate to fairly slow speed, a little faster than a normal walleye trolling speed. At such a speed, $\frac{1}{4}$ to $\frac{1}{2}$ ounces of lead will be perfect in most cases.

The best way to add this weight to your line is to use a sinker such as a rubbercore sinker made by Water Gremlin. Attach the sinker about three or four feet ahead of the lure, farther ahead if the water is very clear. With an outfit like this there is no reason not to catch lakers, if the fish are there. Other rigs that work are Mepps spinners, Chicos and Storm's large Hot-N-Tots.

Many spring lakers have been taken by using trolling spoons such as the Doctor spoon, Swedish Pimple, Daredevle spoons and the Whitefish Wobbler. Or you can troll plugs. I've had success using Lindy Shadlings and Baitfish, Rapalas in size 13 to the magnum version and other minnow-type baits.

Even though lake trout are common and easy to catch in parts of Canada, some preparation is necessary to ensure a successful trip. The first step is to make sure you bring a complete array of lures to cover any conditions you may encounter.

Spoons, diving plugs, spinner/bucktails, and jigs all will take lakers when they are shallow in spring and fall.

Spinning, baitcasting and spincasting rods and reels all work well for trolling. Use whichever one feels most comfortable to you. It is important, however, to use a fairly stiff rod. For that reason I'd suggest a graphite rod, such as those made by Lew Childre. Lake trout will hit your lure with gusto and you need a strong rod to fight them properly. It also helps to have a strong rod to set the hook solidly. I suggest using a six-foot moderately stiff graphite rod.

Live bait fishing is another excellent way to pop some of those early season lakers. Many folks do well by casting out a dead smelt or chunk of sucker or ciscoe and letting it lie on the bottom. Simply position your boat so that you can cast to a likely looking trout hot spot and heave it out. This method works very well casting out from shore too. Obviously, points dropping into deep water are the best place to shore fish. It's really nice to set up camp, eat your meal, then slip down to the shoreline and cast out your bait. After bouncing around in a boat all day, this is a relaxing way to fish.

The best terminal tackle for live bait laker fishing is a Lindy Rig with a treble hook and a ½ to ¼ ounce slip sinker. You can cast this rig easily and present your bait on or near the bottom where the fish are. After you've cast, open the bail on your reel and prop up your rod. When a hunting lake trout comes along, it can scoop up your bait and take off without any hesitation because the line will flow freely through your slip sinker. The trout can run with the bait and feel no unnatural drag with this rig. Once you notice the line peeling off your reel, let the fish run for a few feet, then set the hooks hard. Even though this method seems simple, many limits are taken each spring by using it.

Remember to be quiet when you are fishing for shallow water lake trout. Spring lake trout have just left the seclusion of the deep holes of the lake and are in new territory when they creep up into the shallows. They're spooky. If you find you can't get the fish to hit and you know they are there, you may have to switch to lighter tackle. Try using a high quality six-pound test line on a sturdy lightweight rod and reel for those tough times. Switching to a lightweight outfit can make a considerable difference at times. Be prepared by having a lighter outfit in the boat all the time.

As we know, summer lakers are usually in deep water. This calls for a different way of presenting a lure or bait. The fish may be over 100 feet down. This seems to turn off many "would be" lake trout fishermen. They assume that deep water fish can only be caught with deep sea tuna fishing tackle. This is not true. Guides in Canada who make their living catching lake trout have come up with a way to catch these deep water trout with the same rod and reel that you use for walleyes and smallmouth. It's called vertical jigging.

Vertical jigging is the most fun and usually the most productive way to catch summer lakers. You have no clumsy weights on your line to dampen the fight of the fish. You feel the strike and enjoy the battle from start to finish. On top of this, you can fish with the same rod that you use for walleyes, smallmouth bass and northerns. Many of these lakes in Canada support several species of fish. With the same rod on one lake, I've caught walleyes, northerns, smallmouth and lake trout by simply changing lures and location.

Vertical jigging is a simple matter of dropping your lure down and reeling it back up, dropping back down and reeling it back up. Actually it's a lot like casting and retrieving a lure. The difference is that you drop your lure and retrieve it up in a vertical line from the bottom, rather than fishing horizontally. Same thing, different direction.

Dropping your lure down to the bottom in deep water can take a lot of time. But even when the fish are suspended over a deep hole, or slot, it's best to let the lure fall all the way to the bottom. In order to get the most out of your fishing time, you need to get the lure down to the bottom fast.

A medium action graphite baitcasting rod works the best for this type of fishing. Lew Childre's Model G56X casting rod seems ideal. Often the strikes are subtle and hard to detect. A sensitive graphite rod will allow you to feel even the gentlest pickup. A graphite rod also has much better hook setting power. This is important for vertical jigging because at times you will have as much as 70 feet of line out, maybe more. It isn't easy to set a hook into the jaw of a laker at any depth, so you need all the help you can get.

You should also try to put the odds in your favor by using a clear or gray-green monofilament line from 12- to 17-pound test. Lake trout have excellent vision and can see lures up to 20 or 30 feet away. Sometimes these fish are line-shy, so it's best to be on the safe side. A no-stretch line will also add to your control for the jig and help set the hook. Don't scrimp on the line quality. After spending all that time, energy and money on a trip, don't lose the fish of a lifetime because you decided to save a few pennies on cheap line. After all, it's the only thing between you and the fish.

When it comes to choosing a selection of lures to use while you are vertical jigging, remember that lake trout are sight feeders. They will hit lures that have flash and action rather than those that are dull and lifeless. Through the years, I've found that vibrating blade baits like Heddon's Gay Blade, tail spinners and Swedish Pimple jigging spoons work consistently well. You'll notice that all these lures have an enticing action when they are on the drop, which goes right along with the vertical jigging concept.

Jigs are very productive when jigged vertically, too. Certain jigs work better than others when fished this way. A lure with a fast drop rate is necessary, so a jig with a large head works best. Depending on how deep you have to fish, jigs from ¼ ounce to four ounces are about right. Attach a "stinger hook" to prevent any short strikers from nipping your jig and getting away with it.

The style of jig head that you use can be very important. Round jig heads will work at times as well as stand-up jig heads like the Lindy Dingo Jig, but there are times when one style will outproduce others by quite a margin. The jig style that has often worked best for me is a planing type head such as Lee's Planing Jig. Planing heads cause the jig to flutter from side to side on the drop in an enticing eratic manner that really can drive a big laker wild. Planing jigs take longer to get to the bottom, but they usually make up for that by outproducing other jigs.

Last summer on Great Slave Lake, we were working some lakers that were holding on some deep water structure. We had shown the fish just about every type of jig we had, with little success. Occasionally we would pick up a smaller trout in the 10- to 18-pound range, but none of the "gargantuans" that we knew were lurking down there.

I had included some new planing style jig heads in my tackle box before we had left home, thinking that I might want to experiment with them on this trip. Their unique flattened head had really intrigued me. After tying it on, I lowered the four-ounce jig to the bottom over 100 feet below us. After I gave it a couple of good hops, a trout engulfed it and took off. I knew then that it was a bigger fish than those we had been catching. And I was right.

After hammering it out with the trout for what seemed an eternity, we finally lifted out a laker that tipped the scales at over 25 pounds. Now, one fish doesn't prove much, so I lowered the new jig once more down into the depths only to have it hit by another trout over 20 pounds. By now we all knew that this neat little jig was a real killer, and it stayed effective time after time that day. We caught more and bigger trout with that particular style jig head than with any other type.

Another big lake trout comes to net. This lunker was taken on a bucktail jig, with a planing jig head.

Before you leave on a lake trout trip, you should make sure that you have an array of jig styles that include round jigheads, stand-up types, banana-shaped heads, airplane jig heads and, of course, planing jig heads. With an assortment like this you should be prepared for any mood the trout may be in.

What is important is getting that jig to the bottom quickly. The deeper the water, the heavier the jig head you'll need. Also, if there is a current you will need a heavier jig to get to the bottom. Experimentation will be the only way to arrive at the best size for your particular situation.

Colors can be important. In some waters the fish will prefer one color over another, while on some lakes it doesn't seem to matter what color you use. White is probably best, though yellow and green are productive at times too. Dark colors seem to be on the bottom of the list. Probably the lighter colors are more visible at the extreme depths where you find the trout. With the blade baits the silver, whites, yellows, golds and greens seem to out do the darker colors. But, as we noted, the color preference may change from lake to lake. Environmental conditions may have a bearing on what color the trout will prefer. So, pack an assortment of different colored jigs, especially the light colors.

Many successful guides and lake trout enthusiasts are taking bragging-sized stringers of lake trout by using downriggers. These ingenious mechanisms were made popular by salmon fishermen who troll the depths for kings and coho in the neighboring Great Lakes. Downriggers enable them to troll the lures at a precise depth where lakers are known to be.

Downriggers work best when used with graph or flasher units. You can locate the fish with the depth finder and see exactly what depth they are using. Then it is a simple matter of lowering the weight from the downrigger to the proper depth and trolling the lure right through the fish zone. While watching a rod, waiting for a fish to strike, may not seem real exciting to some folks, to me it is a real blast. The anticipation of knowing your lure is being watched by possible dozens of sleek, silvery lakers can keep you on the edge of your boat seat waiting for your rod to "go off." Not only is it exciting, but fishing with downriggers is an effective way to take trout.

Several companies make high quality downriggers. Choose a smaller sized model because they are more convenient and suitable for small boats. Some good ones are made by Riviera and Penn.

By using the methods and equipment discussed here, it is entirely possible to take stringers of lake trout consistently . . . even to the point of overfishing a population of trout in a lake. You need to realize that with increased fishing know-how comes increased responsibility, a responsibility to fellow anglers and to the fish themselves. The lake trout is a slow-growing fish that has frequently been hurt by careless fishing pressure. So release the fish you catch rather than stringing them up, especially if you catch lake trout. In my opinion, the person who practices catch and release deserves every fish he catches . . . and more power to him!

Trophy lake trout are one of Canada's greatest resources. However, it takes many years for one to reach the size of this one. So you can see how indiscriminate harvesting of big trout could severely deplete their population. All anglers are urged to keep one or two for mounting or eating, but all the rest should be released.

LAKE TROUT SEASONAL LURE SELECTION

Season	Bait or Lure Type	Size	Color	Remarks
Spring	Jig & minnow	¼ to ½ oz	White, pink/white	Very early, shallow
	Spinner & dead smelt	#4 to #7 Blade	Various	Good for reluctant fish
	Minnow baits	Shadlings	Blue, green, silver	Use "S" type trolling pass
	Spoons	Thin Doctors	Chromes with red, blue, green or chartreuse	Vary sinker size & boat speed
	Sucker meat			Great for shore fishing
	Crank baits	Large Hot-N-Tot	Chartreuse – chromes	Early mornings
Early Summer	Planing jig & sucker meat	½ to 2 oz	White, yellow	Use low stretch line
	Tail spinners	⅜ to ¾ oz	Various	
	Crazy Spins	4 to 5 inch	Silver, gold, red	Good on down riggers
	Spoons	Finsel Spoons	5 of diamonds red/white, brass	Vary weight & speed
	Down riggers & plugs	4" to 7"	Chrome, orange, green	Best for deep suspended fish
	Jigging spoons	½ to 1½ oz	Chrome	Drop & rip retrieve
Late Summer	Down riggers & various plugs	Poptail	Pearl, red, green	*Most fish deep & suspended must exactly control bait depth
	Spoons	Various	Various	
	Dodger and fly	Various	Various	
	Heavy jigs - airplane or planing type	1 to 4 oz	White, yellow	Don't be afraid to go deep
	Jigging spoons	1 to 3 oz	Red, green & blue chromes	Most hits on the drop
Fall	Jig & minnow	⅜ to ¾ oz	White - pink/white	*Note! most areas have
	Spoons	Medium	white, silver, blue	closed trout seasons in fall

In many Canadian lakes, lake trout this size are the rule rather than the exception. Give them a try on your next trip to Canada.

Chapter 5
Northern Pike: Keeper of the North

We hoped Lake Despair would not live up to its name that afternoon. The gray water was dead calm and the air was heavy. Distant rumblings foretold a summer storm, so we knew we didn't have much time. But had we known then what this mysterious Canadian Lake had in store for us, we wouldn't have believed it.

We decided to try for some walleyes on a large flat that lay next to a small island. We had heard rumors that some "goshawful" big fish roamed the area.

We found a spot where the flat plunged off into deep water and decided to start our fishing there. I tipped a small Fuzz-E-Grub with a minnow and cast it out. No sooner had it started to settle to the bottom when I felt a walleye scoop it up. I set the hook and began to bring it in. About 15 feet from the boat my walleye suddenly became very heavy ... too heavy for a walleye. In the dark water a huge northern materialized, holding the walleye crosswise in its mouth like a dog with a stick. The big fish was completely unaware of my existence. I gently pumped it up to the surface and led it toward the net. I knew the fish wasn't hooked, just grudgingly hanging on to the walleye. As quickly as he could, my dad scooped up the fish. All heck broke loose. Water flew like a geyser as the fish suddenly came to life. You can only appreciate the power of one of these brute fish after you've tried landing a "green" one. Rods were flying and people shouting as the fish tried it's best to reduce our gear to shambles.

With one unexpected fish down, we tried for some more walleyes. This time it was Dad who hooked one. As he started to bring it up another pike streaked in and grabbed the hapless walleye. This northern, a 15-pound fish, didn't wait to be led in, but tore and slashed the walleye until it was shredded. Once it realized something was wrong, the pike let go and dove.

While all this was going on, another monster northern had hit a hooked walleye that my brother was fighting. But during all the excitement we had not been able to hook either. But the pike were there, still waiting for a helplessly struggling walleye to show itself. No sooner would we start bringing up another fish than one of the wolf pack of 15- to 20-pound pike would come out and slash it. We still weren't able to get another pike in the boat and we must have fought with a dozen northerns over 10 pounds.

We finally tied on some small jigs and caught some perch, which we hooked on the back of spin rigs. With these we started to hook some of the northerns.

The big fish were coming in as fast as the storm was approaching. The closer the storm got, the more frenzied the fish became. Several times we had more than one gigantic northern on at once. And then the storm hit. The wind and the heavy rain forced us to pull into the island and wait out the blast. But, like many north country summer storms, it was soon over.

Without any hesitation we raced back out to the rocky flat to nail some more northerns. But we couldn't raise a fish. Like the storm, they had attacked with a savage force and then left as quickly as it came. But I know I'll never forget the way those huge brutes slashed and churned the water into a foam. It almost scared me.

But that's the type of creature we are talking about here. One that feeds furiously and with no qualms. No wonder so many fish stories have been told over the years about monsterous pike that bust up tackle, break heavy lines, and scare the socks off unsuspecting anglers. Want to know the interesting part? Many of them are true.

Legend has it that when Great Spirit created the northern pike he called it the "Keeper Of The Waters." The "keeper" was to hold all the other fishes in check to make sure they didn't become over-populated. Thus he was equipped to go to all depths and inhabit all types of lakes and streams. His nasty disposition and savage nature led him to feed on all types of fish, at any time. Believe me, the keeper lives up to his name.

Northern pike have an elongated body with a pair of duckbill-like jaws that are lined with razor sharp teeth. They are usually colored dark green, green, bluish-green or brown. The sides are profusely marked with elongated spots that are white or yellowish-white. The northern has a pale belly that is creamy white or yellowish. The tail, anal and dorsal fins are usually green, yellow-orange or red, with irregular dark markings on them. This coloration makes this "eating machine" practically invisible when they lie in the weeds, timber or other cover.

Northerns can reach huge proportions. But, how big is a really big northern? Well that depends on what part of the country you're from, and how big the tales they tell. Big northerns go over 20 pounds, one over 30 pounds is a trophy anywhere and some super giants will tip the scales over 40 pounds. Right now the all-tackle record is a monster caught in the Sacandaga Reservoir in New York that weighed 46 pounds 2 ounces.

Northerns can be confused with their similar cousin, the muskie. The northern has light markings on a dark background, while the muskie has dark body markings on a light background. One sure fire way of differentiating the two is by counting the mandibular pores found on the underside of the lower jaws. The northern never has more than ten, while the muskie has never less than eleven (see Figure 1). Additionally, the northern will have scales on their cheeks, while the muskies will only have scales on the upper half of their cheeks.

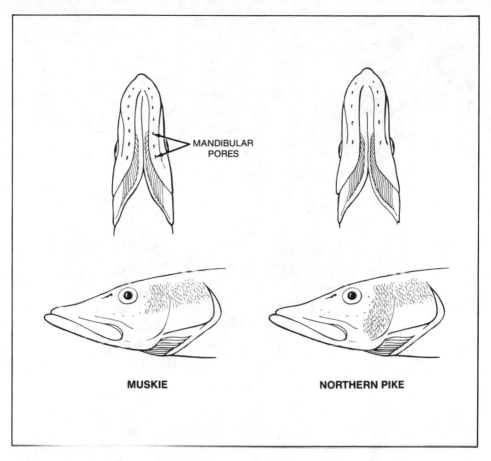

MANDIBULAR
PORES

MUSKIE

NORTHERN PIKE

Figure 1. *At times the northern can be so similar to a muskie that is nearly impossible to tell them apart. However, there are subtle differences that make it easy. The northern never has more than ten mandibular pores under the lower jaw while the muskie never has less than eleven. In addition to this, the northern may have scales on the entire cheek area while the muskie will only have scales on the upper half of the cheek.*

The northern pike is perhaps the most common and well-distributed gamefish in Canada. They can find suitable habitat in some oligotrophic lakes, but really flourish in mesotrophic (more fertile, weedy) lakes and even eutrophic (extremely fertile and weedy) lakes. Actually the northern will be found in just about any lake as long as the lake has suitable spawning areas and something for him to eat. The same is true of Canada's rivers and flowages.

The range of the northern pike includes an area from Labrador south of Ungava Bay through much of the Maritime Provinces, throughout Quebec, Ontario, Manitoba, Saskatchewan, Alberta and in the extreme northeastern corner of British Columbia. Northerns abound in the Yukon and Northwest Territories, except in the northern and eastern coastal regions and arctic islands.

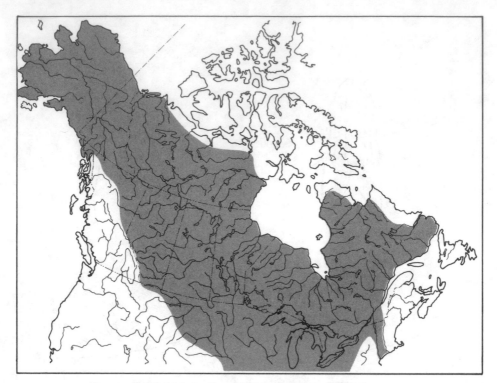

The Home Range of the Northern Pike

Northerns are spring spawning fish that begin to move into the shallows when the water temperature reaches 40 degrees F. Vegetated, flooded shoreline, marshes and bays are prime spawning areas. At times, the water in these areas will be quite shallow, possibly only six inches deep. The spawning urge is so strong that northerns will push themselves over shallow bars and barriers until they can find the proper bottom content for spawning. At times you will see pike up to 20 pounds in water so shallow that their backs are sticking out of the water.

The spawning run will begin in April and run through early May. Usually a larger female pike will be attended by one or two smaller male fish. No nests are built but the eggs are just scattered at random on the bottom vegetation.

About 12–14 days after the eggs have been laid, the young fish hatch. These tiny fry exist on their yolk sacs for a few days until they are able to fend for themselves. The young pike are extremely aggressive right from the start, feeding on sucker fry and even on each other. Commercial fish hatcheries find it hard to raise northern pike from eggs because of their cannibalistic nature. Perhaps it is because of this aggressive nature that the northerns are such successful predators.

Once the northerns have completed spawning they will move out of the rivers and flooded areas to rest in the bays. Some pike may also head for deep water in the main lake to recuperate after spawning. One of the best early season, post-spawn places to find northern pike is in rivers that flow through marshy bays. This is prime Canadian pike spawning grounds.

These marshy, wind-protected bays are among the first to warm up in the spring, bringing up the first weed growth and insect hatches. The minnows, small perch and other forage species will move into these bays to feed on the newly emerging plankton and insects. So many post-spawn pike remain in the bays to feed. On warm days you may find pike cruising the shoreline ready to nail some unfortunate morsel, or some lucky angler's lure.

Even though these marshy, stream-fed bays attract northerns like a magnet, some will pull in more pike than others.

The key elements to look for in a prime spring northern pike area are: 1) a shallow, sandy bay that is bordered by vegetation such as reeds or a marsh, 2) protection from cold winds, and 3) direct exposure to sunlight to warm the water. Find an area with these three ingredients and you'll find the fish. An area with only two or three ingredients usually turns out to be only so-so, maybe even a complete waste of time.

Many times as the northerns begin to return to the lake from the rivers they will run right into suckers entering the rivers to spawn. The pike will then remain in the river mouths to feed heavily on the schools of suckers (see Figure 2). This special feeding situation can pull in some of the biggest pike in the lake. As the schools of suckers move up the river they are stopped by a barrier — two impassable waterfalls, in our illustration.

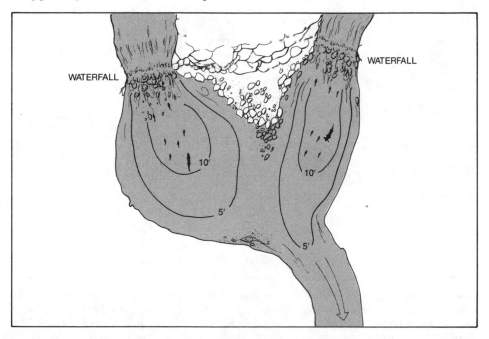

Figure 2. *As big pike leave their spawning areas they will often encounter suckers just beginning their run. When the suckers congregate below falls or in deep holes the northerns will often take advantage of the situation and have a feast.*

With these conditions, you can count on some real monster pike hanging in the deeper pools, feeding on the suckers. Once I fished the area illustrated in Figure 2. There were a mixture of walleyes and white suckers in the pools so we knew the big northerns were there somewhere. We cast to the area with Bagley B Flat Shiners and Magnum Rapalas, picking up several four- to seven-pound northerns, but none of the big "sleds" that we knew were there. However, it wasn't long before one of the neighboring boats had come in and landed an 18-pound pike, gorged with small walleyes and suckers.

Not all bays attract early season pike at the same time. Several factors determine which bays will attract pike earlier than others. The map of a section of a northern pike lake shows how bays will often be located (see Figure 3). The first bay to shed its ice and attract northerns would most likely be bay A, since it is an area of moving water from the river. If you encounter bays with water flowing into or out of them, fish them before looking for any other spots.

Next would be bay B. Since this bay is more exposed to west and south-westerly winds, it will warm up before C, which is protected from the warm winds and will be the last to warm. The north shore warms before the south shore since it is exposed to the direct southern rays of the sun and warm southerly winds.

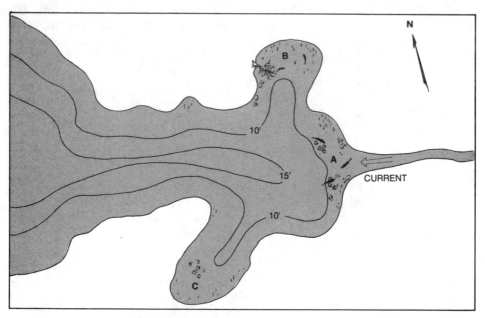

Figure 3. This is a typical bay on a Canadian lake that will attract early spring pike. However there are spots within the bay that will be better than others. Area A would be the first to attract fish because of the inflowing stream bringing in warm water. The second area to draw in northerns would be area B which is exposed to warm southerly breezes that warm the water. Area C would eventually attract some pike because it is shallow and would warm before the deep central bay, but would not be as nearly productive as A or B.

Early season pike fishing in these bays will be better if there is some sort of cover. Flooded timber, fallen trees, bullrushes and cabbage weed beds are perhaps the most common types of cover found in the back ends of these bays. After the pike have spawned, they will move into the first available cover they encounter as they move out of the marshy areas. This would make a cabbage bed or area of drowned timber at the mouth of a river a perfect place for trophy fish. If these areas hold enough forage food for the fish, the pike may stay all summer.

When you move around by boat looking for prime early season pike hangouts, keep an eye out for beaver dams. These can pull in big fish like magnets, especially if there is some deep water close at hand. Mix in a nearby cabbage bed or some drowned trees, and you have trophy fish water. Beaver dams are quite common and easy to find. You don't need any depth finders or other special gear.

Spring pike fishing is a fairly cut and dried matter. You know the fish will be in shallow water, probably in the bays that are adjacent to good spawning areas. Once you've located a productive looking bay, concentrate on the pike holding areas such as stream mouths, cabbage beds, beaver dams and flooded timber. If an area has a combination of these, that's all the better.

As spring merges with summer, the northerns will not change their location much, especially on oligotrophic, trout-filled lakes. Stumpy bays, bays with flooded timber, marshy bays and bays with cabbage beds will all hold summer pike. Stream mouths also continue to hold their share of fish from spring throughout the summer on these rocky lakes.

We should make special mention of weeds. Pike are ideally suited to living and feeding in weedbeds. While they can enter open water to chase down prey, their preferred and most effective feeding style depends on launching a short-range ambush. Timber and even rocks can serve as pike ambush points, too, but pike obviously prefer weedbeds. This can make life easier for the pike fisherman. If you find weeds (and if those weeds aren't in water too warm or cold for pike) you're not far from pike. Crack out the steel leaders.

The best weed for pike is what fishermen call the cabbage weed. It is a group of weeds that have fairly full, curly leaves. Cabbage weeds look like they'd be good to eat. They will grow in fairly deep water, making them more desirable for northerns than, say, the thin fringe of light rushes that often ring Canadian lakes. Cabbage weeds tend to grow in distinct clumps or beds, which can be small or almost as extensive as a bay.

In summer, the key areas for pike are cabbage beds and points. These beds hold forage fish and offer protection from hot weather. Whether the beds are located in bays or out in the main lake, they'll usually hold pike. Even the thin weedbeds that have sparse growth on them can attract northerns. Many times smaller walleyes and smallmouth bass hang in these thin weedbeds, chasing small minnows and forage fish. The pike in turn feed on the bass and walleyes.

Since pike are temperature-sensitive fish, weather can be a factor. A basic rule to follow, however, is the hotter the day, the deeper the fish will be in the weeds. Many people don't realize that the northern pike is a cold water fish. Given the chance, pike seek out cold water. This comes as a surprise to many because northerns are found in some of the shallowest, warmest lakes in the country. Yet it's true. One pattern that some very good northern fishermen use is to locate cold water springs that flow into a warm body of water, such as mesotrophic (middle-aged lakes of medium fertility) or late mesotrophic lakes. By trolling over these springs they've taken dozens of huge trophy pike from an area no larger than a living room. Remember the pike's preference for cool water when fishing shallow, sprawling lakes that have little or no depth. If the lake has plenty of deep water the fish will most likely just move to deeper water to find cool temperatures. It is not uncommon to find big northerns down with the lake trout feeding on ciscoes and small lakers.

Another example of the northern's fondness for cool water is the move they make into river mouths during the summer.

Many Canadian lakes have cold rivers and streams flowing into them. When these conditions exist, you may find the northerns just packed into the river mouths. If cabbage beds are also present, you have the makings of a real "honey hole." At times I've found pike under just about every river weed clump. Never bypass a river mouth if you're hunting for hawg pike. If you do, you may be bypassing the fish that was meant to hang in your den.

Pike will also suspend off small islands, weed covered humps and cabbage beds throughout summer (see Figure 4). These structures may be found in bays or out in the mid-lake expanses. When hungry, these

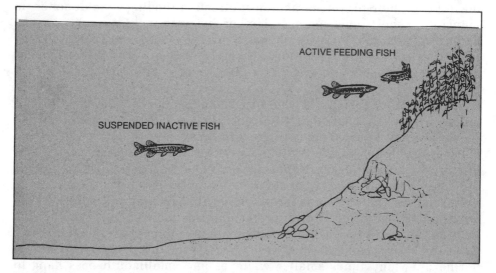

ACTIVE FEEDING FISH

SUSPENDED INACTIVE FISH

Figure 4. Summer pike will often look for the best of two worlds. For example, areas where weed beds border steep dropoffs offer a feeding area, plus the sanctuary of deep water.

suspended fish move up to the shallow edges of these structures and attack small walleyes, perch, minnows, or even small northerns. Once they have eaten they move back out to deep water and suspend again. This simple daily cycle happens over and over on these Canadian lakes.

This movement to cabbage beds is accelerated during the hot, humid days in August and early September. Rather than making forays to the weeds to feed, pike will stay for longer periods of time. Huge stringers are possible during this period which lasts all the way up until the fall turn-over.

In addition to the cabbage beds, pike use weedlines toward the end of summer. One of the favored forage foods of giant northerns is the jumbo perch. They cruise along the weedlines, offering a tempting target for a hunting pike. Sometimes pike can be found in huge numbers hanging off the weedlines.

As the weather gets cooler and fall sets in, northerns move into shallows following spawning ciscoes. These high-protein forage fish are a favorite food of northern pike, and the northerns take advantage of the concentrated ciscoes and feed on them heavily. Gradually tapering shorelines with a gravel bottom are the preferred spawning site of the ciscoes (see Figure 5). Never pass up one of these prime spawning areas without giving them a try in the fall.

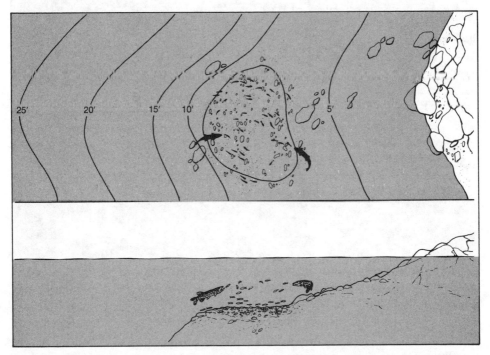

Figure 5. *During the fall, northerns will follow spawning ciscoes right up in their spawning areas and feed heavily on them. Look in areas with gradual, tapering shorelines with gravel bottoms for the small fish. Once you find them, the northerns won't be far behind.*

Lake trout are also fall spawners and they will seek out spawning areas similar to the gravel shoals that the ciscoes spawn on. However, the two species will not spawn together. Try to fish the areas where you know ciscoes spawn rather than lake trout. The pike prefer the smaller ciscoes. Really big pike will feed on small lakers however; you certainly won't find any "hammer handle" pike feeding on lake trout. But if you could see what I have seen come out of the stomach of some giant pike, it might scare you. They can eat just about anything, including some good sized lake trout.

Like the rest of the year, fall is a good time to fish the river mouths for northerns. On any type of lake in Canada you can always find some big pike around the rivers, especially those that attract spawning trout or ciscoes.

Rivers also contain a lot of trophy pike. Look for places where the current forms eddies and chances are there will be a hungry northern waiting there. Notice the small points along the right bank of this river. Each of these provided a perfect spot for a fish and at least one good northern was caught from each one.

Obviously, there are more locational factors than we've mentioned here. But with the guidelines we've laid out, you should be able to put together a successful presentation. There are a few more things that you need to take into consideration. Because of Canada's sprawling wilderness there are places where you can throw just about anything and catch northerns over 20 pounds. But, when you're dealing with lakes that have been fished to any extent you'll have to use some fishing savvy and the right presentation.

This fact reflects the extremely aggressive nature of northerns. They run around with a mouth full of knives, fearing nothing, perhaps because there is no predator in the water that can make a sizable pike back down. So the pike are cocky and voracious, making them an easy mark for the angler who gets a lure out in front of one.

Northern Pike have a reputation as voracious, lure gobbling predators. This may be so with smaller pike, but big ones, like the one Babe Winkelman shows here, can be very difficult to catch. However, with a little knowledge and understanding you can consistently catch them, especially in Canada.

With this in mind, some pike anglers take special pains to select water that hasn't been hit hard by previous parties or water protected by modern conservation policies. Lakes and rivers that have seen much fishing pressure will just not kick out the lunker fish that were taken by those who fished there first, unless a good share of those fish were released. Some Canadian fishing camps operate in the not-so-grand old tradition of killing everything that comes to net; they don't keep lunker pike very long. Other camps are doing everything practical to limit the kill of fish, a policy that gives them a chance to enjoy great pike fishing for generations to come.

The first step in unraveling what's and why's of northern pike fishing is to adapt the locational factors discussed previously to the particular lake you are fishing on. Then you decide what the fish are feeding on. Once you dope out the predator-prey relationship, you can pick a suitable bait or lure and be all set for some fantastic pike fishing. So let's cover some of the presentations that go along with the different locational factors.

Let's say that it's early spring and the pike are still up in the bays. The fish are not feeding on anything specific, but are plenty hungry. It's a perfect situation to catch a lot of pike. So let's cover some good lures.

First you'll want to use smaller baits or lures in the early part of the fishing season. The water is still cold, so the pike will look for small meals. As the season progresses it's best to switch to larger baits, but for now stick with the smaller sizes.

One way to put a pile of northerns in the boat is to troll the bays with spoons. Some of the best choices of colors are orange-copper, red-white, and brass. Attach the spoons to your line with a steel leader. If you use anything other than a steel leader you can forget putting many northerns in the boat. They have a dental set up that will slice through mono like a hot knife through butter.

Also make sure you have some sort of hook remover or needle nosed pliers to take the hooks out. You definitely do not want to take a hook out with your fingers.

During this early period you can get away with lighter line. I suggest spooling on some 15 to 20 pound test Stren or other high quality line. Normally a big pike could break line like this, but in the cold water of spring the pike are sluggish and slower.

If there happens to be a lot of cover such as timber, weeds or brush you should try a bass-sized spinnerbait. These little rigs are so snag resistant you can toss the lure into timbered areas where pike like to lie. The flash of these lures really turns on the northerns. Even though they are effective on their own, you can increase their effectiveness by tipping them with a 4-inch sucker minnow.

When these bay roaming northerns move into the cabbage beds and points it's time to toss a tempting minnow-imitating bait such as a Lindy Baitfish or a Rapala and work it back over the tops of the weeds. If you want to get a little deeper down, use a small bucktail such as the Mepps Giant Killer and retrieve it over the weed tops. Either method can really call up those ol' pike in the weeds.

82

Many northerns, like this one, fall for the flash of a tandem spinner bait. These versatile lures can be retrieved many ways, which is perfect when you're faced with changing conditions.

The perfect rod for this would be a five-and-a-half foot graphite bait-casting rod such as a Lew's 6X Speed Stick. It's a light, easy to use rod but has enough backbone to fight an angry, saber-toothed pike.

If you find out that some big northerns have moved into the river mouths to feed on spawning suckers, you have an exciting time ahead of you. A properly fished sucker is by far the most effective way to take a wall-hanger during this sucker run. And perhaps the best method is the old, but highly effective bobber and sucker minnow. This rig has probably accounted for more big pike than any other rig. If there are twenty-pound-plus pike in the lake, I will use an 8- to 12-inch sucker hooked lightly under the dorsal fin. If the pike run smaller, I'll use a 6- to 8-inch minnow.

Just cast this rig up into the river mouths where the suckers are congregating. The hooked minnow will struggle against the bobber, giving off signals to any hunting northerns. I've seen big pike slowly cruise by suckers, or other baitfish, without showing any sign of attacking. Suddenly, when the hooked minnow begins to get frightened and struggles against the bobber, the pike will rush in and grab the minnow like a dog grabbing a bone crosswise in its mouth. Talk about getting the heart pumping!

Another highly effective live bait method is free-lining a sucker using a Northern Pike Lindy Rig. These specialty rigs are similar to the normal Lindy Rig, but have a larger hook and a steel leader in place of the mono snell normally used.

With the Lindy Rig you can let the pike take the sucker and run with it. This is especially important when you're dealing with a trophy pike. Big pike have an irritating habit of grabbing a big sucker or minnow and just chewing on it rather than swallowing it. At times they may swim around for as long as half an hour before taking the minnow completely so you can hook them when you set. It's frustrating to watch your bobber slowly go down and be towed around the weedbed for twenty minutes, set the hook and get nothing for your efforts except a chewed up minnow.

Big pike can be very tempermental and they don't like the unnatural drag from the big bobber. With the Lindy pike rig you can allow the fish to freely take line with no drag, and the fish will swallow the bait much more readily.

However, there are times when big fish just won't swallow the bait no matter how careful you are. Yet there is a trick that I have used successfully many times to hook these big devils. Early season pike will often lie in the shallows to sun themselves. Many times they won't take a bait, and if they do they won't swallow it so you can hook them. In this case I'll long-line a Lindy Pike Rig tipped with a 6- to 10-inch sucker.

Using my Minn Kota electric trolling motor, I'll slowly snake my way through the shallows, presenting my bait in an ultra-quiet manner. Once I get a hit I'll immediately let out line, and lots of it. I don't want the fish to feel anything. After I'm sure the fish has got the minnow in its mouth, I'll quietly sneak back over the fish until I'm directly above it. With an open bail I'll gently lift up on the fish. Surprisingly enough, a big pike will usually let you lift them right up to the boat, if you take it easy. Once the fish sees the boat it will take off and you must give it free line immediately. Now that Mr. Pike has been semi-hooked, he will usually swallow the minnow in his haste to get out of there. After the fish has run for a bit, tighten up and hit him hard. Usually you get a good set because the fish has taken the bait solidly, plus you are setting the hook from straight up above the fish, the best way to sink a hook into the tough roof of their mouth. Even though this method may seem exasperating and time-consuming, it is exciting. You feel twice as good after landing the fish because you matched wits with a big fish and beat him rather than just hooking him and bringing him in. It is one of the biggest thrills in freshwater fishing.

Other effective baits are dead smelt or ciscoes. These dead baits are often easier to keep and transport than a bunch of live minnows. Besides, they are just as effective at times.

One final way to fool these sucker-eating pike is to use a jig tipped with a sucker minnow. My favorite is a Dingo Jig. The stand-up style head sinks to the bottom quickly and can be ripped through cover easier than any other style jig head. Cast the tipped jig up into the river mouths and retrieve it with a hopping technique. Just fan-cast the entire river mouth, retrieving the jig past any waiting fish.

During hot, sultry days, pike will take large baits readily.

Even though many northerns move out from the bays in summer to main lake cabbage beds or go down deep to feed on ciscoes and small lake trout, some will remain in the bays. For these, the same tactics that were used for spring pike will work, but you will want to use larger spoons, spinnerbaits, and other lures.

But for those fish that move out to deeper water weedbeds and points, you will want to use some different techniques and presentations. What I usually do is begin at the deep water weedlines (see Figure 6). I slowly work along the edge with a ³⁄₈- or ¼-ounce stand up jig such as a Dingo Jig, Stand Up Fuzz-E-Grub or Mr. Twister Pow-RR Head tipped with a minnow. Work this combo along over the top of weedlines so that it occasionally ticks the weed tops, then let it drop down the front face of the weedline. Or, you can let the jig settle in the weeds, then snap it up. This can trigger some tremendous strikes. Remember to be ready when you lift your jig up from the weeds. Many times pike will suspend just above the weeds and will nail your jig when you least expect it.

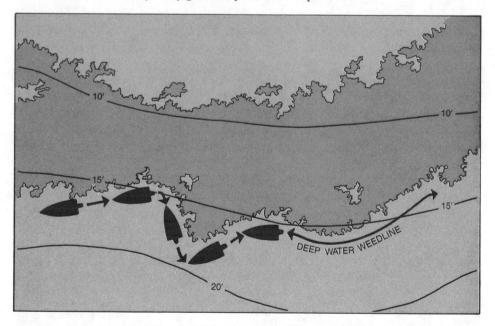

Figure 6. *A good place to begin your search for northern pike is the deep water edge of weed beds. This seems to be a reference point for them so work the weedline thoroughly with a deep bait such as a jig and minnow.*

If the pike aren't in the weedbeds, try moving out toward deeper water along the breaklines in 30 to 40 feet of water (see Figure 7). A perfect rig for working these breaks is a Northern Pike Lindy Rig with a #5 or #6 Colorado Spinner added to the snell. Tip this with a 5- or 6-inch minnow and hang on. The fish tend to really gobble these smaller minnows down rather than toying with them as they do when you are using a big sucker for bait.

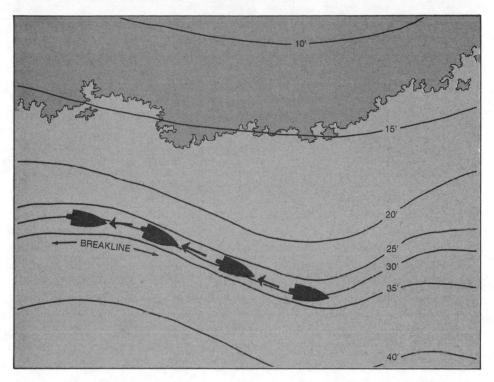

Figure 7. *If you don't score along the weedline, move out to the next reference point, the first major breakline. Many times the breaks will be in 30 to 40 feet of water.*

For this type of rigging, I like to use a hefty spinning rod with a fairly heavy action, such as a 6-foot Speed Stick spinning rod in a #6 action. Match this with a Speed Spin 3, a reel with a large line capacity and you'll be able to handle even the biggest fish.

Backtrolling is the best way to present the rig to any northern. Backtrolling is a newer twist to the age-old practice of regular trolling. By simply putting your boat in reverse you can stick to a weedline or contour like glue. Also, by running in reverse you can crawl along at a snail's pace, which you can't do going forward. The deeper you wish to troll, the slower you should move. If the water is very deep you may have to shift between reverse and neutral in order to stay slow enough.

Another way to ensure your lure is deep enough is to use a down-rigger. It is a simple matter of lowering the cannonball to the desired depth and attaching the desired lure to the line release. Having a flasher sonar unit will make it even easier to set the depth; by watching the dial and raising and lowering the cannonball, you can glue your lure right to the bottom no matter what the depth is.

Toward the latter part of summer, the weedbeds begin to fill out and become huge, drawing in big pike. These lush beds are the real key for summer pike. During these hot, sultry "dog days" I like to use bigger baits because the fish become more aggressive and prefer to feed on something a little more substantial. So muskie-sized jerk baits, bucktails and spoons become the normal late summer pike ammo (see Figure 8).

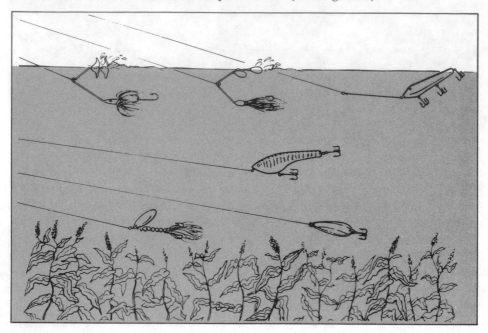

Figure 8. *The saying "big fish like big baits" is true many times for northerns, especially in the summer when the fish are most aggressive. Muskie-sized spinnerbaits, jerkbaits, big stick baits, bucktails and large spoons are normal summer fare for these big toothy critters.*

Lure color is important. You need to keep in mind what type of forage fish you wish to imitate, so I like to use perch and sucker finished Teddies, Suicks, and Bobbie Baits. Another excellent choice is a small Bagley B Flat Shiner in a walleye or ciscoe color. Work these lures over the top of the weedbeds in normal jerk bait fashion, popping the lure to make it dart from side to side.

Big bucktails and large spoons also take their share of big pike from the cabbage beds. One of these lures quickly retrieved over the weed tops will bring up some really big fish from down in the weedy jungles.

But, perhaps the best way to call up some of these gargantuan pike is to use large buzzbaits or muskie tandems. These lures have an alluring action as they sputter and gurgle across the surface, ringing the pike's dinner bell as they move along. I have found that the best colors to use are black and orange, black and chartreuse, black and silver, and sometimes white if the water is very clear during the later part of summer.

Some pike may still stay suspended off from the weedbeds or go deep during the late summer period. These open water fish can be hard to locate, but once you do they can be taken on a properly worked lure. One very successful way is to weight a plug so that it sinks down to the depth of the pike. Some lures that I have found to work very well for this technique are magnum sized Rapalas, Creek Chubs and jointed Pikies. Just add a ³/₈- or ¹/₂-ounce rubbercore sinker about 18 inches in front of the lure.

Most pike do not reach trophy proportions by being foolish and reckless. While many smaller pike are attracted to flashy, gaudy lures, most big pike fall for more subtle bait-imitating lures. A little trick to use when you're weighting down these plugs for deep water northerns is to color the diving bill with a dry marker to disguise it in the clear water of their environment. You may also replace any silver shiny hooks with bronze hooks. These subtle changes can be the difference between catching a bunch of small "hammer handles" or something so big it may remind you of Jaws.

Springtime northerns love suckers, but summer pike have a weakness for them too. Bobber rigs and Lindy Rigs are good ways to place a sucker minnow in and around the weedbeds. Or you can try a sucker harness.

There are several commercial sucker harnesses, but one good one is the Bucher Sucker rig. There are many ways to fish these rigs, including trolling, bobber fishing or free-lining. The best way, however, for summer weedline pike is to cast them and work them like a jerk bait. Big northerns love to lie near gaps, holes and pockets in the weedbed so they can ambush any unfortunate critters that look like lunch. You can chuck the sucker harness rigs up into these spots and work them in jerk bait fashion. You might even find yourself hooked to a big muskie on some Canadian waters, or a big walleye.

Regardless of what method you use for summer pike you need to use a rod and reel that can handle a battling northern. Use nothing less than a good stiff musky rod. A 20-pound-plus northern in the middle of a cabbage jungle is not a place for light line and wimpy rods. To land your fish you need to be in control. To do so, I use Lew Childre's SG6X-159. This rod has the backbone for setting the hook and wrestling monsters out of the weeds. Match this with a BB 1N or a BB 2N Speed Spool filled with heavy dacron line. Don't scrimp on the quality of your line. Both Cortland's Musky Master and Berkley's Green and White are good choices.

During those hot, glass calm days of summer, pike may bury themselves deep in the cabbage beds and almost become dormant. It takes quite a bit of work to get them to move, let alone take a lure. Many methods for taking these fish have come and gone, but one works best for me. It's called speed trolling. You may have visions of a boat streaking across the water at water skiing speed. While speed trolling may be new and unorthodox to some, it's not quite that far out.

Speed trolling allows you to cover a lot of water in a short period of time, stirs big fish into striking, and works well around cabbage beds. In short, it's a great summer pike technique for Canadian waters.

The method is simple. Just let out about 20 to 30 feet of line behind the boat and begin to troll. If there are two of you, use the buddy system. One should troll just behind the prop wash, while the other trolls farther back.

The idea is to follow a depth contour, staying exactly at one depth, until you are sure the fish are not there. Keep changing depths until you find the fish. The term "speed trolling" implies that the boat must be moving fast, but this is not always the case. You troll, instead, at a speed that will trigger the fish into striking. The proper speed might be very slow at times, quite quick at others. Five or six miles per hour is a good speed to start with, then work faster. Keep running at different speeds and depths until you find the right combination to trigger the fish. Once you've determined this you can work a large area in a short period of time. That's the beauty of speed trolling.

As you troll along, take note of any irregularities in the weeds. A little dip, bed, point or greener clump in the cabbage may be all it takes to hold a number of big pike. This is where a pair of good polarized glasses will be worth their weight in gold. I never leave the dock without mine.

Pike will often hit your lure on the turns. On turns the lure will hesitate, then speed up, which may be all it takes to make a big pike hammer your spoon. Or you might get more hits because an S-shaped trolling pass will pull your lure over areas that the boat hasn't passed directly over. If the fish has moved away from the boat when you moved over it, the serpentine trolling will get them (see Figure 9). Whichever the reason, it pays off to use a few turns when your lure enters key areas.

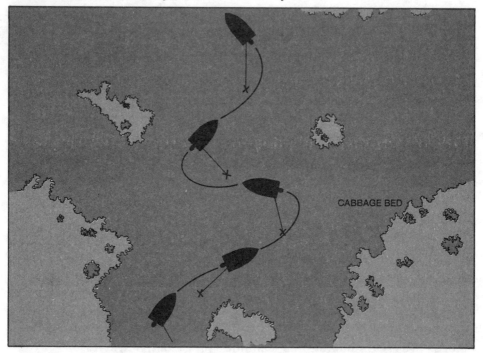

CABBAGE BED

Figure 9. An old speedtrolling trick is to use a "serpentine" pattern when you troll. This causes your lure to hestitate briefly then speed up with a fish attracting action. Also, this pattern will cause your lure to swing out over water the boat hasn't passed directly over.

Many lures will work for speed trolling, some better than others. Spoons with a wide, floppy action, such as Doctor spoons, Daredevles, and Five Of Diamonds do the job.

Certain colors are better than others, with orange being probably the best. Combinations with orange, chartreuse, and black and white are also proven giant killers. Other lures to try are bucktails, such as Lindy Hot Spots, the Mepps Giant Killers and Windell's Harasers. Jerk baits like Teddies, Suicks and Bagleys will also do a number on big snakes when speed trolling. Spoonplugs are another good choice. They were specifically made for speed trolling, and help you hold the lure at a specific depth.

Another version of speed trolling that works exceptionally well in these summer conditions is trolling a Musky Tandem across the weedbeds. This "buzzing" technique will turn pike inside out as they tear up the weeds trying to get at the lure. Just roll the lure at a speed where it will just brush the tops of the weeds...and get a good grip on the rod handle.

A good, stiff musky rod is definitely needed for speed trolling. When you are fishing northern pike in weeds you need to remember the pike is boss. Use a weak "buggy whip" rod, and the fish will tie you up in seconds. With a strong graphite rod like the Childre's SG6X-159 you can control the fish and steer it out of the clumps that would normally spell disaster. Top this off with a good quality casting reel loaded with 15 to 20 pound test dacron line, and you will be set.

Don't be surprised if a big ol' snake looms up out of the weeds and engulfs your lure with a mouth the size of a wastepaper basket.

Early fall brings a change in northern pike activity. The pike move in shallower to feed on spawning open water baitfish and perch along the weedlines, as well as other fish that congregate around river mouths. You'll have to try some new methods and presentations to catch fish now.

Use live bait rather than artificials. One dynamite presentation is to troll a Northern Pike Lindy Rig tipped with a sucker minnow or shiner. Work along the breaklines near gravel shoals and reefs where these open water baitfish are known to spawn.

When the northerns are up around the river mouths feeding on sucker or other small fish, sucker harnesses on a bobber rig are deadly.

As the pike move in from their deep summer haunts to feed on the spawning baitfish, they may stop along the weedline and feed on jumbo perch for a short period of time. This is an ideal time to work a jig and minnow along the weedline. Use a ⅜- or ¼-ounce jig tipped with a large, 4- to 6-inch minnow. Jigs with a standup head are easier to work in the weeds, so I prefer jigs like standup Fuzz-E-Grubs, Dingo Jigs, Pow-RR Jig Heads tipped with a Twister Tail or Magnum Tinsel Tails. Cast these into the beds and retrieve over the weed tops, or let the jig settle into the weeds and use a lively, snapping retrieve.

Most of the big pike I've caught have been during the fall period. Pike, along with many other gamefish, go on a feeding spree just before freeze-up. It's as if the fish anticipate the lean times ahead. Fall is an exciting time for the pike enthusiast.

But, really, it doesn't matter whether it's fall, spring or summer, the mighty northern pike is usually willing to bite and to fight once hooked. A real gamefish through and through. And talk about vicious!

I recall one day several years ago when some friends and I were fishing along a breakline just out from a large cabbage bed. We were trolling using Lindy Rigs tipped with 5-inch sucker minnows. It hadn't been too long before I had a fish pick up my minnow and race off like a torpedo. I fed it line, being careful not to let the fish feel anything unnatural. Then, with a powerful sweep, I drove the hooks home, only to feel a dead weight on the end. For a minute I thought I had a good one on until the line came free and a hammer-handle pike came in with cabbage weeds wrapped all around it. Disappointedly I gave the small fish some slack, hoping he would shake himself free so I wouldn't have to harm the little fella by handling him. Suddenly, out of the corner of my eye I caught the movement of an ominous shadow moving toward the small pike still on my line. The huge northern clamped its jaws around the small pike. My heart was in my throat as I watched the long, sinuous body shoot down toward the bottom. But I was able to keep my head enough to give the fish free line as it dove.

For twenty minutes the lunker pike poked around until I was sure he had swallowed the hammer-handle. With all the strength I had, I leaned back and drove the hooks home into the tough jaws. I was really glad I was using my Lew's musky rod because that fish decided he didn't want to give ground. There is nothing more exciting than battling it out toe-to-fin with a big fish. And this time I was the winner. The fish was just short of twenty pounds, a lunker in anyone's book. But typical enough for Canada.

To many people, the whole idea of a Canadian fishing trip is to catch big fish and lots of them. Northern Pike have made this dream a reality more than any other fish.

NORTHERN PIKE SEASONAL LURE SELECTION

Season	Bait or Lure Type	Size	Color	Remarks
Spring	Small thin spoons	3" to 4"	Silver, blue, gold	Fish will be very spooky in clear water. Make long casts with no leader
	Minnow baits	Baitfish size	Perch, shad, silver	
	Small bucktails	3" to 4"	Black/orange, yellow	Timber and heavy cover
	Spinner baits	¼ to ⅜ oz	Various	Cold front days
	Live bait rigs	Moderate		
	Bobber & dead bait	6" to 12" Smelt		Excellent for river mouths
Early Summer	Spin rig & minnows	⅜" to ¾"	Chartreuse, silver, red/white	Fish with "helicopter" retrieve
	Jig & minnow	Heavy Dingo	Green, brown, black	May need to add stinger hook
	Crank baits	Bass size	Various	Fl. orange is very good in dingy water
	Spoons	Medium	Various	
	Bucktails	Small musky	Black, red, orange, brown	Work at moderate speeds
Late Summer	Jerk baits	Big Teddies	Cisco, black, sucker	Work fast, cover water
	Bucktails	Largest	Black, orange, red	
	Musky tandem	Largest	Chartreuse, yellow	Might need to add pinch-on sinkers for fast trolling
	Buzzing baits	Bass size	Various	Excellent for heavy overcast
	Speed trolling divers	Hellbenders	Chrome, yellow	Excellent in hot weather
	Large crank baits	4" to 6"		
Fall	Jerk baits	Large	Cisco, yellow, black, red/white	Steep breaks with green weeds
	Big minnow baits	#18 Rapalas 7" Hellcats	Various	Follow the ciscoes
	Jig & minnow	5" to 8" bait		Midday, deep
	Live bait rig & suckers	1 to 3 lbs		This is only for trophy fish

Chapter 6
Walleye: Fillet Mignon of Canada

The early morning fog was still rising, drifting in patches across the clear water. The sun had peaked over the treeline enough so, with the aid of my polaroid fishing glasses, I could see the bottom quite easily. And it was alive with walleyes...huge fish, slowly ambling along, scrounging for breakfast.

As we sneaked quietly through the bay with our electric trolling motor, I noticed two giant fish swimming parallel to the boat. I flipped over a small yellow Fuzz-E-Grub and minnow about two feet in front of them. We watched in amazement as the smaller of the fish swam over, rolled partially over on its side and snatched the tiny morsel up in one easy motion.

Quickly, I set the hook hard and saw the huge fish shake her head and turn back for deep water. But it was over for this nine-pounder. A few seconds later she joined another half dozen already swimming in the live well. And the fishing was just beginning.

As we returned to our cabin that morning, my brother remarked, "Babe, if we tell anyone else about this kind of walleye fishing, they'd say we lost our marbles! I know I saw 300 walleyes in that bay this morning."

Now, don't get the wrong idea. Fishing like this is hardly an everyday occurence, even in Canada. And it doesn't happen on all types of Canadian waters. Yet certain types of lakes really produce trophy fish. You have to be at the right place at the right time, and you have to understand Canadian walleye fishing.

Of all the popular sport fish, the walleye is surely one of the most sought-after and widespread throughout Canada. The walleye is a favorite fish partly because it is so plentiful. Walleyes are also often easy to catch on a variety of lures and baits. Walleyes are a schooling fish, so when you catch one you can, many times, catch more from the same place. But perhaps the biggest reason that anglers chase the walleye all over the north country is they are simply delicious to eat. The thought of fresh walleye fillets sizzling over a campfire will make anyone's mouth water.

Normally, the walleye is an easy to identify fish, though at times can be confused with it's close relative, the sauger. Walleyes have an elongated, cylindrical body that is commonly 13- to 20-inches long, or about two to eight pounds in weight. The dorsal spines are stiff and rigid with a black spot at the base of the last three spines, something that is unique to the walleye. The background color is usually olive-brown to golden brown, though it can range to yellowish and even silver. The back is dark, almost black, with sides that are

paler and usually flecked with gold. The bottom or ventral portion of the walleye is milky-white or yellowish. A trademark that identifies the walleye every time is the large conspicuous white spot on the lower lobe of the tail fin. If you ever drift up on a school of walleyes in shallow water, you can usually see their white tail spots as the fish glide over the bottom of the lake.

The closely related sauger also has a white mark on the tail fin, but it is not nearly as large or conspicuous. There are other differences to help you tell them apart. The sauger lacks the walleye's black mark on the dorsal fin and only has some dark, oblique rows of marks. The sauger also has dark rhombic blotches on it's sides that the walleye lacks.

The walleye takes its name from its large opaque eyes. This over-sized eye is quite a mechanism in itself, with light gathering power that allows the walleye to be a very efficient low light predator. That is why walleyes tend to feed more aggressively during low light periods such as nighttime, dawn, dusk, cloudy and windy days. If you think back to some of the best walleye catches, it's a good bet they came during one of these low light periods.

Walleyes inhabit many types or bodies of water, from rapids to flowing rivers, to small pothole lakes, to large cold lakes. Walleyes will live and survive in any body of water that provides them with sufficient depth, forage foods and spawning areas. There are some lakes with walleye in them and lack sufficient spawning areas, but these are stocked artificially rather than being supported by natural reproduction.

Even though the walleye can be found in various types of lakes and rivers, some waters will consistently produce better walleye populations and larger fish. For example, some lakes will hold walleyes but have so little habitat that the fish exist in low numbers, while the fish in others more agreeably structured can be quite numerous. If a lake is made up of all sharp, cliff-like drop-offs and is full of ciscoes and whitefish, the chances that there will be a lot of walleyes are remote. On the other hand, if there are a lot of extended flats with rises and humps in the medium depth ranges, of 10 to 40 feet, and the lake supports lots of small bait fish and insect larvae, it will hold quite a few walleyes.

The average fish size can vary dramatically from lake to lake. Some lakes tend to produce tons of walleyes, but rarely one over five or six pounds. Yet on another lake, sometimes right next door, people pull out trophy walleye with regularity. The answer to this puzzle lies in the make-up of the lake's forage base.

In many of the shallow, sprawling, off-colored Canadian lakes, walleyes mainly feed on insects, nymphs and larvae, even though there might be some minnows present. An insect forage base is usually associated to a lake with a limited walleye growth. There may be a lot of fish, but no eight-pounders.

On the other hand, in the gin-clear lakes that support lake trout in addition to walleyes, there is generally a combination of forage types. At times the fish will feed on the abundant insect forage base, while at other times they are free to switch to small perch, ciscoes or whitefish. Add to this some crayfish, a few leeches, an occasional shiner...and the walleyes have a virtual smorgasbord. Because of the diversity of this food base, these lakes usually produce large healthy fish in the trophy class. Though there usually aren't a lot of fish by comparison to the first lake type, the ones present are real dandies.

These prime walleye lakes can be found throughout the extensive range of the walleye in Canada. And it's large, running from Quebec south into the United States, west to the Alberta-British Columbia border, north to where the Mackenzie River meets the Arctic coast, then southeast across James Bay to Quebec.

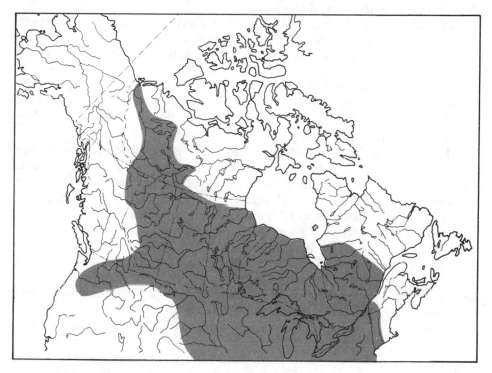

The Home Range of the Walleye

At times fishing for walleyes in Canadian lakes can be frustrating, but not for the angler who understands walleye seasonal movements and who can change the plan of attack to cope with the times when the fish aren't where they "ought" to be. While many wilderness lakes look as though fish should be just about everywhere, the fact of the matter is they're not. On some lakes there will be a small area suited for walleyes. The rest of the lake will turn out a big fat zero. Even with the latest in modern fishing gear, you can't catch fish if they aren't there!

Walleyes are a very patternable fish. They make seasonal movements and migrations which, in most Canadian waters, follow basic rules. That can only help the informed angler; he can look for fish where they are, not where they were two weeks ago.

Walleyes are a spring spawning fish. Thus spawning controls the early spring location of the fish. Shortly after the ice goes out, when the water temperature is 39 to 42 degrees, the walleyes make a pre-spawn movement into the areas where they will spawn. The male fish are the first to move into the spawning grounds.

Walleyes, like all fish, have a definite preference in spawning grounds. If it is available to them, they seek areas with a bottom content of gravel and rock. The rocks would range from pebbles to fist-sized rocks. The adhesive eggs stick to the rocks and gravel. A gravel bottom is necessary to keep the eggs from being silted over and destroyed.

If the walleyes make their spawning run up a river or stream, they still seek out areas with a gravel, rubble bottom, preferably near the shoreline. But if the fish can't find that bottom type, they turn to their second choice, rubble and boulders. The female drops her eggs at random. Some adhere to the rocks, while others will fall in between the rocks and in the cracks. The eggs that fall into those nooks and crannies are generally missed when the male attempts to fertilize them. Sand, the fishes' third choice, is the least productive of the three walleye spawning sites.

Most of Canada's better walleye lakes are connected by rivers and streams that offer prime walleye spawning areas, especially throughout the Canadian Shield. The usual habit of the walleye is to enter these rivers when the water temperature reaches the 38 to 42 degree mark and move upstream until they can go no farther, being blocked by impassable rapids or a barrier waterfall. Often the fish congregate right below these areas, spawning at night and slipping into the deeper holes during the day to rest.

Another prime river spawning area is a gravel bar that forms behind an island. You can often find huge congregations of walleyes on these bars. When active, the fish move up on top of the flat bar, then slip into the deeper pools and slack water during periods of inactivity.

If there are no rivers with the right conditions for spawning, the walleyes will make use of areas in the lake such a shoreline points, bars or gravel shoals. These areas are more attractive to the walleyes if there is a wind-pushed current going over them to keep the eggs oxygenated and free from silt.

Spawning can take place as early as April in the southern reaches of Canada, but in May or even mid-June in other areas. In some regions, because of unfavorable temperatures in a given year, walleyes may not spawn at all.

Spawning activity starts early in rivers because the water is warmer, while lake-spawning walleyes may not respond until much later. All Canadian walleye spawning does not take place at the same time. Depending upon if it is an "early" or "late" spring, each of the different spawning areas could be holding fish in different moods. If spring came early, you may find the spawning run in the larger streams is over and the fish that spawned there will have moved out before fishing season even opens in mid-May. However, this doesn't mean that all of the walleyes have completed spawning. Other fish groups, like those that spawn on shoals or reefs, might be just starting their spawning cycle, while those which will spawn in bays and on shorelines, might already be in the spawning stage.

Main lake flats and reefs add up to make prime spawning grounds for walleyes, if the bottom content is right.

If you plan an early season fishing trip, be advised that timing your trip to catch the fish in an active period is crucial. If it's a late spring, you can sometimes hit walleyes feeding savagly in a pre-spawn period. Fishing can be superb! But most of the time the fish will have already spawned by the time season approaches and the majority of the fish will be in a slow post-spawn mood.

Again, this doesn't mean that all fish have spawned already. Remember, different fish groups may not be in the same stage of the spawning cycle. Some fish will probably be active at any given time, though not necessarily in any numbers. However, if you happen to time your trip just right and find that the fish are over their post-spawn doldrums, you've got it made. After this post-spawn layoff the walleyes go on a feeding spree, producing the type of fishing that Canada is famous for, the type described at the beginning of this chapter.

By now it should be clear that early spring walleye fishing takes place near the spawning grounds. We should be able to recognize these areas by their bottom content, depth and current flow. But what about the rest of the year? Where do you begin to look in all that water?

The key to walleye locations during the rest of the fishing season is the predator-prey relationship or, in other words, the availability of food. When the predators—the walleyes—switch from one forage type to another, they are often forced to relocate. At times this results in migrations that take them long distances. A walleye that feeds primarily on insects during the summer is apt to hang out near the weedbeds and backwater bays most of the time. On some types of lakes this is as far as you have to look for walleyes all summer. Yet on other lake types, where ciscoe, whitefish, herring, or perhaps even some small trout are the summer table fare, you'll probably have to fish the points and main lake humps that attract these small fish.

To make it even a bit more complicated, the best walleye lakes normally have some of each type of forage available, so the walleyes will work the shallow weed areas for a while, then many of the fish, usually the larger ones, will head for the deeper water. In this case its possible to find schools of smaller fish shallow and other schools considerably deeper, both actively feeding on a given day. You may think them hard to pattern because of it. But realize, there's normally a reason for what the fish are doing. Because you don't understand it doesn't make it weird!

After the walleyes complete their yearly spawning ritual, they begin to filter out of the spawning areas, relocating to their summer haunts. This movement does not happen overnight. In fact, sometimes it can take quite a while before you'll find the fish inhabiting their normal summer habitat. This period, the transition period, can be most frustrating. When the fish are still around the spawning areas they're easy to find. Then, during that 10- to 20-day transition period you'd think the walleyes had packed up and left the lake.

They don't, of course. And they can be caught, if you understand this period of transition and how it affects walleye movement.

The first thing to know about transition is that the walleyes aren't going to be in their normal, classic locations. This will all make sense once you understand why this transition phenomenon happens.

A huge, spawn swollen female is escorted by three anxious males in a spawning river. Notice the gravel/rubble bottom which is the walleyes' first choice to spawn on.

First, the larger female walleyes will generally leave the spawning areas and find a place to recuperate as soon as they can. The smaller male fish are the first to arrive at the spawning areas and last to leave. They may remain in the area for sometime and can still be caught with some consistency. Usually you'll find that an early season stringer of walleyes will be mostly made up of male fish, simply because they are easier to find and are much more aggressive than the females at this time. But even the males leave, eventually.

How far and how fast the fish move out of the spawning areas depends on the conditions they encounter. If there is a slow gradual taper to the bottom where the fish exit out of the spawning areas, they will disperse much slower than if it is a steep plunging taper. Given a gradual taper, the walleyes might take a week or more to filter out. Given a sharp taper, the fish may all be gone in a few days.

Weather also affects how quickly the fish leave the spawning area. If the weather has been warm and stable, the fish will leave faster than if cold temperatures have prevailed after the fish have completed their spawn.

But where do they all go? Basically the fish will be looking for something to eat after their spawning fast, as well as a place to hide and rest. Chances are, if you can find a spot that has all that to offer, you'll find a lot of walleyes. And the most logical place to start searching is in the closest place adjacent to the spawning area where the fish can find an easy meal.

These guidelines must be related to the particular body of water you're fishing. Many lakes offer different structures and places where a walleye can satisfy it's needs during this transition period. We'll take a good look an some of the most common ones that you'll encounter in Canadian walleye lakes.

On an oligotrophic (rocky, infertile) Canadian Shield lake, perhaps the most common walleye lake in Canada, early season walleyes will be drawn to three basic kinds of areas: 1) an incoming stream of fair size and some depth, 2) a shallow bay that is fed by a smaller, shallower in-flowing stream and 3) an extended shallow flat or plateau in the main lake that has a rocky/gravel top (see Figure 1).

As we've noted, the larger rivers are the favored spawning grounds for the walleye. Once spawning is completed, the females usually retreat outside the river into the feeder arms. Sometimes they will congregate near the mouth of the river for an extended period of time. After the females have left, the males will follow and likewise congregate near the mouth of the river where they may feed actively for a period of time before moving out to their summer haunts (see Detail 1).

This brings us to the second area that you can expect to find our post-spawn walleyes, the bays with inflowing streams. Whether they are used for spawning or not, the transition period walleye will be attracted here. Detail 2 shows a typical small stream entering a bay located off a long arm.

These bays offer many of the things that a post-spawn walleye are looking for, mainly preferred water temperatures, subdued sunlight and forage food. These dark-bottomed bays are usually quite a few degrees warmer than the main lake. The dark bottom absorbs the sunlight and holds the heat rather than reflecting it like a light sand or rock bottom. Secondly, the shallow water

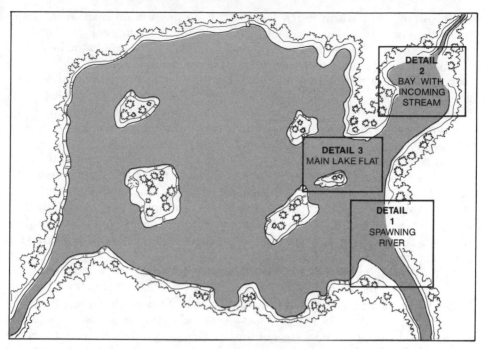

Figure 1. The make-up of a typical, shield walleye lake is such that early season walleyes will be drawn to three kinds of areas: 1) an incoming stream of fair size and depth, 2) a shallow bay that is fed by a smaller, inflowing stream and 3) an extended, shallow flat in the main lake that has a rocky/gravel top. This map shows how they can be laid out in "close" proximity to each other.

Detail 1. It is common for walleyes to congregate near the river mouths after they have returned from spawning up river. They may stay there for an extended period of time, or just briefly, depending upon weather and other conditions.

103

of these bays will warm much faster than the deep main lake. Also, many times the small inflowing streams will be draining a tamarack swamp. This stream water may be stained, and thus will add warmer water to the bay.

Another thing that a bay has to offer walleyes is a ready supply of food. The warmer temperature of bays will kick off the weed growth. The new weed growth starts the ball rolling, and soon the whole food chain comes alive. Small organisms will begin to congregate around the new weeds, then the small minnows will show up to feed on them, and soon you will have the larger fish coming into the new weed growth to eat the minnows.

Insects are another food source found in the soft-bottomed areas of the lake, which usually are the bays. Insect nymphs, larvae and adult forms are an important part of the walleye's diet in many of these Canadian lakes. Out of all insects walleyes will feed upon, the mayfly is most important, though the fish will also feed on caddis flies and dragonflies in their various life stages. This fondness for bugs explains the walleyes' unusual choice of habitat during the transition period.

When the major insect hatches come off you can count on having the walleyes switching their feeding preferences from other feed to the bugs. Just how do you tell when a hatch is coming off? Well, it's unmistakable. There will be countless numbers of shucked larvae cases floating on the surface, while the air will be filled with swarms of the flying insects. While these hatches are taking place don't be surprised to see walleyes acting like trout, swirling the surface chasing nymphs and adult mayflies.

This feeding pattern dawned on me a number of years ago when we were plying the depths of a walleye lake trying to scratch up a few keepers. We were backtrolling along a gravel finger that stretched out from an island, but not getting much cooperation from the walleyes we knew were in the lake. So, trying to be versatile, I tied on a Lindy Baitfish and chucked it out in hopes of picking up a northern before we moved on. One side of the gravel bar we had been working leveled off into a mucky bottomed area that was just beginning to have some weeds pop up. A few casts produced nothing. I threw out one final cast and started a shallow retrieve in the area of new weed growth. Something thumped my lure solidly. Rather than coming to the surface to battle like I expected a "snake" would, this fish headed for the depths. After slamming it out in the deep water for a while, the fish finally started to let up and I drew it up to the surface. We couldn't believe what we saw. There beside the boat lay eight pounds of golden walleye, caught from a mucky area on a shallow water lure. It just didn't seem to fit anything I knew about walleyes. But then, I didn't know about the mayfly hatch that had taken place the night before either. I made a point to find out more.

Beaver dams are another hotspot for early walleye action. While some of them are built on steep rock banks that plunge off into really deep water, most are built near the right type of bays. The debris around the dam really attracts insects and minnows, bringing in walleyes in droves.

Expect the runs in front of the shallower beaver dams to hold the fish. The presence of suckers here will be a dead giveaway that the walleyes will be

Beaver houses often attract aquatic insects and minnows which in turn draw in walleyes like a magnet. By working the surrounding area with a jig or live bait rig you can take some hefty limits of "marble eyes".

feeding here sometime during the day. If the suckers are not there when you first find the spot, come back every hour or two until you can set up a pattern.

The deeper beaver dams are usually built near a deep water weedbed of some type. Not always, but often enough. This can really help you narrow down your search in a hurry!

While not all beaver dams in Canada hold schools of walleyes during the transition period, I never pass one up before checking it over carefully. These easily-seen fish magnets have saved the day many times for me on a strange lake.

To understand the details of the walleye-mayfly relationship, it's necessary to learn two stages, an underwater nymph and a free flying adult. Mayfly eggs are laid by the flying adult female as she drops down to the surface of the water after the mating flight. The eggs sink to the bottom, where they adhere to various rocks, weeds, twigs or other bottom debris. Here they stay until they hatch into a nymph, complete with gills and a mouth looking like something out of a horror movie. In the nymph form, the critter will then either build a small case or they burrow into the soft bottom of the lake. The types of mayfly common to Canadian waters seek out soft-bottomed bays where they can dig their burrows. Thus you have the walleyes coming into soft, mucky bays rather than rocky bays. I don't think there is a variety of mayfly nymph that is up to drilling holes in solid granite!

Most of the mayfly's life is spent in this nymphal stage, crawling along the bottom. When the nymphs mature they leave the bottom of the lake and swim to the surface. This is the time they are most vulnerable to predation by a roving walleye. When you clean one of these paunchy shield walleyes that have been gorging themselves on mayflies, you'll find their mouth, throat and stomach packed with them.

Upon reaching the surface, the nymphal case splits open and a free-flying adult breaks free and soon flies away. This activity is heaviest on warm nights when there is little or no wind to disturb the surface of the water. Smart fishermen should be right there along with the walleyes to take advantage of this special moment.

Another walleye holding area would be a small rocky outwash section where the small stream enters the bay (see Detail 2). If any successful spawning took place in this bay, it would be right here because this is the preferred bottom content of spawning walleyes. Even if there had been no spawning here, it would attract early season walleyes. Often there will be a washed out hole located between the mouth of the stream and the point where the bottom of the bay starts to flatten out. If so, the area will be even more attractive to walleyes. Again, the fact that the stream will be bringing in warmer water will draw in early season walleyes.

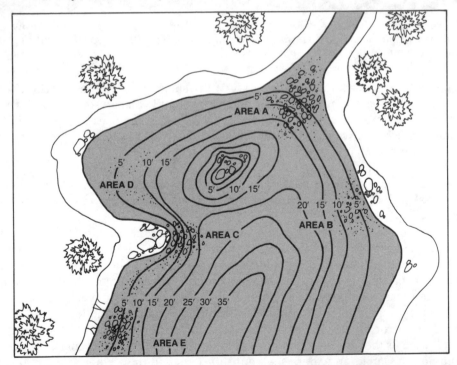

Detail 2. *Bays with small, inflowing streams are excellent places to find post-spawn walleyes. These bays, especially dark-bottomed ones, will be warmer than the main lake and will harbor newly hatched insects and feeding baitfish. Of course certain areas within the bay will be better than others, and knowing the how's and why's of these spots will help you find the schools.*

106

Off to one side of the stream lies Area B, a hard-bottomed area. Although this area is structurally much the same as Area A, there is no current flow there. While this spot doesn't attract walleyes in their spawn cycle, it is often used by post-spawn fish while they recuperate from their rigorous spawning activities. If the bottom content between Areas A and B makes a transition from sand to silt, some of the larger walleyes that spawned in other areas might come back here to rest.

Area C is a hard bottomed finger-like point. This would be the prime area when the walleyes regroup and begin their feeding spree after the post-spawn recovery period. Often walleyes use areas like this as daily holdover areas after a day of roaming around the bay. Check this type of area thoroughly when you cover the different areas in a bay like this one.

Area D is a shallow flat. This section would be a prime feeding area for big walleyes as they regroup and start feeding again after the post-spawn recovery period. In fact, even during the recovery period you may find some schools of fish in here. The peak of their activity in a site like this will last only about a week or two at most.

Area E is a lip area located near where the bay meets the main lake or deeper area. This spot will probably hold many walleyes later on when they disperse from their early spring locations, but it has little to attract the fish before and after spawning.

This brings us to our third primary area of early spring walleye location, the main lake sites. While the spawning streams and bays experience seasonal periods of walleye activity, the shallower main lake sections are used throughout the spring and early summer.

The key factor to locating elusive spring walleyes on the main lake sites is locating shallow areas that will warm faster than the acres of cold water that dominate the main body of the lake. An example is Detail 3, a shallow plateau area with rises on top where the water is primarily 25 feet or shallower.

Area A and C are examples of rises on a flat. Some lake spawning might take place on such a structure if the wind is right. But whether spawning takes place or not, the post-spawn fish will be attracted here. Because it is large, and closer to deep water, Area C will probably hold more big fish than Area A. But both these areas can be dynamite for early season walleyes.

Area D is a shallow lip that is separated from the larger plateau by a stretch of deep water. This spot wouldn't get nearly as much fish activity as a spot like Area B because of the lack of shallow water adjacent to it. It would not hold walleyes long during the early season.

Area B is a gravel and rock bar that runs between two land masses such as points or islands. This area would serve as a resting or recuperating spot for post-spawn walleyes. Schools of fish will often regroup in areas like this before moving to their summer haunts. The walleyes would probably stay in an area like this longer if baitfish were present.

Area E is a large, shallow, dark-bottomed flat in a protected area. This would be a prime spot for walleyes actively feeding during the post-spawn period. In fact, sections like this can be the spot of all spots during the early season! This area is similar to the dark-bottomed bays discussed earlier because it is a prime area for insect hatches and baitfish congregations. Mornings will probably be best for working this area, although great catches can come out of here after dark, too. If the bottom in Area B has intermittent sandy spots with some muck patches and weed growth, large walleye groups will roam and mill about this area all day long. It's common to see some white suckers mixed in with the walleye schools and swimming about the area with them. If you spot the suckers, you can be assured that the walleyes are not far away.

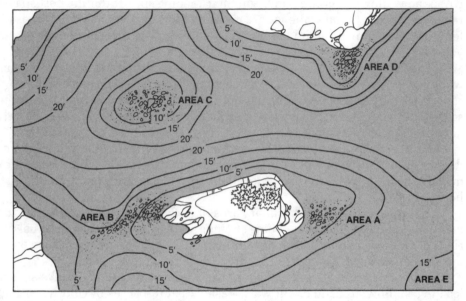

Detail 3. *While large, inflowing rivers and bays will experience brief spurts of activity, the shallower main lake sections will be used throughout spring and early summer. Like the other areas we discussed, the key to these main lake sites is their ability to warm faster than the main lake.*

While early season location of walleyes appears to be a fairly cut and dried situation, summer location is not quite as simple. Research and tough fishing experience has shown us that there are many factors involved that determine where Mr. Walleye will park his fins during those long summer days.

The factors that control summer location of walleyes are basically the same as those governing spring location. Of course, spawning is a thing of the past, but the fish will always be concerned with where their next meal will come from. In addition, they'll seek out suitable water temperatures and relief from high light intensities. Put all of these factors together, and you'll find the fish. But keep in mind that even though these Canadian lakes appear to be a virtual walleye paradise, with fishy looking structures everywhere, you won't find the walleyes all over. You've got to put it all together first.

I've done a lot of research—some folks call it fishing—on summer walleye location on these lakes, and I've found some patterns that should aid you in your search for fast action.

As we learned in the previous section on spring location, walleyes have to seek out areas that meet a set of basic needs. It is no different in summer. As the weeks roll by, walleyes move out from the spawning areas to take up their summer haunts in the main lake where deeper water will provide the preferred temperature range, food and security. Some of the deeper water structures used by walleyes are sunken islands, bars, rock piles, small humps and weedbeds.

The fish will hold near these for a variety of reasons, predominantly, because this is where cool water is. These structures attract, and hold, the forage fish so important to the walleyes, especially if there is some sort of weed growth on top. Structure such as these also offer a fast depth change so the fish can move up and down as they please in response to temperature changes without having to move any great distance.

To find summer walleyes you first find the first typical walleye structure near a known walleye spawning area. A perfect place would be one similar to Figure 2, which is a saddle or point leading out from shore to a hump or island. Walleyes dispersing from the shallow spawning area will follow the connecting saddle out and, if enough forage fish are present, they may spend much of the summer there. The fish will often be found on the saddle between the two structures during the day, migrating to the hump later in the afternoon or evening. Check out these structures closely located to the spawning areas, especially during the early summer.

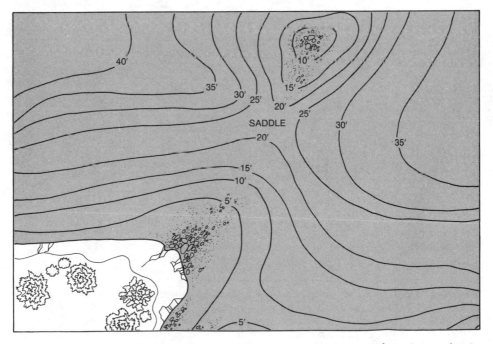

Figure 2. *A saddle formed by a hump on the end of a point is a perfect place to begin your search for summer walleyes, especially if it connects to shore near a spawning area. The post-spawn fish will follow the connecting saddle out and stay there if there is enough forage food. If so, the walleyes may stay there all summer.*

Often these infertile oligotrophic Canadian lakes offer very little food for the walleyes. On some lakes that food will be in the mucky bottomed bays discussed earlier, particularly if there is a deep water weedbed near the mouth of the bay and deep water. These bays can offer some of the best summer fishing you'll find, especially at night.

On some lakes, usually those without extremely deep water and lake trout, thermal stratification will have an effect on summer walleye location. When the lake begins to layer it forces walleyes to leave their deep water haunts because these areas lack sufficient oxygen. When that happens, "old marble eyes" is faced with only two choices: either move to shallower water with cover such as weeds or wood or suspend off the bottom in mid-lake. On some lakes an incoming stream may also provide oxygen as well as cooler water, and this will draw some fish.

Since it has been the theme of many articles, some readers may be familiar with thermal stratification. But it is important when dealing with summer walleye location and deserves a brief review. Water is most dense or heaviest at approximately 39 degrees F. Any water that is warmer or colder will, consequently, float. As the summer wears on and the upper story of the lake is continually warmed by the sun, the lake begins to stratify into three distinct levels or layers: the epilimnion (warm water upper level), the thermocline (or middle layer) and the hypolimnion (the cold water lower level). See Figure 3.

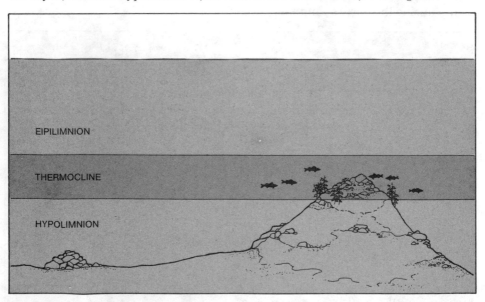

Figure 3. *Understanding stratification is important to the angler, especially on these deep, shield lakes. In some lakes the only layers that will get any amount of oxygen rejuvenation is the upper level and thermocline, which of course forces the fish to use only certain areas. But the knowledgeable angler will use this to his advantage by fishing only those spots above or in the thermocline and ignoring anything below it. Notice how the fish are using the hump that comes up into the thermocline while the deep hump is completely void of life.*

To realize the significance of this layering effect, you must understand that oxygen enters the water in only so many ways: through rain, wind action on the surface, photosynthesis (the life processes of aquatic plants) and through ground seepage water. Therefore the only layer to receive oxygen rejuvenation is the epilimnion, or the upper level, unless there is some deep water seepage.

It all boils down to this: on some lakes the layering effect and its consequent stratification of oxygen will force the fish to locate in specific areas. So it's possible to find fish in areas where normally they wouldn't be. And that fact confuses many Canadian anglers.

However, though almost all bodies of water in Canada (with the exception of the northern-most lakes), stratify, that does not mean this layering effect has to affect the fish adversely.

In other words, in some Canadian lakes you'll see thermal stratification without finding oxygen depletion in the depths. In these lakes, walleye location might be affected by the temperature of the water, but the fish would be free to roam down into the depths because there would be plenty of oxygen for them there. These lakes hold deep water oxygen both because they are so big and because there isn't enough decaying vegetation in the depths to consume the oxygen there. You can tell these lakes fairly easily. If a lake holds lake trout, it must have deep water oxygen, and in such lakes the thermocline is not such a powerful influence on walleye location.

There are a couple of ways that you can find out where the thermocline lies. The easiest is with a fishing temperature probe like Lowrance's Fish N Temp. This device has a probe you can drop in the water telling you the exact temperature at the depth you are at. When you get to the drastic change of about one degree per two feet, you've hit the thermocline. Also, with a powerful flasher or graph like Lowrance's 2360 or the X-15, you can visually spot the thermocline by the layering of suspended particles right above it. This method is undoubtedly the fastest, but neither tell you if the oxygen supply below is sufficient. You'll have to use an oxygen monitor to find that out.

For the most part, however, don't worry too much about this phenomenon. Even though the water has layered, it simply may change the choices the walleye has offered to him on a particular lake. As a rule of thumb use this. If the lake is fairly shallow, say under 40 feet, then the thermocline could pose some locational changes. If it is deeper than that, probably not.

If you're fishing a lake where the thermocline has forced the fish to move shallow, they normally head for cover, namely shallow water weedbeds. For that matter, the main lake weedbeds will be one of the hottest summer walleye hangouts on any type of Canadian lake. This is where the food chain is usually at its highest concentration; where, because of the plants, the oxygen is at maximum levels and where old marble eyes can find some shade and security. It's a natural.

As a rule, when you find weeds of any type in Canadian lakes, you'll find gamefish. But some types of weeds draw fish most of the time, namely cabbage and coontail.

"Cabbage", "celery", "musky weed", "red tops"—or whatever you want to call it—is a type of water weed that offers everything the fish is looking for. You'll find cabbage growing in the backs of bays, on dropoffs near the mouths of bays, on the sides or tops of points and around or on sunken islands. The weeds themselves will often draw in fish, but if you find cabbage weeds growing on the right type of structure, you've found a summer walleye bonanza.

As a rule, the more complex the structure, the more fish it will hold. My favorite structure would be a sunken island or long shore point with a heavy cabbage growth on top and lots of small fingers, cuts or irregularities on the side of the structure. Ideally, the weed growth should cover the top of the island and follow the dropoff down to 15 or 20 feet. Deep water weedbeds generally hold the biggest walleyes. No doubt about it! And you're apt to run into all kinds of toothy critters in the same weedbeds.

If you're fishing the type of lake that has insects and shore minnows as the primary forage base, then it's almost a sure bet that the weedbeds or shallow structures with weeds on them will hold almost all of the walleyes in the lake. This is not the case, however, when you are dealing with a primary forage base of ciscoes, whitefish and the like. These small fish seek out the cooler water of the depths. They spend much of their time suspended, but move up on the side of deep water points, or the sides of tops of sunken islands to feed. They are often met head on by the walleye, as well as other major predators.

Usually the walleyes won't migrate out to these areas until the dead of summer. That can be mid to late June in some areas, or even near the end of July in more northern lakes.

While it's possible to find some walleyes in depths greater than 60 feet in the warm summer months, most of the catchable fish will be hanging out from about 12 to 30 feet. Often they will change the depth they are feeding at, dropping from the shallows to deep water from early morning to mid day, and moving up to the shallows again in the evening. The astute angler simply follows them up and down the structures, searching out all the tiny nooks and crannies that might attract them along the way.

When you're dealing with walleyes on deep water summer structures, you should look for weeds and rocks. If you can find weeds and rocks together, you could really get your string stretched.

But perhaps you are thinking "everything is rock in Canada, especially in the Shield areas." While that might be true, all rocks are not all the same by any means. A cliff-like wall with a rock slide tumbling down from it may be good for trout, but not walleyes. This is also the case with gigantic boulders, though if placed right these can hold some fish.

What kind of rocky structure, then, attracts summer walleyes? Look first for a food shelf. If you find a sunken island with a little round top, that's no shallower than 20 feet, dropping steeply to real deep water around it, you probably won't find walleyes here in summer. Fall, possibly, but not summer. But if the structure say tops out at 8 to 10 feet, with scattered weeds over a fairly large flat top (the "food shelf"), small rock piles and fingers or points protruding from the side, you're apt to find all kinds of fish, big and little (see Figure 4).

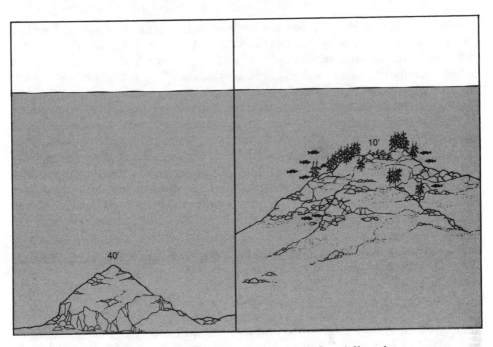

Figure 4. *While searching for summer walleyes remember "all sunken structures are not created equal". Notice the one sunken island that tops off at 10 feet with plenty of weeds, rock fingers, and irregularities has all the fish. The deeper island has very little weed growth or cover, thus, no fish.*

Usually you'll find many more walleyes on structures with a gradually tapering drop to deep water than on those with cliff-like sides. If you want to be proficient at finding these different tapers, a good electronic depth flasher is a must. A graph recorder makes the job even easier. I use and highly recommend the units made by Lowrance. I'd never think of going fishing without them; it's like trying to go deer hunting with a blindfold.

Just finding the island or hump is often not enough. Sure, if you're dealing with one of those virgin Canadian fly-in lakes, you won't have to worry much about doing things that right. The fish will usually be all over any bait you can throw in shallow water. But more often than not, you've got to work harder than that. Too many anglers think that catching fish in Canadian lakes is unbelievably easy, but such fishing is rare even in Canada.

You have to find the fish on the structure. Usually they'll be in a tiny area, perhaps on the side of a big rock, or the very tip of the point, or that small cut in the deep water weedline edge. Look for something small or different on the structure you're fishing and you'll probably run into the biggest fish in the area.

Locating these summertime walleyes is often exasperating, especially if you don't follow an orderly search procedure. Remember, the spot you are fishing could be the best looking on the lake, but if you simply can't catch fish from it at the time you are fishing it, you should leave! You have to find catchable fish.

113

Don't die in one spot. Once you get hooks in a few, figure out as much as you can about exactly where and why you caught them. Then start running the lake and fishing similar situations. You'll probably find a number more schools doing the same type of thing on the same type of structure. This is called "patterning" the fish. Very simply, the more you understand about a "hot spot" the more you'll realize that the fish weren't just there by accident. Normally they are drawn to a particular structure or area by a given set of conditions. Let me give you a recent example.

Last year my dad and I were fishing trout on Great Slave Lake as guests of Chummy Plummer. Chummy mentioned that he knew of some decent walleye lakes, so we decided to fly out and try one. Because of weather conditions, when we finally hit the water, we had less than four hours to fish before the plane had to come back for us. Just a few hours and five thousand acres of water we had never been close to in our lives. It was a challenge. I had brought my Lowrance "Green Box" with me, so we started running the lake, looking for structures. The lake was fairly shallow, so I guessed the walleyes had to be using the shallow water weedbeds.

They were, but not where you'd expect them. The only thing we could catch on the deep water side of the weeds were northerns...loads of them. Figuring the presence of the "snakes" had moved the walleyes right into the weeds, I ran up on top and started fishing the inside edge of the cabbage bed that lay in less than three feet of water. First cast, I hit a fish! The walleyes were stacked in there like cordwood. We boated an even 100 fish in less than three hours and fifteen minutes on Quiver jigs, keeping a limit that averaged out near five pounds.

Easy fishing? Well, not quite. The very next day some others from Chummy's camp went to the same lake and nearly got skunked. Dad and I had patterned the fish exactly, then capitalized on it. The other fellows trolled deep water dropoffs as they always had for walleyes, and they missed the fish. There was no reason for the fish to be deep. If you'll look for patterns, it can make all the difference in the world.

That's also the case in fall. When the cool northwesterlies start to howl, a change comes over the Canadian wilderness, not only on the surface, but in the depths as well. With the return of the cool weather the insect hatches have all but disappeared for the year. There's still some larvae trucking around, but the pickings are slim. The baitfish population has been fed upon heavily for the summer months and is much diminished now. That vast smorgasbord enjoyed by predators like the walleys a few months ago is gone. Time for another major change!

During the first onslaught of colder temperatures, most lakes undergo a fall turnover. The previously stratified lake begins to mix until the thermocline is broken up and oxygenated water enters the deepest portions of the lake. In these conditions the walleyes can go just about anywhere they want to in the lake, and they do. Those fishy-looking deep water structures are no longer off limits as they are in some of the lakes in summer. The walleyes sense the coming long winter. Like most of nature's creatures they go on a heavy feeding spree before the leaner times of winter hit.

The walleyes, especially the big females, are now aggressive hunters and feeders. Even though they may be more scattered now than they were in summer, they are easier to catch. Fall is trophy time. On certain days the big fish really go.

Fall walleyes react a little differently in the two types of lakes that we have been dealing with: the deep, cold trout/walleye lakes and the shallow, somewhat off-colored flat country lakes. But forage fish are still the major key to finding walleyes in both types of lakes.

In the shallow lakes the small minnows and fish that walleyes will feed on are attracted to a variety of structures (see Figure 5). Small rock piles or humps (Area A and B) will hold some fall walleyes, as will points and coontail clumps.

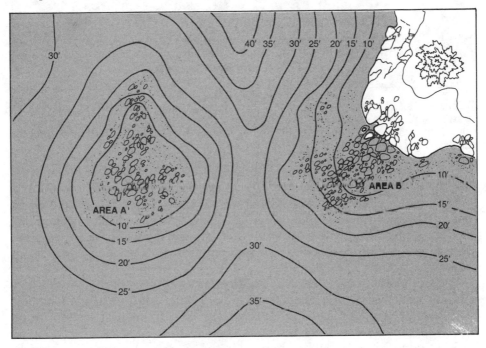

Figure 5. *In shallow, flat bottomed lakes there is very little structure for the fish to relate to. During summer the fish will roam quite a bit, but in the fall they will be more prone to relate to any structure they can find. Little rock piles like areas A and B will probably hold fish as well as weed clumps and points.*

However, areas with current will be by far the most productive during the fall periods on these shallow lakes (see Figure 6). Current areas draw both walleyes and baitfish to a small area where anglers can get at them effectively. The big fish will lay off to one side of the current areas in the deeper water during the day, moving in to "pig out" at night. Of course, all current areas do not have the same potential. Those that have bottom content similar to the preferred spawning bottom, such as gravel or rock/rubble bottoms, usually are best.

Figure 6. *As fall winds cool the lake, you may see another movement of fish into the spawning rivers, especially in shallow lakes. During the day the big walleyes will school up in deep holes and cuts, but under the cover of night they will move into the shallows and "pig out".*

The shallow off-colored lakes will be the first bodies of water to enter the cold water stage. A week or two after these lakes have cooled off, the big, deep, clear trout lakes will also cool down enough to enter the fall cold water period. This is the time to find those big ol' sow walleyes chasing around like the young'uns. The classic location for these deep lake walleyes are often on the steepest dropoffs of shore-connected points or flats, or the steep sides of mid-lake sunken islands.

The key question is "What are they feeding on?" Some of the yearling ciscoes and whitefish will still be using the deep water sunken islands. The best reefs usually will be located adjacent to the largest, deepest section in the lake. And, ordinarily, the more rocks, the better!

Some adult whitefish will be headed in the opposite direction. These high-protein, soft-finned fishes are fall spawners. They seek out gravel shoals on flats and points, from 2 to 10 feet deep, that are adjacent to deep, open water areas of the lake. This spawning ritual could take place on mid-lake islands and sometimes does under the right conditions, but for the most part the best areas will be connected to the shore in some way. Big walleyes, looking for easy pickings, move right in after them and chow down at will. Members of the whitefish family provide the richest source of protein for the walleyes, but not the only source.

Many Canadian lakes have perch as the primary walleye forage species. The population of these fish was recently replenished in spring. Come fall, the new crop of perch are about good eating size. And that's enough to bring in the hungry walleyes. Of course the real lunkers will prefer a big meal, at times seeking out forage that is up to one-half their own body length. That means the adult perch better watch where they go. Perch like weedbeds (if there are remaining green ones) flowing water areas and mud bottom bays with insect larvae. Consequently, that's where walleyes on these types of lakes go in fall.

Fall is definitely lunker time. By understanding where and why the big fish use a certain area, you can rack up some heavy stringers.

One last point: if the lake you are fishing doesn't have any members of the whitefish family or any perch present, you should move to another lake. Shore minnows and insects rarely sustain a healthy population of walleyes year 'round.

You can buy truckloads of different baits and lures for walleyes, and they'll all produce some fish. On the other hand, no one lure type will be the "most effective" all year long. The only rule is that most often you'll catch more and bigger fish on live bait or some combination of live bait and artificial (such as jig and minnow).

Without a doubt, jigging is one of the best—perhaps the best—way to take walleyes on Canadian waters, particularly in early season. Admittedly, there are times and circumstances where live bait rigs, spinners, crankbaits, minnow immitators or even slip bobber rigs might be the big producer for the day or moment. But, day in and day out, jigging will be the most productive on most lakes, most of the time. Don't think for a moment that you can just drag around any old jig and slay the fish. There is quite a bit of technique involved. Unless you are lucky enough to find the fish committing suicide, you must choose your tackle with care and fish it intelligently.

A jig, more than just about any other artificial lure, requires a certain technique and a finely tuned "touch." Concentration and common sense are a big part of it. Knowing what to do and plenty of practice make up the rest.

First, it simply isn't true that "a jig is a jig." Browsing around your favorite tackle shop, you'll notice there appears to be every size, color, length and shape of jig one can imagine . . . plus a few more. To tell the truth, most are made to catch the fisherman's eye, not necessarily the fish. They deal in basic principles.

Without a doubt, the plastic bodied jigs are the best for most walleye fishing. Not that bucktail or feathered jigs don't work, because they do. But walleyes will hold on to a plastic bodied jig longer because of its natural feel. And that helps alleviate one of the trickiest things about fishing with jigs: hooking fish. Those big old walleyes did not get big by being easily fooled.

With a bucktail jig you need extremely fast reflexes to set the hook before the walleye spits it out. But with a jig dressed with plastic like Lindy's Fuzz-E-Grubs, walleyes will give you a bit more time before they spit the jig. That can make all the difference between a full stringer or just some scarred-up minnows.

Right from the start, think small, especially during those times when the walleyes are not feeding aggressively. Small jigs in the one-eighth or the one-quarter ounce range are just the ticket, unless you are dealing with current. Then you may have to use up to a one-half ounce or even heavier jig. The rule

Having an assortment of jigs can be one of the best ways to ensure early season walleye action.

is that you need to control your bait in the situation you are facing. I use the lightest jig I can while still feeling what I'm doing.

Color is very important too. During the early spring fishing, light colors seem to be the best. During the pre-spawn stage white is the best choice, with hot yellow and pink/white becoming more productive as the fish enter the end of the spawn. Later, during the post-spawn when the fish start using the soft bottomed bays and preying on insect larva, colors like brown/orange, yellow or chartreuse become more productive. A guideline for the rest of the season would be to use dark colors like purple and black for dark water. If the water is clearer, light colors such as hot chartreuse or orange may be best.

Tipping the jig with a minnow or other bait will tend to put the odds more on your side. Again, if the walleyes get that familiar "meaty" taste, they will hold on to the jig longer, thus giving you more time to react and sink the hook. This is especially true in clear lakes, which so many Canadian lakes are. However, in some regions of Canada, it isn't legal to use live bait. Here the plastic bodied jig, like the Fuzz-E-Grub or a small Mr. Twister can really make a difference.

You can stick just about any form of live bait on the back of a jig and catch fish. Nightcrawlers, leeches and even water dogs have been used! But a minnow about two to four inches long, hooked through the lips, is still the most popular way of tipping a jig.

118

There is one "secret" that will double your catch when jig fishing for walleyes. No, I take that back...it will triple your catch! That's right, triple it, if you remember to do one thing: keep your line taunt at all times. Each year thousands of walleyes escape the frying pan because unsuspecting fishermen hopped their jigs sloppily, letting their lines become slack when they let the jig fall to the lake bottom.

Most fishermen don't know how a walleye takes a jig. Walleyes very rarely take a jig when it is being pulled up off the bottom, striking instead when the jig is falling back to the bottom. If you are just jerking your offering from the bottom and not paying attention to the fall, your probably missing a minimum of three-fourths of the walleyes that hit your bait. It is easy to overcome this. Hop or swim your bait from the bottom. Then keep the line taunt while it's dropping back down. You should be able to feel your jig at all times. I can't over-stress how important this is.

A good jig fisherman is an artist. In order to be a good artist you must use good equipment. First, because jig fishing is mostly feel and control, graphite rods, quality ones like those made by Lew Childre, are a must. But not just any graphite rod...you need a specific type for jig fishing. I favor a short rod, around 5½ feet, with a light tip and a medium heavy butt. Most of the control when jig fishing should be from your wrist and the top 1½ feet of your rod. If you are using a noodle, you have no way of knowing what your bait is doing. Lew Childre makes a couple of rods that are really suited for this type of fishing, model G56LS for light jigs and a model G56S for heavier ones. At least that's what I use.

A small to medium sized spinning reel, is best. The better ones, like Lew's Speed Spin have a skirted spool and an excellent drag system. Your drag system is critically important. I can't tell you how many big walleyes have been lost near the boat because the drag stuck. In the end it might be better to play them a bit longer than to lose the fish.

The last portion of your equipment, but surely not the least important, is your line. You don't need 40-pound braided rope to land a walleye. For jig fishing I normally use either 6- or 8-pound line, although I'll go to 4 in extremely clear water and 10-pound or heavier if snags are a serious problem. For most of my fishing I favor a clear premium like Stren. Quality equipment is always the best investment.

The larger in diameter your line is, the more it's affected by friction as it moves through the water. This will dramatically impair the action of the jig. Also, with heavy line it is hard to get to deep water, especially if you are using a light jig. Use the lightest line you can for the conditions you are fishing. You're bound to get more action.

Let's get fishing.

There are a number of types of retrieves you'll need to practice to become adept at working a jig. My favorite method is to swim the jig. The trick is to swim it within a foot of the bottom without continually scraping bottom. You'll be jig fishing early season on rocky bottom areas. If you are on the bottom too much, it'll cost you a fortune in jigs. If you are too high off the bottom, it'll cost you a stringer of fish. Your concentration must be absolute. Use a light jig, making as long a cast as you can. Put your rod in the 10 o'clock position and watch your line till your jig touches bottom. The instant it does, close the bail and snap your wrist so the jig swims up a foot or so. Then, with a steady pumping action, bring it back to the boat, allowing it to tick the bottom every few feet so you know where you are (see Figure 7). The strike will most often come from behind, and it will be hard to detect. The jig just sort of gets heavy, even though you can still retrieve it. The problem is that the walleye has it in his mouth but is swimming toward you. When you sense anything out of the ordinary going on, drop your rod tip and sock it to 'em! Often you just won't know if you've had a pickup for sure until you set the hook.

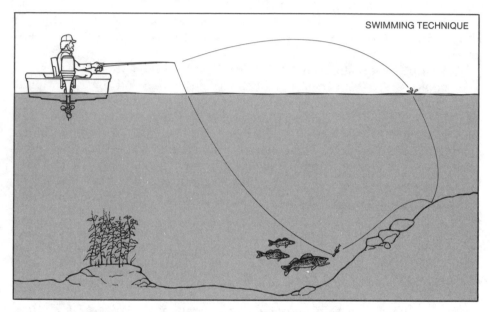

SWIMMING TECHNIQUE

Figure 7. Just tossing a jig out and reeling it back is no way to catch fish, there is more to it than that. My favorite retrieve is to "swim" the jig back to the boat. The idea is to swim the jig within a foot from the bottom without continually dragging it across the bottom. You want to occasionally tick the bottom just so you're sure you are deep enough.

A couple of years ago while fishing Pipestone Lake with a fishing buddy, Kevin Hoffman, this retrieve really saved the trip. Pipestone is an excellent lake, but on opening day had found the fish right at the end of the spawn period. "Tough" wasn't the word for it. I checked 35 places that usually held fish and scrounged up only a couple of loners. Finally I found a bay in it with a primarily mud bottom, except for one short rock/gravel point. All the active fish in this bay were using this point. In the course of three hours we managed to catch over 40 walleyes from the spot, while all the boats around us didn't have a half dozen between them. The walleyes were so spooky that they were spooked if we used a slightly too-heavy jig or a bottom-bouncing retrieve. Of course, the other fishermen thought it was the bait we were using. One guy offered me $10.00 for my Fuzz-E-Grub!

If you find the walleyes in the pre-spawn period or just when they move into the back water bays to feed on insect larvae, a slow, crawling type retrieve is called for. Cold water makes the walleyes, particularly the big ones, lethargic. They're not going to chase down some tiny fly that goes whizzing by. But crawl it right in front of their nose, and a few will come over, roll slowly on their side and scoop it up (see Figure 8). The hit feels like your jig just dropped into a cup of syrup. Again, concentration is critical. Usually the fish won't hang onto the jig for more than a split second. They're just not very hungry.

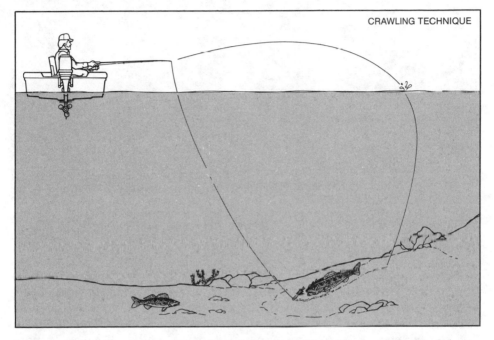

CRAWLING TECHNIQUE

Figure 8. *When the water is real cold and you're dealing with slow, lethargic fish, you should use a crawling retrieve. These slow fish are not into chasing down a jig that whizzes past. By just slowly dragging the jig across the bottom you'll tempt a few into scooping it up.*

Later in summer when the water warms the fishes' metabolism gets going. Then a faster, jumping retrieve will be more apt to trigger them (see Figure 9). At this time of year you'll probaly get more strikes on a stand-up type of bucktail jig like Lindy's Dingo or the Mr. Twister Pow-RR head. A piece of crawler or fat leech on the jig will normally out-produce a minnow ten to one, in the late spring.

Although jigs can be quite effective in summer months, on many lakes there are more effective methods and lure systems. But, unquestionably, good jigs have earned their place in every serious walleye fisherman's box. Don't be caught on the lake without them.

As I mentioned earlier, walleyes normally prefer live bait in some form —nightcrawlers, various types of minnows, water dogs or leeches. The trick is knowing how and when to present each type of bait.

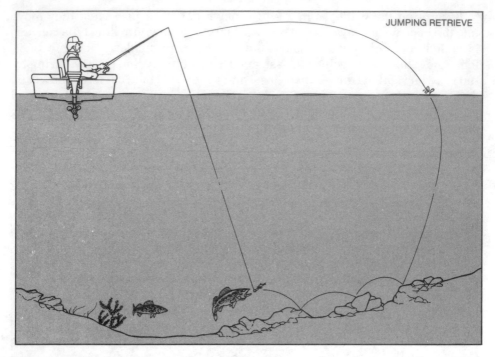

Figure 9. Later in the summer as the fish get more active, a faster, jumping retrieve will trigger more fish. But remember to keep a tight line as the jig is dropping or you will miss most of the fish that do bite.

The famous Prescott Spinner, the Weller Strip-ON and the Little Joe June Bug Spinner have all sacked up their share of lunkers over the years. But in recent years, since the invention of the Lindy Rigging system, many of these old favorites have found their way to the bottom of the tackle box. The Lindy Rig, invented in the mid 60s by the Lindner brothers, Al and Ron, is usually more effective. This system incorporates numerous rigs into an easy, extremely effective method that allows the angler to present his offering in the most natural way possible. And that's normally the way giant walleyes prefer their lunch.

The Lindy rigging system incorporates a specially designed "walking" slip sinker, thread-like line and tiny hooks. The bait is allowed to swim freely without the incumbrance of clumsy terminal tackle. When the fish strikes, simply feed him line. The walking sinker will rest on the bottom, allowing the line to run freely through its large hole so the fish won't detect any drag or unnatural sensations. He'll usually swim off a few feet, swallow the bait and be on his way. About that time is when you come in. When the fish first hits, freely give him all the line he wants, but watch your line. You'll notice that he'll swim a short distance, stop, then take off again. When that happens, close the bail, and drill him a good one! The set should be hard—very hard! You've got to take up all the slack caused by the fish's first run at the bait, and then you have to bury the hook (see Figure 10). That usually takes more "umph" than most anglers give it.

122

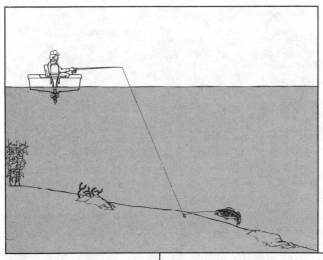

Figure 10. Lindy rigging has evolved to the point where it is the "bread and butter" technique of many walleye fisherman. However, knowing how to handle a "rig" properly is imperative if you are going to be successful.

The whole idea of this concept is to allow the fish to pick up the bait and run with it without feeling anything unnatural. So, when you feel a hit, freely give the fish all the line he wants. The fish will normally peel off several feet of line, then stop, and after a brief moment take off again.

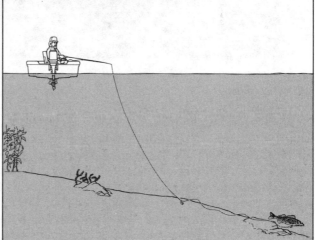

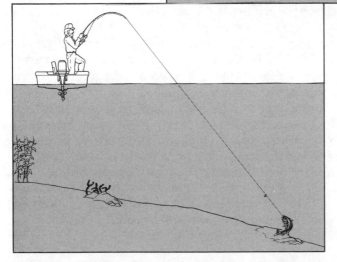

When that happens, close the bail and drill him a good one. You've got to use a long sweep set in order to take up all the slack line the fish peeled off as well as set the hook. So do it with authority.

A well stocked, live bait tackle box will cover many fishing situations you'll face when pursuing walleyes.

When outfitting yourself for Lindy rigging, there are a number of components you'll need. Start with an assortment of "walking" sinkers, ranging in size from ⅛ to ¾ ounce. That should allow you to work your bait on the bottom in nearly any depth or current conditions you'll encounter on your trek to the Canadian wilderness.

Get an assortment of snells in both the minnow and nightcrawler leech sizes. They come in two lengths, 36 and 60 inches. A versatile angler has some of each. Also, you'll need some of the special swivel slips and a "worm blower" for nightcrawlers. Crawlers are usually most effective when you put a small bubble of air in the collar of the crawler to float it off the bottom a bit.

This will round out your basic tools for "rigging" walleyes. Personally, I also carry an arsenal of floating Quiver Jig heads, some floating rigs, and an array of Little Joe Spinners. Colors like chartreuse, white, green orange, gold and silver are best in both the spinners and floating equipment.

For rig fishing I usually start with 8- or 10-pound line. In stained or off-colored water I prefer the fluorescent blue Stren. This line is easier to see. But in clear water, I'll switch to clear Stren. Make a point of cutting off 10 or 15 inches of line after every other fish you catch. This last bit of line gets weakened.

Many anglers like an open-face spinning reel outfit. A good choice is a smaller model reel, such as Lew's Speed Spin 1, matched with a 5 foot-plus rod with a light tip and strong backbone, something like Garcia's G56S. Other anglers use modern free-spooling baitcasting outfits. Both kinds of outfits allow you to release line freely to a walleye running with the bait.

Summer walleyes often school together so tightly they are easy to miss. Besides which, walleyes don't often chase baits very far. You have to put your offering right where they are, with precision. To do that, you need to apply the locational principles detailed earlier, and you need superb boat control.

"Boat control" is not at all the same thing as "running the boat." True boat control means putting your boat—and thus your bait—exactly where it should be, even in a wind. This kind of control is only possible when the boat is run backwards, what is often called backtrolling. Backtrolling permits slow, precise boat maneuvering. You'll get wet on windy days unless you use splashguards on the transom to turn back waves.

You'll also need a means for staying at the right water depth level, some sort of sonar device. Lowrance's 2360 and 2330 are excellent examples. Turn on your sonar as soon as you begin fishing and never take your eyes off it. With your boat at just the right level and moving slowly backwards, drop a Lindy Rig with a crawler (or some other bait) down to the bottom and get ready for some action.

Before you can start catching walleyes, you've got to find them. On a normal walleye summer haunt—such as the tip or sides of a point, or the deep water weedline edge on a sunken island—you just start at one likely depth and keep trolling systematically at various depths until you find how deep they are. If you have a partner, each fishes different baits. After a while you'll have the pattern—where the fish are and what they want.

The better the population of a species in a lake is the more you'll notice they'll school by size. If you've located a school of one- to three-pound fish, the odds are the bigger ones are someplace else. Look for *big fish patterns* if you want to really stretch your string!

If one of your goals on your Canadian excursion is to go after a "wall-hanger," a few tips will help shift the odds in your favor.

There are usually few giant fish compared to the number of smaller ones. Don't expect the trophies to be everywhere. Small spots with ideal conditions are often the best. Take your time and seek them out, then start looking for patterns.

Big fish are normally much more sensitive to light. During the day, look for them in slightly deeper water. In the evening, expect them to enter the shallower water along the route with the best available cover.

You never know just when a huge marbled-eyed monster is going to clamp down on your bait, so be ready at all times. When you are fishing, fish; when you are relaxing, relax. Of the thousands of trophy walleyes that are hooked and lost each year in Canada, most are caused by the angler being too relaxed.

Remember that a trophy walleye's strongest run will usually be immediately after seeing the boat for the first time, so set your drag properly and don't be in a hurry. After all, how long was it that you've been working for that trophy? Can't you wait another couple of minutes?

A favorite big fish bait, at times, is some sort of minnow-immitating plug. Baits such as Lindy's Baitfish and Shadling, Cordell's Redfin, Rapalas and other similar minnow type baits should definitely be in your walleye box.

After putting it all together and taking a trophy, you'll know why people come back year after year to get in on the world's finest walleye fishing.

Early in spring, when the walleyes come up to the shallow bays, slow trolling a Baitfish with a couple of split shot in front can be devastating in the low light periods of early morning and evening. This method is particularly effective on big fish after dark, from the time the walleyes reach the transition feeding peak all the way into the early summer patterns.

But you must be extremely quiet. If I'm fishing a drive-to lake, I always take my own boat because of the twin Minn Kota trolling motors mounted front and back. That way I can stop short of the bay with my big motor, then sneak in with the noiseless electrics. Being quiet is important because big fish are usually ultra-spooky anytime they are in the shallows.

If you fish a lake where you can't bring in a trolling motor, bring the boat down to a low idle speed before entering the bay. Once in the bay, *don't rev the motor!* Just keep it at a calm and steady pace.

These minnow-type baits also work well casting over shallow rock piles in early spring, then again later in summer once the big fish move out to the shallow main lake sunken islands. They'll usually move up sometime after dark, often into only a couple of feet of water. This will be especially true if part of the forage base is shiners.

When you want to get down deeper during the middle of the day, switch to a deeper diving bait, like the Rebel Wee "R", Lindy's Snipes or a host of other brands. Again, like the minnow baits, they are easy to use. Either cast and retrieve, or troll, either way, these lures have a built-in action.

I like to use a small rounded snap (*not* snap swivel) in front of the lure. Makes it easier to change, besides giving a looser action. A loop knot, like the granny knot, works well.

Most crank baits will run deeper, up to a point, the smaller diameter line you use. For most conditions 6- to 8-pound are fine. But if you are fishing primarily after dark, then I'd go to a bit heavier line just to be on the safe side.

One last thing. When a behemoth walleye comes up to smash your Shadling in the wee light hours of evening, you'll wonder how they ever got the reputation of being doggy fighters. These brutes make ferocious runs in shallow water. Matter of fact, about the only thing they're not into is acrobatics. And that's probably just as well. They know plenty of line-breaking tricks already!

When you are pursuing walleyes in these multi-structured Canadian lakes, you should add another weapon to your arsenal. This can almost be your "ace in the hole" when things really get tough...which can even happen in Canada.

Bring along a slip bobber rig. That's right, the same old system that our grandparents used, back when the walleyes "were dumb." Well, some of those dumb walleyes must still be around, because tons of walleyes are caught on bobbers down in the walleye lakes in Minnesota and Wisconsin.

Much of the future of sport fishing depends upon what we as fishermen do today. Catch and release is just one way we can ensure good walleye fishing for a long time.

Slip bobbers are a simple system utilizing a sliding bobber with an adjustable stop. You set the depth by just moving the sliding bobber stop. With this slip bobber system you can cast with ease and reel in a fish without having to contend with the problem of having 14 feet of line between your bobber and bait. Lindy/Little Joe Tackle markets slip bobber rigs complete with bobber, hooks, sinkers and adjustable line stops. No one else does, to my knowledge, on a national basis.

Slip bobbers are probably the simplest method of contending with the old problem of suspended fish. When you find a school of walleyes suspended off a reef or sunken island, simply tie the bobber stop at the depth the fish are and you are all set. The catching part is easy, just let the bobber drift to the school of fish, watch your bobber go down, count to ten and drive the hook home.

This system is beautiful for many different types of walleye fishing conditions. When fishing sunken timber in the back of a dark-bottomed bay, you are able with a slip bobber to put the bait right in front of the walleye's nose without continually getting snagged. And that works the same way when fishing on boulder-covered sunken islands and reefs. When you find a school of spooky walleyes that has set up over a reef or island, the slip bobber really comes in to its own. By letting the bobber rig drift downwind into the school, you can offer them the bait in an ultra-slow and natural way.

Probably the oldest, most widely used bait for catching Canadian walleyes is the Little Joe Spinner. Paired with a simple sinker and minnow, crawler or leech, these rigs have been wreaking havoc with walleye populations for centuries. And like most other bait types, innovation and improvements have developed over the years.

The straight spinner snell, like the famous Little Joe or the Mighty Grip, can be easily used as part of the Lindy rigging system. Simply replace the plain snell with the spinner model. For some reason, fluorescent orange and chartreuse are apt to be your best color choices, although others will catch some fish. But switch around until you find the color the walleyes like best at the time you are fishing.

Recently, a few variations of the spinners have been making headlines. The most popular is the weight-forward spinner like the Tom's Walleye Lure, the Charters Choice and the Wall-Eye Catcher. These lures have a built-in weight ahead of a spinner/hook. All you do is add the live bait.

This type of lure is quite versatile. You can fish it by casting or trolling around points, islands, shoreline cover or weedbeds. Because of their design, they are somewhat weedless.

They really gained popularity a few years ago with the walleye explosion on Lake Erie. On Erie, most summer walleyes are in great suspended schools, and that's where this bait system works best. To use it, cast out and count the lure down once it hits the water. These lures usually drop at the rate of one foot per second. When your bait drops to the desired depth, start the retrieve in a slow pumping manner...and hang on. These baits appeal to all types of fish. You probably won't know what's on the other end until you get 'em to the boat!

Most anglers would give anything to catch just one of these fish, let alone five of them. By using the methods and techniques described here, it's entirely possible to match this stringer.

By now it should be clear that I prefer live bait, either by itself or in combination with some type of artificial. That's primarily because that's the way the walleyes want it. Keep your offering close to the bottom and move it slowly along.

Seasonally, you'll notice that walleyes usually prefer smallish minnows in spring, then make a switch to crawlers and leeches for the summer months, finally switching to crawlers and minnows again in the fall. But during the colder fall months, the old rule of "big bait, big fish" often holds true, so I'll go for minnows in the 4- to 8-inch range if I'm after a biggie, which is usually what I'm after in Canada. Sure I enjoy the acrobatics of a five-pound smallie doing his thing, or the deep water bull-dogging of a giant lake trout as he heads back for the bottom. And I love to catch big northerns, toothy muskie and brook trout too.

But there is something about a giant walleye—one with those milky eyes the size of half dollars, a deep belly and golden sides; one who holds deep, just shaking her head when you can't do anything about it; one who comes up slowly at first, then with the speed of a torpedo heads straight back to the bottom; one who is so tasty, yet eludes thousands of anglers each year. One who . . .

Remember that one?

I do. And she still swims in Canada!

WALLEYE SEASONAL LURE SELECTION

Season	Bait or Lure Type	Size	Color	Remarks
Spring	Fuzzy Grub jig & Minnow	1/16 to 1/4	White, pink/white, chartreuse	Use slide retrieve
	Lindy Rig & minnow	1/8" to 3/8" sinker	Various baitfish colors	Short snell often best
	Minnow baits	3" to 5"		Heavy current — hold in place trolling at night
	Floating jig & minnow	2" to 3"	Fl. green, fl. orange, red	Big boulders
	Rig & crawler			Only after spawn
Early Summer	Floating Quiver jig & leech	Vary snell	Chartreuse, blue, orange	Excellent in new weedbeds
	Jig & minnow	1/16 to 3/8 oz	Brown/orange, yellow	Swim or jump retrieve
	Lindy Rig & leech or crawler	Various weights		Most productive under most conditions
	Jig & twisters	Various	Yellow, white, black	Night trolling shallow
	Minnow baits	Medium	Silver, blue, orange	Shallow rock piles
	Slip bobber rigs			Murky water
	Spinner & crawler		Various - orange is good	
Late Summer	Live bait rigs	Jumbo leeches and crawlers	Vary	Vary snell lengths
	Weight forward spinners	3/4 to 5/8 oz	Various	Great for suspended fish
	Crank baits	Bass size	Chartreuse - brown	Use for edges of weedbeds
	Minnow baits	Shadling or Baitfish	Blacks - blue	
	Speed trolling divers	Shadling - Hellbender	Various	Good during hot muggy days
	Large spinner & crawler	#4 to #6 blades	Chartreuse	Fish at night over weedbeds
	Slip bobber rigs	Jumbo leeches		Use for fishing pockets in weedbeds
Fall	Jig & minnow	1/8 to 1/2 oz	Yellow, brown, grape, white, chartreuse	Fish slow
	Lindy Rig & minnows	4" to 8" redtails		Best bet usually
	Lindy Rig & crawler			Cold front days
	Minnow baits	6" to 8"	Silver, gold, blue	River mouths or narrows at night

Chapter 7
Smallmouth Bass:
The Bronze Bombshell

Much has been said for the fighting qualities of different species of gamefish. A stalwart member of the trout fraternity may tell you that no fish can match the leaping, acrobatic and brilliantly colored rainbow trout. The angler that pilots his 20-foot craft out on the Great Lakes will tell you no fish can compare with the king salmon with their long, drag-smoking runs. Musky fishermen, northern nuts and largemouth freaks will all defend their favorite fish. And the list goes on.

All these fish deserve the respect they win. However, one spunky fish that will always rise up out of the commotion of these arguments as a top contender is the pugnacious smallmouth bass. This Sugar Ray Leonard of the fish world will put on a show, once hooked, that will impress the fans of any other species.

The smallmouth is very common in certain parts of Canada. In fact, in some areas, it is the "bread and butter" gamefish. Many people truck on up to the north country with lakers, muskies or northerns on their mind, only run into a bunch of smallies. Before they know it, they've completely forgot about the fish they've come for because they are having too much fun catching smallmouth.

Recently, I was with a group that returned from a spring fishing trip to an Ontario lake where we hoped to string up some really big walleyes. But luck was not with us. The huge marble-eyed fish that we knew were there just plain turned off. Try as we did, we couldn't turn them. However, the same weather that turned the walleyes off triggered the smallmouth into moving to the shallows.

After cruising the shoreline and watching with polarized sunglasses, we spotted some smallies hanging under timber, rocks and other cover. In order to tempt the fish into coming out from the cover we knew that it would take some pinpoint casting with something very tempting, like a jig and a wriggling leech. We then pulled up to one of the spots where we had seen a big smallmouth under a log and flipped out the jig and leech.

The Fuzz-E-Grub slowly filtered down until it rested on the bottom right next to the hidey-hole of the bass. It was exciting to watch. After the jig had settled to the bottom, the leech began to stretch out and wriggle in a way that would turn any fish inside out. Soon a nose and two eyes slid out from the log and studied the jig for only a second. With a tremendous rush, the fish snatched up the jig and ran back for the log. The fight was on! The bass fought with leaps, jumps and all kinds of aerial tactics. It took some time before we boated the bronze-colored, robust fish. And that fish was just the beginning. For the next few days, this scenario was repeated many times. And you can believe we soon forgot about the walleyes. We were just having too much fun.

The smallmouth bass is a moderately large fish, usually 12- to 20-inches long. They have a typical bass-like body that is laterally compressed, much like its near relative, the largemouth bass. Smallies can get up to six or seven pounds, but usually run up to four pounds.

The overall coloration of the fish can vary with the age and habitat the fish live in. In darker bodies of water the fish tend to be darker. In clear waters the bass will be lighter.

The background color of the fish can be brown, golden-brown or olive colored. Smallies have vertical markings running along the fish's side that can be quite pronounced or only vaguely visible. Like most members of the bass and sunfish group, the smallmouth has orange or red eyes.

As common and prolific as the smallmouth can be in parts of Canada, it is not native to much of this area. The original range of the smallie is primarily the eastern, fresh waters of the United States. This included parts of the Great Lakes and the St. Lawrence water systems. Through early and sometimes very primitive methods, the bass were carried into these new waters and released. Many smallmouths found themselves living in milk cans or pails until they were released in their new homes.

The area where most of the stocking was done are the lakes northeast of the Lake of the Woods. These lakes and rivers proved to be ideal for the fish, and today the smallmouth flourishes in the clear, rocky lakes of this area in addition to other sections of the Shield region. This beautiful land now boasts of perhaps the best smallmouth fishery in the entire world.

One of the main reasons the smallmouth has become so prolific is the ability of this fish to adapt to any situation. The smallmouth flourishes in the gin clear, oligotrophic lakes that are so common in the Canadian Shield. But surprisingly enough, smallmouth also multiply in the shallow, darker water lakes that can be just across the road.

Presently, the range of the smallmouth bass stretches from southern Nova Scotia eastward through southern Quebec and Ontario. In recent years the bass have pushed westward into central Saskatchewan and established isolated pockets in Alberta and British Columbia. Upon looking at a map, the angler from the United States will be pleased to note that this smallmouth belt is conveniently located all along the U.S./Canadian border. That makes it easy to take a vacation by car to sample some of the fastest action a fisherman can find.

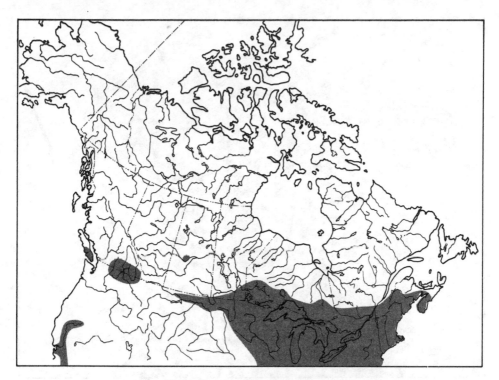

The Home Range of the Smallmouth Bass

Smallmouth bass are a spring spawning fish. They move into the shallows to spawn when the water reaches a temperature ranging from 55 to 68 degrees F. In southern Canada, where the smallmouth are most prevalent, this usually happens in late May to early June, but can be as late as July during a late spring. The length of spawning will vary depending on whether spring is early or late.

As the water nears the temperature that triggers the spawning urge, the fish move into their pre-spawn locations. The ideal place for pre-spawn smallies is the first breakline (dropoff) out from the areas where they will eventually spawn. Usually these breaklines occur in 8 to 15 feet of water. An ideal situation is shown in Figure 1. As the fish move in from the main lake to spawn in the bay, they encounter a sharp rise in the lake bottom from 15 to 10 feet. There are scattered boulders where the fish can feel protected and secure. All in all, this is an excellent place to begin your search for pre-spawn smallies.

The smallmouth bass may hang around the breaklines for a few days or as much as ten days if the weather turns cold. But, if the sun shines and bays warm up, the bass will soon venture into the spawning areas. Prime spawning habitat is a sand or gravel flat connected to shore in about 2 to 5 feet of water. If the shallow flat is adjacent to deeper water, like about 6 to 10 feet, that's all the better. At first the bass will move in and out of the spawning areas until conditions are prime.

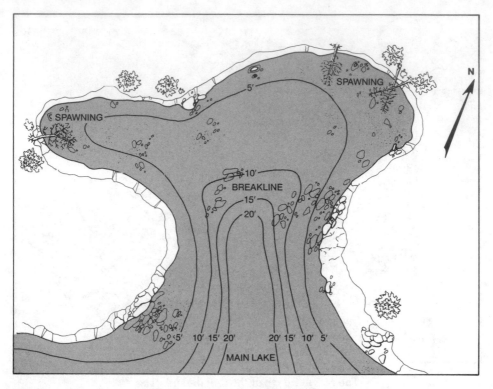

Figure 1. *Pre-spawn smallies can be quite confusing, but they needn't be. This is an ideal example of where you should find pre-spawn fish. The bay shown here is a prime spawning bay connected to the main lake. Just outside the spawning area is a sharp dropoff which will hold fish prior to their move to the shallows. There is enough depth and scattered boulders present so the fish will feel safe and protected.*

During the spawn, the large female fish become very difficult to find. Most of the spawning is done at night. During the day the females head for deep water, where they are shy and inactive. Actually, the females are hard to find during the pre-spawn period all the way up until they enter their summer locations and habits. So you see very few stringers with big bass on them during this part of spring. Most of the fish you catch will be smaller "buck" bass.

The spawning area will be more attractive to the fish if there is cover present. Objects such as large boulders, logs or pieces of wood seem to further enhance the sand, gravel or rubble area. Many times I've studied the bass in spring to check different areas out and see what they preferred. Shoreline with gravel and sand bottoms but no cover would have few, if any spawning beds. Shorelines that had sand and gravel bottoms along with scattered boulders or stumps and logs would often have beds every 10 to 15 feet.

Some lakes have no decent spawning areas for the bass to use. Then you might find bass spawning on sand flats where there is no cover available. Or, on lakes with only areas of muck or silt bottoms, the bass may build nests on rocks, logs or other hard surfaces.

Earlier in the season, smallies will use the shoreline, rock points shown here. Later, many of them will move out to the rock piles in the lake.

The male bass are the first to move into the spawning areas. Upon arriving, they will fan out a nest in rock/gravel bottomed areas. This fanning clears away any silt and leaves a clear place on which the female can lay her eggs. Many times these nests are visible, and with polaroid sunglasses you can spot them easily.

Whenever possible, the male bass will fan out a nest under, or near some sort of cover. It is very common to see a bed, or nest, along a submerged log, or right underneath the log if there is enough space there for the fish. Other places where you may find beds are crevices between boulders, places where logs rest on each other, or other protected areas.

Smallmouth bass prefer those shorelines that catch the early spring sunshine, which is the northwesterly shore. These shorelines may be several degrees warmer than a southerly shore or the main lake water. For example, if you traveled along a bay that was attractive to spawning bass, you'd find few, if any, beds on the southern shore. The number of beds would increase until they became very frequent as you traveled north. However, any wind-protected area will warm quickly, so don't pass up any likely areas, no matter what direction they're facing. Keep your eyes open for small bays, channels and other areas that warm quickly.

After the arrival of the females, spawning will take place. Once the eggs are laid and fertilized, the females will move out of the shallows into deeper water to rest. Now an interesting thing takes place. The male bass remain with the nest and guard the unhatched eggs. The fish will chase predators away and gently remove silt or any other foreign matter out of the nest until the young are hatched. This unique prenatal care greatly increases the number of young bass fry that survive the vulnerable egg stage of their development. This is probably the reason smallmouth bass have become so numerous in this area in such a short time.

I've come to believe that bass not only have flourished because of extremely protective guardians, but because they are extremely cunning.

One still evening, my friend Jeff and I were fishing smallmouth along a shoreline where we had some nice action the day before. We were slowly working our way along when Jeff noticed a dead smallmouth on the bottom. It was pale and still, perhaps dead for a couple of days. Naturally we passed by the fish, looking for something a little more lively, when the little guy suddenly came to life. It righted itself, saw that we had gone by and then raced off toward deep water. Needless to say, we were surprised and out-smarted by him!

Early in the season, the male smallmouth are fearlessly defending their nests. You can find the fish by looking for their fanned out nests with a pair of polarized sunglasses. Once you spot a nest, the bass will not be far away.

After the male bass completes his paternal duties, he too moves out into deeper water. The location of bass is now, and for the rest of the summer, controlled by water temperature and the availability of food. If you find the right combination of the two, you will find summer smallies. The prime summer prey of the smallmouth during the summer is the crayfish. This small crustacean is quite common in the lakes and rivers throughout much of Canada, living in the nooks and crannies in rock piles.

Crayfish prefer to inhabit rocky areas like crumbling granite walls, high rocky bluffs that drop into gradually sloping shorelines or rocky points and islands. These areas are preferred because most of the rocks found there are small. Any area with rocks that are fist-sized to basketball-sized will hold crayfish and, almost surely, smallmouths.

Once the bass find an area with crayfish, they will nose around among the rocks searching for the delectable little crustaceans. Smallies love the crayfish so much that they will literally stuff themselves to the gills with them. At times I've pulled in smallmouths that regurgitated crayfish all the way to the boat. They really go for them.

Where you find broken rock you will probably find smallies scrounging for crayfish. Often you can fool one into taking your bait instead.

Prime summer habitat for smallmouth bass is an area where you have rocks and fairly deep water, perhaps 8 to 20 feet. Good examples are sunken islands with rocky tops, deep water points and submerged rock piles. In a typical smallmouth lake in Canada, the bass leave the bays where they have been spawning and move into the main lake. Once there, they set up along the deep water points, islands and rock-strewn bottoms. The number of smallies that will hold around prime areas will astound you. I remember fishing a lake in southern Ontario that is well-known for it's excellent smallmouth fishing. After a little exploratory fishing, we noticed a definite pattern. The fish were on the main lake rock piles, prowling over them looking for food. We could flip a jig out over the visible top of the rocks and work it in with a lively retrieve...and the fish would nail it nearly every time. In the crystal clear water we could see the jig hopping across the rocks until a bronzeback would come and hit the jig like a blitzing linebacker. I couldn't believe how many fish were in that area.

This is a common summertime pattern, one that you will find successful on most lakes and rivers for that matter. Simply find an island, point or rock pile that will hold crayfish, minnows, or other forage foods, and that is in close proximity to deep water. If you find these conditions, you should find the warm weather smallmouths.

A typical smallmouth lake is shown in Figure 2. It has a section of the main lake body close to a spawning bay. Upon leaving the bay when the main body warms up to about 65 degrees, the bass will take up residence in the first structure they encounter that will supply them with a food source, depth and water temperature.

Areas B and C will first attract early summer smallmouth bass. Both spots have points coming off from shore that extend out into deeper water. The rocks on them will attract minnows, crayfish and other foods. These in turn will attract the fish. These places also offer the necessary deep water nearby.

Area A is a rocky tip of an island that extends out into deeper water. These areas are very similar to areas B and C and will just as likely attract summer smallmouth. Whenever you come across an island, you should always check for points that will extend out from it and pull in fish.

Area D is an underwater rock pile, which is common in many lakes in smallmouth country. Whenever you come across one of these, make sure you fish it. These rock piles often come up out of deep water to top off from one to eight feet of water. They are often visible to the naked eye, especially if you are wearing polarized sunglasses. But be careful because these rock piles can be treacherous and really do a number on the hull of your boat or your motor's lower unit.

Once you have located a summer holding spot for smallmouth bass, take note of it. Smallmouths are notorious homebodies. The fish often stay around the same structure throughout the entire summer. The same is true of river smallies. They will often set up in one hole and spend much of their entire lives there. The only movement they make out of the spot is to spawn.

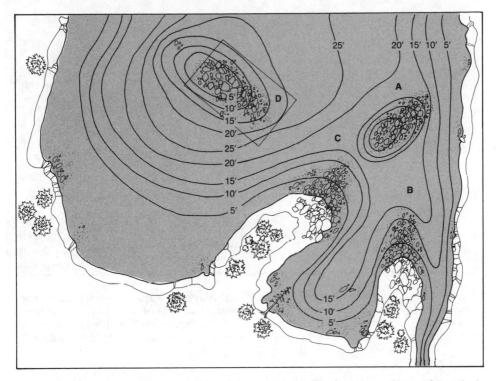

Figure 2. Finding summer smallmouth is easy, if you take the time to learn about their needs and what attracts them. As the bass leave the spawning bays they will stop at the first place that offers food, proper depth and water temperature. This shows a typical situation found in many Canadian lakes. Areas B and C will be the first spots to attract fish because they are the first prime habitat the fish find as they leave the bay. Gradually the fish will disperse out to areas A and D which offer the same conditions the smallies are looking for.

Another key summertime hangout for smallmouths are the cabbage weedbeds that are common to many Canadian lakes. Many times these beds are located at the mouth of incoming rivers, on top of sand bars or on sunken islands.

The smallies will move to edges of these beds after the water temperature warms and the weeds begin to fill out to form thick, green beds. There are plenty of minnows, forage fish, and insect larvae living in these beds, besides which the weeds offer shelter. No wonder they can be real "honey holes" for summertime smallmouth bass (see Figure 3).

Don't overlook other cover such as flooded timber and bulrushes. There have been times I've caught smallies in a stretch of rushes until my arms ached.

Another factor that makes summertime smallies a real treat to fish is their schooling habits. In areas of prime habitat, the bass may school up by the dozens. When you get over one of these huge schools, you will know it. Sometimes

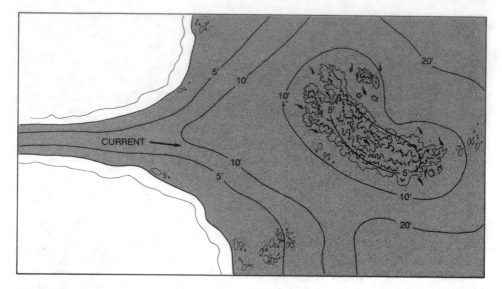

Figure 3. Cabbage beds are another excellent place for summer smallmouth. These beds are often found just outside of river mouths, on tops of sand bars, or sunken islands. As the weather warms and the beds fill out, they attract smallies like a magnet. Concentrate on small pockets, fingers of weeds and other ambush spots along the edge.

when you hook one and bring it to the surface there will be six, eight, ten, even a dozen other bass following it, trying to steal the bait. At times I've even caught two on one lure. Those are the days you talk about around the winter stove.

As the first cold winds of fall come whistling out of the north, the bass make a move for deeper water. Most of the time they will not leave the structure they were holding near during the summer, but simply move farther down the edge of the point or sunken island or other structure they were using. But, believe me, they will go deep. By the time the water temperature is in the mid-40s you can find the fish in the 20 to 30 foot range. When the water reaches about 37 degrees, the fish can be 40, 50 even 60 feet down. While 60 feet may be an extreme, it is common to be fishing in 20 to 50 feet of water in the fall.

To help put this all in perspective, let's take a typical smallmouth lake in Canada, such as the one in Figure 4. There are many areas that will hold smallmouth bass, but some are much better than others. Area A is an excellent spot for fall smallmouth. It is an underwater point that juts out from the shoreline to 40 feet of water. During the summer the fish will be found up higher on the point in the shallows, but when the water cools they will move down the point to the deep water. This is a perfect place to catch bass in the fall.

Area B is a sunken island that tops off at 25 feet. Fall smallmouths move out from the shoreline related structures that lack any deep water to deep water humps like this. Notice that the entire hump is between 25 and 45 feet deep, so the bass could be located just about anywhere on the hump. However the bass will most likely be on the southern edge of island B where it drops off into the deepest water. Also look for small rocky fingers, or points, that come off from the main hump. Chances are if there is a change in the contour like this, some bass will be there.

Area C is another sunken island or hump, but in this case it is connected to shore by a "saddle." In situations such as this the bass will move out from Area D, which is ideal summer habitat for smallmouths, and follow the point out to Area C. Here they will scatter along the deeper edge of the island and stay for the fall. Area C has the potential to be a real smallmouth hotspot.

Area D can also be a good bet for fall smallmouth fishing. Even though it may prove to be better during the summer, it still has water deep enough to hold bass during the fall season. The rocky bottom will also be attractive to bass and will hold fish there much of the year.

On the other hand we have Area E, which will not likely hold smallmouth bass in the fall. Even though it has a few boulders on the bottom and is adjacent to deep water it lacks the typical fast drop that attracts smallmouth in fall. Concentrate your efforts on rocky points and islands that drop fairly rapidly into water that is deep enough, like 20 to 40 feet deep, or even deeper at times.

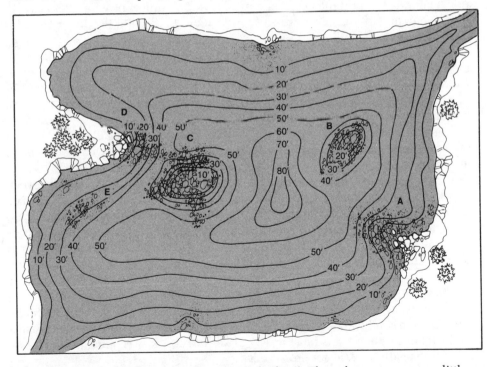

Figure 4. Smallmouth are notorious "home bodies". They choose to move as little as possible. As fall approaches, smallmouth will not normally leave the points and structures they inhabited all summer, but will go down much deeper on the edges. But if the structure does not have thirty, forty, or even fifty feet of water nearby you might as well forget it. You'll notice that areas A, B, C, and D, have steep dropoffs to deep water. On the other hand, area E, which does not have much of a "fast drop" to the deep water, will probably be marginal fishing at best.

If I had a choice of what season I would fish for king-sized smallmouth bass, it would be fall, hands down. Most species of gamefish have a definite spurt of activity during the fall, and this is especially true of the smallmouth bass. I have seen more stringers of monster smallies taken in the fall than any other season. So, if a wall-hanger smallmouth is your goal this year, try fall fishing. I'll guarantee you'll have some hot fishing during some cool days.

The smallmouth bass fishery in Canada is an almost untapped resource. Only ten years ago many anglers considered them trash fish and would totally ignore them. This is one of the reasons why Canadian smallmouth fishing can be perhaps the angling experience of a lifetime for you.

Smallies are usually quite aggressive and will strike at a host of lures and baits in spring, summer or fall. Even though the smallies are usually ready and willing, certain lures and techniques will produce the best at different times.

Spring smallies can be taken on several lures or baits. When the fish have moved up to the edges of rock shoals and bars in their pre-spawn movements, you need to remember that you may be fishing in water that is fifteen to 25 feet deep. It is necessary to use a rig that will get down to the fish, such as a Lindy's Flikker Snell in gold or silver colors, tipped with a minnow. The type of minnow is not that important so you can use fatheads, shiners or whatever is available. Year in and year out, I have found this to be the top producer for very early pre-spawn smallies.

The technique is quite easy to use (see Figure 5). Often the fish will be situated along a breakline in 15 to 25 feet of water prior to their move into shallow water to carry out their spawning ritual. Once you have located a school of fish, troll the Flikker snell along the break, making sure it gets down to where the fish can see the rig. As you troll, give the bait action by lifting your rod tip one or two feet in a pumping motion. This causes the spinner blade to rise and fall in a helicoptering motion and will trigger some vicious strikes. This is an unbeatable combo for pre-spawn smallies.

When the water gets warmer the fish will move right up onto the rock shoals and points. One day you may fish these spots and get very few fish and the next day it will be full of them. Since the water is more shallow now you must adapt by using more subtle methods and seductive presentations. I normally switch to a light spinning rod and load my reel with a clear, light line, such as clear Stren in six pound test. Time and time again I've seen people using four- or six-pound line catching fish like crazy while a person with eight- or ten-pound test line will catch only a few.

I usually switch to a jig tipped with a minnow, crawler, water dog, or leech during these shallow conditions. Of all these live baits, however, I love to use a leech. These little rascals have a way of slithering and wriggling that drives a reluctant smallmouth absolutely crazy.

Another reason why I prefer jigs for this type of fishing is that many times these shallow areas are littered with rocks, boulders, logs and brush. You would be pulling your hair out in frustration if you used most lures because you would be getting snagged continually. With a jig you can cast your offering up along the debris and let the live bait "call out" the fish. Many times the tipped jig will lie next to a log for a few moments until the bass hiding there

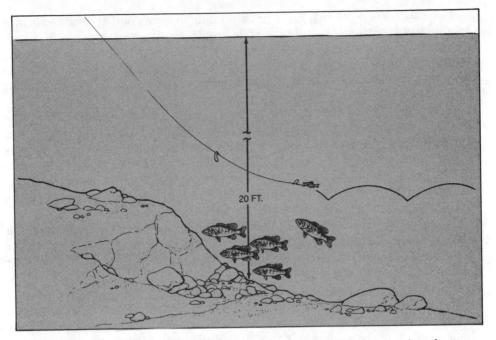

Figure 5. *Since pre-spawn smallies hang on breaks that may be 15 to 20 feet deep, you need to use a bait system that will get down to them. A favorite technique is to troll a flikker snell tipped with a 2-3 inch minnow along the breakline. As you troll, give the bait action by lifting your rod tip 1 or 2 feet in a pumping motion. This causes the light spinner to flash and fall in a hellcoptering motion, triggering some vicious strikes.*

can take it no longer and will rush out to scarf up the morsel. It's an exciting way to fish.

Many types of jigs will work for this type of fishing, but I prefer Lindy's Fuzz-E-Grubs, Lindy's Quiver Jigs and Mr. Twisters. Colors such as brown-orange, crawfish, or chartreuse work best for me. They seem to match the natural food that the smallmouths are accustomed to. If you prefer to use artificial baits, try a 1/8 ounce jig/spinner or a small floating minnow (such as a Rapala) with a small split shot attached to the line.

Small straight-shaft spinners can also really turn these crafty bass on. Small Lindy's Chicos, Mepps Spinners and Rooster Tails are all excellent choices. Again, use light, clear line and make long casts so you don't spook the fish. The best way to maneuver yourself into position when fishing these spooky fish is with an electric trolling motor. I have two Minn Kota electrics, one mounted on the bow and one on the stern, so I can work my boat quietly even in the most demanding situations.

Once the water temperature starts to warm up, these shoreline bass become a little more aggressive. Not only will they still take small spinners and jigs, but they now will really go for minnow baits. Lures such as Rapalas, Lindy Baitfish, Redfins and Hellcats have all proved to work well. Experience has shown that natural colors such as silver and browns work very well. But, orange or fluorescent orange seem to be the best colors.

145

If the water is quite shallow, work a floating minnow bait across the surface in a pumping retrieve. It will take your breath away when your minnow suddenly disappears in a gusher-like strike. Or, if the water is deeper, retrieve the bait faster so that it dives down near the range of the fish. Sometimes even bumping the lure on rocks or tree stumps will trigger fish into bashing your lure.

Hot, sultry days of summer are the time to put on the crank baits. This is the formula for some of the biggest catches of smallmouth bass for the entire year. Typically, the bass will be concentrated around shoreline structures such as rocky points, talus piles, crumbling granite walls, and brush piles. These spots can be great, but only if they are shallow. Of course this depends somewhat on the water clarity. If the water is murky the fish will probably be in water less than fifteen feet. In ultra-clear water the fish will be deeper.

The best structures are those that top off right at the surface. However, a sunken island that tops off right at the surface also should have some sort of cover to attract the fish and provide protection for them. Usually this cover is in the form of boulders or cabbage weeds.

There are so many crankbaits on the market today that deciding on a particular one can be confusing. Just remember that each style has its own unique action and gives off a different vibration. Gamefish pick up on these vibrations. And, at certain times, one vibration will turn on fish more than another vibration. Some plugs have tight actions and long bills that cause them to dive down deep. On the other hand, there are shorter, fatter plugs with short bills that have a loose action and run shallow. Then you have the longer baits that have a very tight, vibration action. Each of these styles can be good at times.

Colors can be important, too. In dirty water with little light penetration, I'll use darker colors so the lure will have a sharp, clean silhouette for the fish to zero in on. In clearer lakes, I'll use light colored baits such as bone with an orange belly, or even chrome. Most fish strike, not because they're in a feeding mood, but because they are in a striking mood. So visibility is very important.

In dark water you may want to consider using a crankbait with a rattle inside. That gives the fish a sound to attract them in addition to a silhouette. However, I feel that a rattling lure works against me in clear water. Just use noisy lures in murky conditions.

When you use a crankbait, never attach it to your line with a heavy, cumbersome leader or swivel. That will only kill the natural action built into the lure. The best way is to use a light snap or a loop knot, such as the Uni-knot. That allows the lure to work naturally, which of course will put more fish in the frying pan for you.

It is very important to use the correct type of rod when you are pitching crank baits. With a soft action "buggy whip" rod it is hard to cast the lure accurately enough. On the other hand, a stiff "pool cue" rod is not the answer either. If the rod tip doesn't flex enough, you'll be worn out from the effort of casting before the morning is over. And believe me, when you are fishing with crankbaits you'll be doing a lot of casting. I like to use a light 5'2" or a 5'6" graphite casting rod.

A good selection of crank baits and minnow baits will help put smallies in the boat under most conditions.

A graphite rod will help you observe the action of the lure and pick up on light strikes. As the crankbait runs it gives off vibrations that are picked up by the rod tip. As long as that quivering continues your lure is running correctly. However, if a smallmouth happens to hit the lure and swim along with it, the tip will stop vibrating. So when that tip stops, set the hook. You may have an angry bronze-colored torpedo on the end of your line.

Proper presentation and retrieves are also essential. When you are fishing rocky points and reefs, remember the bump-and-go retrieve. After you've cast the lure, reel it in as fast as you can and make it dive down deep. This will make the lure run right into the rocks and boulders. When you feel the lure smack a rock, stop reeling and let it suspend for a moment. Then quickly start retrieving it again. Often the bass will hit it when you let it suspend after hitting the rock, or when the lure takes off again.

Try varying your retrieves. Many times it takes a certain speed or action to turn a school of smallies on. Try fast, medium and slow retrieves. You may want to try stop-and-go retrieves, or a pumping action. Just keep experimenting until you find whatever trips their trigger.

Good boat control is also important. If you can't position the boat properly it is not possible to work the point, island, or structure correctly. Often the bass will school up in one small area of a larger piece of structure. If you don't get your lure or bait to that one spot, you may not catch anything (see Figure 6).

From the illustration you can see that this particular point could only be correctly covered by moving the boat at least once. If the anglers had only given the point a lick and a prayer from position 1 they might have gone fishless, but from position 2 they were able to hit the pocket that held the fish.

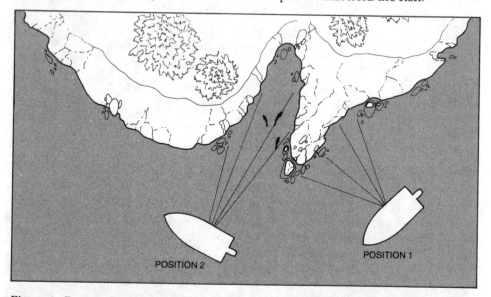

POSITION 2

POSITION 1

Figure 6. *Boat positioning is critical when working shallow water fish. If you casually drift along, giving each spot a "lick and a prayer", you may miss out on much of the action. A person in Position 1 may think he has covered the point well enough, yet, unless he moved his boat to Position 2 he would never reach the fish that were there.*

148

A properly presented crankbait has proved to be the undoing of many prized smallmouth bass.

The ideal way to move your boat along the shoreline and effectively cover all potential spots is with an electric trolling motor. Usually outboards will be too noisy for use in shallow water and will spook all the big fish out. With an electric you can creep along and really cover an area (see Figure 7). I personally use a Minn Kota that has variable speeds that I can turn down for just barely creeping along to work a fallen tree or turn it up on high for beating the wind as I come around a point. If you couple this electric motor with a good deep-cycle battery such as a Gould Action Pack you can troll all day on a charge. You just can't beat a system like this for creeping up on bronzebacks along shoreline structures.

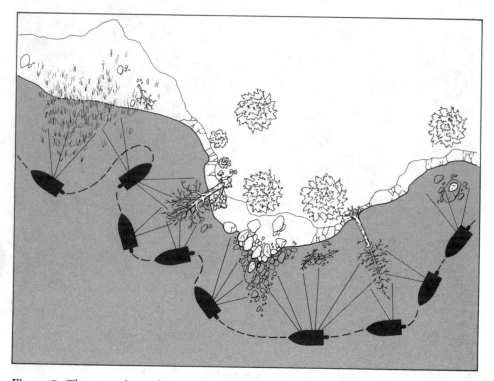

Figure 7. *The use of an electric trolling motor can make shallow water casting and positioning a breeze. In addition, you can silently creep along without spooking any fish, and thoroughly work the area.*

When the bass are along rocky points, sunken islands, or just about any type of structure, you can take them with Lindy rigs. These rigs are as deadly on smallmouth as they are on walleyes. You can troll them around sunken structures such as islands, reefs and rock piles. Or, you can cast them around shoreline-related structures such as logs, rocks and other debris. Just let the bait sit for a moment and then slowly bring it back to the boat. This works especially well when the bass are not very aggressive.

I have had success using all types of live bait on rigs. Leeches will work, crawlers are great, and minnows have their place at times too. But, during the summer, it is hard to beat a crayfish for smallie bait. Crayfish make up as much as 90 percent of a smallmouth's diet during the summer, so you can see why they are so effective. If you are interested in trophies try fishing with a water dog. Small fish normally won't bother them, but big smallies love them.

Jigs are also an excellent choice for summer smallies. By casting the jig around these summer hangouts, you can often catch a bunch. One super method is to cast the jig up on a point, sunken island or rock reef and then reel it off the edge, letting it slowly fall down the steep sides.

The idea is to position your boat so you can work the area completely and cast to the edges of the structures. After you cast do not engage your reel but allow the line to play out as your jig sinks toward the bottom. If you engage the reel there will not be enough line out to let the jig fall freely down, so it will swing back toward you and not even reach the fish. Let the jig fall until it hits the bottom or stops. When it does, tighten up the line and feel for a fish. If you feel any life at the other end, set the hook immediately. Often a pot-bellied smallmouth will inhale a jig as it free-falls down toward the bottom.

You can further enhance the effectiveness of the jig by tipping it with some sort of live bait. Minnows, nightcrawlers, leeches, crayfish or water dogs all will take fish. Regardless of which bait you use, make sure that it is fresh and lively. Many times it is the action and movement of the live bait that will make the difference between no fish and a stringer full. So don't settle for dead or shriveled-up bait.

If you don't have any live bait, or can't find any available in wilderness regions, try tipping the jig with a twister tail, shad tail or piece of pork. Not only do these work as well as natural baits at times, but they are much more durable and will stay on your hook longer. Also they don't require any special care; just tuck them in your tackle box for safe keeping. Yellow, chartreuse, brown and orange tails all work well on these Canadian fish. But, my favorite is a silver tail. Pork rinds come in different colors too, but I usually bank on the natural white or frog finish for best results.

Spinnerbaits have proved to be extremely effective and versatile for smallmouth bass during the summer. Often when I come across a shallow weedbed, or a rock pile that comes up from deeper water, I'll throw spinnerbaits. A brisk retrieve across the tops of these structures can really drum up some heart-stopping action.

One day I spotted a big red and white bobber floating out in the middle of the bay. As I got closer I saw the bobber marked a rock pile that came up to within a foot of the surface. There were a few broken boulders littered across the top, so I figured I'd give it a whirl with a spinnerbait. The water was extremely clear. With my polarized glasses I could easily see the white spinnerbait as I retrieved it back to the boat.

As I watched the action of the lure a huge wake suddenly appeared as at least half a dozen bass followed the spinnerbait. As the distance between the biggest fish and the lure rapidly closed, I got all set for the best part. It finally came in a huge showering splash. The charging bass must have crossed 15 feet of water before he finally got to the lure. As I reared back on the rod it bent in a dangerous circle and I knew I was onto a real tackle-buster. Up he came again, gills flaring red and bronze sides flashing in the brilliant sunlight. Finally I landed the chunky little gladiator, a fish of about five pounds. I love to catch smallmouth like that and fry them up golden brown, but I was happy to slide that bass back into the water. He sat there for a moment and worked his gills before swimming for the deep water next to his boulder pile. It was hard to believe the number of smallmouth bass on that rock cap. Cast after cast resulted in smashing strikes. Experiences like that keep me coming back for more spinnerbait fishing.

Usually the bass will be quite aggressive when they see a spinnerbait pulled over a rock pile or weedbed. However, at times they can develop a case of lock-jaw. Sometimes you can turn these fish on by "helicoptering" a spinnerbait. This technique works extremely well when you're working rock piles and cabbage beds. Just retrieve the lure across the top of the structure until it reaches the edge. Then stop the lure and let it fall down the edge, spinning and fluttering seductively (see Figure 8). When things go right, the lure may fall into the jaws of a waiting bass. Helicoptering a spinnerbait has turned my luck more than once. When the water is clear, I'll use a white spinnerbait with chrome blades or green with copper blades. In dark water I'll switch to a black skirt with orange blades.

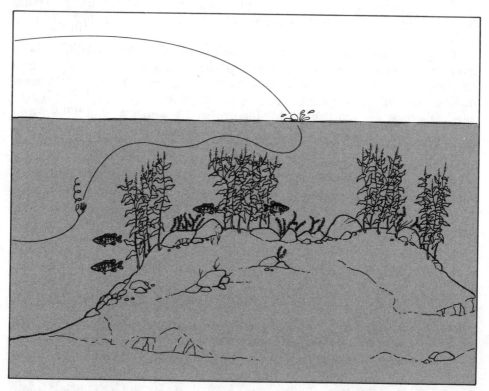

Figure 8. *Another little trick to add to your book is "helicoptering" a spinnerbait. This works especially well when you are casting to a rock pile or weed bed. Just retrieve the lure across the top of the structure until it reaches the edge. Then stop retrieving and let the lure fall down the edge, spinning and fluttering in a seductive manner. When things go right, your lure might helicoper right into the waiting jaws of a big bass.*

Sometimes the smallies will be found in places that are so hard to get at you wonder how they got there. They will sit in thickly matted cabbage beds, or in between logs where no conventional lure can be thrown. Then I do what the largemouth fishermen do: tie on a plastic worm. You can rig these up to be weedless and chunk them into the heaviest timber, reed beds or cabbage jungles without getting snagged. Stick with the four- to six-inch lengths in purple, grape, brown and black for smallies. A little variation to this that also works is a jig head with a plastic worm. An excellent combination is a weedless jig head with a Reaper tail.

When these fish are up in the shallows, the fly rodder can really have a ball. An 8½- or 9-foot rod with floating or sinking tip line is perfect. These fish look for the majority of their food on the surface or sub-surface, so I use muddlers, hair bugs, bushy looking streamers, or popping bugs. This type of fly rodding can get so exciting that I've seen sophisticated trout men quiver at the knees and babble away when a wild smallmouth bucked on the end of their rod.

Once the sun goes down, many anglers head for the camp with visions of shore supper and a comfortable sleeping bag. But, if you have a trophy smallie in mind, I would suggest that you grab a quick bite and get back out on the lake for some night fishing. After the sun sets in summer those big female bass venture out and begin to prowl the points looking for something to fill their big bellies. This is especially true on still, hot evenings when the air is so heavy you could almost cut it with a knife.

The big bass will usually be cruising the points that are in water about 8 to 12 feet deep. The best way to catch them is to "call them up" to the surface with a noisy surface lure such as a floating minnow bait with propeller baits or some noisy surface plug. Some of my favorites are big musky sized Jitterbugs, small Teddies and Heddon Torpedos. These lures can really do a number on huge smallmouth that prowl the shallows at night.

Colors are important even when fishing at night. Black is best, but other dark colors will work too. Use dark baits so the fish can pick out the silhouette of the lure against the lighter surface and zero in on it. Lighter colored baits will blend in with the surface and be practically invisible to the fish.

Big blackspinner baits will work, as well as buzz baits and balsa or plastic minnows. Just work them across the surface, pumping with your rod tip to make the lures dance, flutter and hop. The splashing and gurgling will sound like a dinner bell to any hunting smallies. But watch out! Any fish that hits during these late hours will probably be big. In fact, you may latch onto a big walleye, northern, or even a musky using these tactics.

Night fishing can produce some really big lunkers, but you need to take special precautions. Take along a powerful flashlight or, better yet, a Q Beam. Take along an effective mosquito repellant, such as Muskol, or those little, bloodthirsty critters will ruin your trip.

Also make sure that everything in your boat is organized so that you can find anything quickly without the use of a flashlight. If you keep turning on your light your eyes will never get used to the dark. Keep things tangle-free and ready, especially the net. When that big smallmouth hits you want everything going your way.

Throwing big baits, like these, requires a medium to medium heavy graphite casting rod with a strong backbone. A rod like Lew Childre's SG4-156 will give you the necessary power to cast these heavier baits, set the hook and steer any big fish away from stumps, logs or other line-busting debris.

Fish do not tend to be as line-shy during the night as they are during the day, so you can use heavier line. Mono in 10- or 12-pound test will put the odds in your favor when you tie into a big one. Using an abrasion-proof line such as Stren will deter line breakage due to nicks and cuts from rocks, stumps and weeds.

But, summers don't last long up in the north country. Before you know it, the days get shorter and there is a frosty chill in the air when you pull your boat up at night. To some, fall can be a sad reminder that summer and the fishing season is waning away. But to the smallmouth fisherman, fall signals some of the most outstanding smallie action of the year. The key to these large stringers is to think deep. Remember, these fish can be as deep as 40, 50, or even 60 feet down.

Without a doubt, the best method to take these fish is with a Lindy rig tipped with a big minnow—preferably five to eight inches long. This may seem rather large to you, but it's important to offer these big smallies something substantial. You may not get as many small "buck" bass gobbling up your offering and supplying you with lots of action, but when you do catch a fish it will be a keeper. The best minnows are red-tailed chubs, if you can get them. If not, you can use dace, shiners or fatheads with good success.

When fishing deep, get your rig right under the boat. You will be able to feel the hits much better and keep your sinker from getting snagged in the rocks all the time. I normally use a ³/₈- or ¹/₂-ounce sinker or a ³/₄-ounce if the water is over 50 feet.

Hook the minnow from below in back of both lips. This way the minnow is securely hooked and the hook positioned for a good set. Big smallies can be quite finicky, so it is important to use fresh, lively bait. If the minnow dies or gets chewed up, change it. It will pay off in the long run.

Once you have located a promising looking structure, troll along the steep edges until you find a fish. Once you've located the fish stick with them. Normally the school will not be scattered all along a certain depth, but will be relating to a certain unique spot such as a rock finger, weed clump or spot of sand grass (see Figure 9).

Finding those little holding spots on a structure is so important. Let me give you an example. This past fall we fished a gin clear, oligotrophic lake in Ontario that had a large smallmouth population. We were specifically trying to catch some of the big female bass that were schooling around the deep water points and islands. Whenever we located a structure that looked like it would hold fish, we would begin to troll, looking for the little holding spot. Without fail, we would only catch an occasional fish until we came across the right spot, then they would come fast and furious. This pattern prevailed for three days. So don't give up on a structure in fall until you've covered it thoroughly.

Figure 9. *In fall, the smallmouth usually will be quite deep on a structure and grouped in a tight school. They won't randomly roam over the entire structure, but will hold tight to a unique spot such as a rock finger, weed clump or growth of sand grass.*

When you are using large minnows for bait, remember to give the fish time to start swallowing the minnow before you set the hook. So many times an angler will get a hit and immediately set the hook, getting nothing but a slashed minnow. After the fish hits, give it several seconds and then slowly tighten up on the fish. Take a moment to feel what it's doing. If you feel the fish still tapping, give it longer. Sometimes you can tease the fish into taking the minnow all the way by applying slight pressure. Once you are sure the fish has got it, set the hook firmly.

You can also catch a lot of dandy smallmouth in fall by using jigs. A $3/8$- or $1/4$-ounce jig tipped with a minnow can really turn on some big ones. I prefer to use black, white, yellow or crayfish colored jigs. The style of jig head can be important. In order to get deep quickly you will want to use a ball shaped head. Or, if it is very rocky, I'll use a stand-up jig head in order to avoid getting hung up.

Fall is a great time to fish for smallmouth. But, then again, all seasons are. Their delectable taste and rambunctious nature will really get you excited. But, a lot of people haven't caught on to this yet, and the smallmouth fishery is still very under-fished. If you enjoy catching lots of fish that fight like the dickens, try Canadian smallmouth. You'll be amazed that more people don't jump in and enjoy it.

By knowing the ropes, like Jimmy Hayes of Pipestone Lodge does, you can string up a bunch of smallies (and bonus walleyes) in no time.

SMALLMOUTH SEASONAL LURE SELECTION

Season	Bait or Lure Type	Size	Color	Remarks
Spring	Spinner & minnow	Small	Silver - gold	Very early, deep
	Quiver Jig & leech	1/16 to 1/4 oz	Black/orange, yellow, brown	Use in shallow cover
	Straight shaft spinners	Small Chico	Various	
	Rig and crawlers			Late spring best
	Minnow baits	Small floaters	Baitfish colors	
	Jig & twister	2" to 4"	Black, brown, yellow	
Early Summer	Live bait rigs with leechs or crawlers			Cold front days or ultra clear water
	Plastic worms	1/8 to 1/4 oz	Grape, black, brown	Food for fish suspended off points
	Jig & grub	1/8 to 3/8 oz	Brown, smoke	Twitching retreive
	Minnow baits	3" to 4"	Gold, orange, silver	Evenings, overcast days
	Top water	Tiny Torpedos	Clear, chrome, frog	Stop & go retreive
	Crank baits		Crawfish	For heavy weeds & brush
	Spinner baits	1/4 to 3/8 oz	Chartreuse, black, white	
Late Summer	Buzzing baits	Large	Black, white, yellow	Evenings, hot muggy mornings
	Big top waters	Zara Spook	Frog, black, crawfish	After dark for trophy fish
	Crank baits	1/4" to 3/8"	Crawfish, bone	Work them fast, bounce off boulders
	Jig & worm	6" worm or Reaper	Black, purple, red	
	Spinner baits	1/4 to 3/8 oz	Various	Add plastic trailer for bigger fish
	Rig & Leech or Crawler	Jumbos		When all else fails
Fall	Lindy rig & minnow	4" to 7"	Suckers, shiners or redtails	Once water starts to cool. Live bait is best overall choice — Work deep - 20' to 60' on sharp rock drops, best if there is weed growth on top of structure
	Jig & minnow	3" to 5"		

Chapter 8
Muskie:
The Maker of Legends

Muskellunge! No other freshwater gamefish can stir the blood and raise hair on your neck quite like the "musky" can. I know because I've had muskies follow my lure up to my boat that looked like they were eyeing me for lunch, not my bait.

One spring I was fishing a scenic Canadian lake with a group of friends and family members. We had a super morning, filling out with limits of smallmouth bass and walleyes. We pulled up to a point near the beaver dam to have shore lunch and take some pictures of our fish. I suddenly heard a tremendous splashing near the boat. A huge muskie, at least 50 pounds, was tearing and slashing at our stringer of walleyes. And those were no small walleyes. The smallest were six pounds or better. So I grabbed on one end of the stringer and tried to pull the fish free from the robber. Have you ever been face to face with a muskie playing tug o' war? Believe me, it's strange!

Finally the muskie let go, but he didn't leave. He just lay there, giving me a cold stare. As I walked back to the group, the fish was still there, and I felt like there were two eyes burning into my back as I walked away. This was all some years ago, but even today when I fish any points near beaver dams the hair will raise on my neck. I can't help but look back over my shoulder and expect to see evil eyes staring at me.

To envision a musky, think of a critter that is a cross between an alligator and a striped torpedo, meaner than a wolverine and armed with enough teeth to make a full grown African python jealous. Fables and legends exist about eight-foot swimming logs, pets being swallowed by an unseen creature and ducks that dive down for feed but never come up again.

However I think a more accurate description of this noble gamefish is pertinent here. Next to the sturgeon, muskies are the largest freshwater fish to swim in Canadian waters. They have been known to exceed six feet in length and 100 pounds in weight, but more often show up in the range of 28 to 48 inches in length and weights of 5 to 36 pounds. Currently, the world record is a 69-pound 15-ounce giant caught in the St. Lawrence River.

The overall coloration of the musky vary quite a bit and are sometimes confused with northern pike. However, muskies have dark markings on a light background, in contrast to northerns, which have light markings on a dark background.

In adult muskies the back, head and upper sides are irridescent green gold, light brown, or almost black. The sides range from green through green gold, to brown, grey or silver. The flanks are marked with vertical bars or spots that are brown or black. At times these markings may be very light, especially in the silvery colored fish.

The musky is limited in range to the waters of eastern North America. In Canada, muskies inhabit lakes and rivers from southern Quebec, westward along the St. Lawrence, then north to the level of Lake Nipissing. The range takes up again in the area from the Rainy River to the Lake Of The Woods, then northward to the Sioux Lookout area.

Though its range is small, the muskie is a very important gamefish. For Canada has most of the world's best muskie fishing.

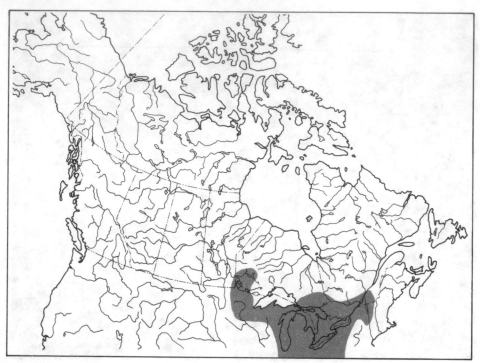

The Home Range of the Muskellunge

The muskie is a spring spawing fish that moves into the shallows shortly after the ice has melted (but not later than the northern pike), usually in late April or early May. When the water temperature ranges from 40 to 49 degrees F. the female fish will move up into feeder streams to prepare for spawning. Usually the males will follow soon after.

When the water reaches a temperature of 50 to 59 degrees F., spawning takes place in vegetated areas that have been flooded by streams. Normally the prime spawning areas are located where the water is only 15 to 20 inches deep. The bottom content is usually matted vegetation and leaves (see Figure 1).

As the water temperature nears 60 degrees and spawning is completed, the male muskies head downstream to the main lake where they will roam the shallows for a period of time. The females tend to stay in the creeks longer and roam the main channel until as late as midsummer in some lakes.

Hatching occurs in 8-14 days, if the water remains in a warming trend. From their first day as a minute creature living off a yolk sac, survival is a moment to moment struggle for baby muskies. First of all, only about 34 percent of the eggs will be fertilized, and those that hatch are immediately preyed upon by previously hatched northern fry. Survival is rare for young muskies, but that is nature's way of keeping the population of muskies low. These predator fish are extremely voracious. According to the rules of nature's game plan, an avid predator must have some sort of population controls or they will throw the whole system out of balance.

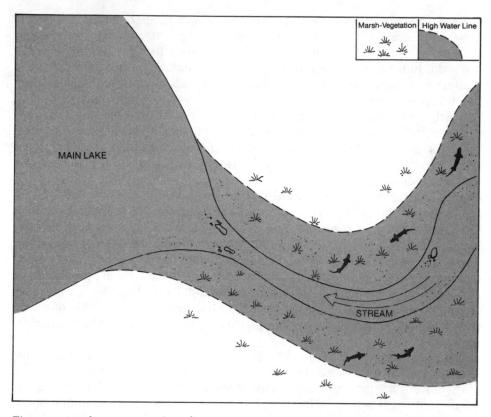

Figure 1. *Muskies spawn when the water temperature approaches the mid 50's. They will seek out areas of flooded vegetation where the water may be as shallow as 15 to 20 inches. A good example are streams that overflow their banks and flood the adjacent shoreline.*

To give you an idea of what a few muskie fry can do, let me relate a tale. Fishery biologists from the University of Minnesota were going to transport 100 small muskies to a nearby lake for stocking purposes. The normal procedure is to place the fish in a small tank on a truck for transportation. Upon arrival at the stocking site, the biologist looked in the tank and to their surprise there wasn't 100 muskies but only about 50 well-fed little cannibals. Just think what a huge muskie population could do to a lake.

Upon arriving back in the lake after spawning the muskies will roam the shallow water for a while. During this time many are very oriented to shorelines. Now is the time that "bank beaters" cash in on their share of the musky action.

However, as the water begins to clear and the temperatures go up above 60 degrees, the fish will usually move out from shoreline structures and go to deeper water. In eutrophic lakes the muskies will move in and around newly emerging weedbeds in the main lake. The fish continue to use these weedbeds and edges for the rest of the summer.

Lately, research has shown that muskies in our deeper, clearer lakes will behave differently after the water clears and the water temperature raises. They don't head for the weed beds as their relatives in older and more fertile lakes do, but they move out to deeper, open water. Some of you old muskie hunters may raise your eyebrows, but tracking studies on different lakes show that this phenomenon exists.

Most major fish movements revolve around, or at least relate to, the predator/prey relationship. On the deep, clear lakes where ciscoes are the main forage base, these muskies probably go down to feed on the ciscoes. However, they may also feed on perch, walleyes, or other forage fish that are found in their range.

And the range of a big muskie can be just about anywhere. A friend of mine, Jimmy Hayes, the owner of Pipestone Lodge on Pipestone Lake in Ontario, was fishing for lake trout in one of the neighboring lakes. He was running his downriggers in about 96 feet of water when he got a tremendous strike. But instead of pulling in a lake trout, he landed a 15 pound musky. Half an hour later they pulled in another musky, this one a nineteen pounder. Both fish were caught in over 90 feet of water. About the only thing for the muskies to feed on in those depths are ciscoes, or possibly small lake trout. Muskies are truly an amazing fish that can adapt to just about any condition you can find in a Canadian Lake.

Summer musky locations, as with all seasons, depends upon where the musky can find something to eat, or the predator/prey relationship. Muskies may move into the lush weedlines during summer and feed on perch, smallmouth, and walleyes. But, these fish don't necessarily stay in one home area. I believe the muskie is a vagabond, roaming the lake at will. Some of the best fish I've caught have been on deep, rocky points. Muskies will come up on these points from deep water to feed on walleyes. Another excellent spot to find summer muskies is on shallow rock reefs that have some vegetation or no weed growth at all. Again, the fish feed on foraging walleyes and smallmouth that move up on the reefs (see Figure 2).

During this time you may even find the muskies in small schools. This may sound surprising, but it happens. On one occasion I caught seven muskies from 14 to 22 pounds on one small point. This all took place in four hours, so it was evident that they were together. Usually they will not be found in big schools, just groups of three, four or six fish. This is something to keep in mind when you catch a muskie because there may be more in one spot than you think. Make sure you fish an area thoroughly after you catch one fish. Or if you raise a fish and fail to catch it, give it a half hour and then go back. These fish that follow a bait are hunting for food. Many wall-hangers have been caught the second time around.

During the fall you will want to hit the same type of structures but have steep, sloping edges that drop into deep water. These key areas consistently hold the most fish when the water gets colder (see Figure 3).

No matter when you go after them, don't expect things to be easy. Musky fishing is rarely a fast and furious sport. Persistence is required, and fast fishing isn't the rule. But once you nail one it's all worth it.

162

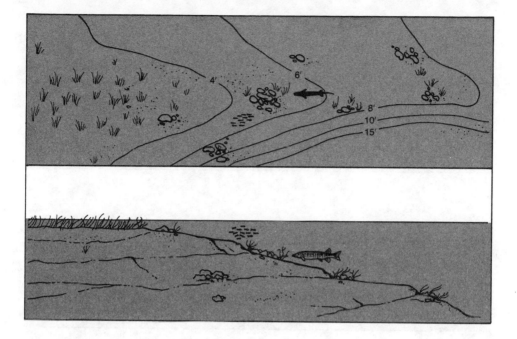

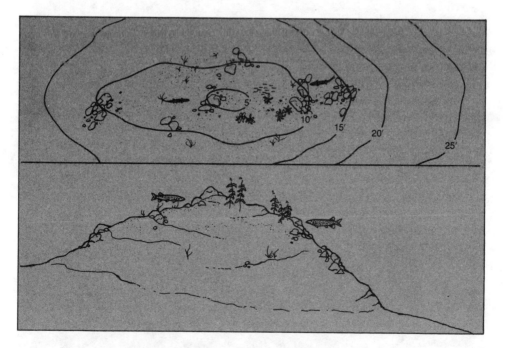

Figure 2. Many people don't realize that rocky points and reefs are super spots to pick up a muskie or two. They can be especially good if they are adjacent to deep water where the muskie can quickly come in from the depths and feed on foraging smallmouth and walleyes.

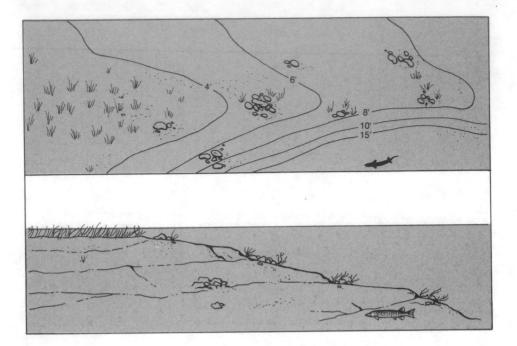

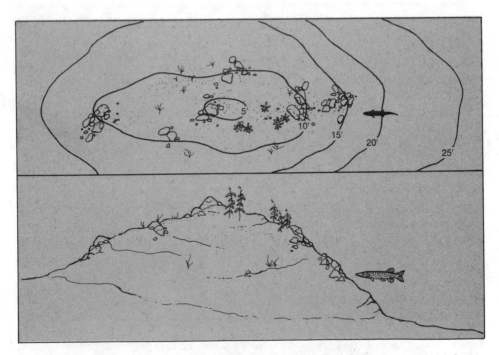

Figure 3. A key fall pattern is to fish the same reefs and points that you would during the summer, but concentrate on the steepest sides that drop into deep water.

Spring is probably the most challenging time to take a musky. The water is cold and the fish are still quite sedentary as they rest after the rigors of the spawn. But many large fish are taken at this time, so it's not an impossible task. One good place to begin your search for them during these cold temperatures is where a stream or creek flows into the lake. These inflowing currents usually bring in warmer water, which in turn warms these portions of the lake faster. This draws in baitfish, who come to feed on the newly emerging plankton or to spawn. Muskies are attracted to these areas because the water is somewhat warmer and because of the influx of baitfish.

In spring you should also concentrate on the shallow bays. These areas also warm faster and attract baitfish, much like a stream mouth does. If a lake has lots of bays, arms or fingers that run off the lake in all directions, concentrate on those that are on the northern shoreline. These are the ones that are warmed by the predominant southern winds that come in the spring. This alone may be enough to draw in a lot of muskies.

Another key area to try is the shallow side of a newly emerging weedbed. Usually by the third week of June the weeds will be starting in Canadian waters. The shallow side will be warmer than the side facing out toward deep water, a difference in temperature that often causes the inside weedline to "green-up" faster than the outside edge. Baitfish will be attracted to these new green weeds and you-know-who will be right behind. Keep in mind that the southerly winds will cause the weeds on the northern shores to green faster than other weeds in the lake.

By now you should realize that one of the keys to spring muskie location is finding the warmer areas of the lake. Muskies have a very sensitive metabolism, and the difference of a few degrees is very important to them. But a musky will not sacrifice its safety for warm water. If there is no cover nearby it doesn't matter how warm the water, they probably won't be there. Cover in the form of weeds or deep water are necessary in order to have any concentration of fish.

Whether you are fishing stream mouths, weedbeds on the northern shore, or other spring hotspots, keep in mind that you should be using small baits. The best action comes with minnows or artificials between three and six inches long. Time and time again I've seen folks using large muskie baits and go fishless while another angler used small lures and came off the lake with more than one legal-sized fish.

Always use a "sloooow" retrieve in the cold waters of early season. The spring musky just is not into chasing down a meal. He really has to be convinced to take your offering. This is one time to use a reel with a lower gear ratio. The popular modern fast-retrieve reels are fine for late season fishing, but for now keep it slow.

Lures that I have found effective on spring muskies are floating minnow baits because they can be worked in slow, darting retrieves that lackadaisical muskies really go for. Lindy's baitfish, Rapalas, Hellcats, and Norman's Linebackers are proven minnow baits. In addition to these, spinners like the Mepps No. 5 work well, along with jigs tipped with minnows or Reapers.

It won't be long before you find out that muskies have an extremely agitating habit of following a lure up to the boat, only to reject it and swim away. This happens during all seasons, but especially during the spring. If you happen to have a musky follow your lure to the boat try working your lure in a figure 8 pattern next to the boat rather than just lifting the lure out of the water. Keep that lure moving! This may just be what it takes to make a fish bite rather than ignore your offering. If you are fishing with a partner, both of you should use the figure 8 technique. The fish is all the more likely to get excited and strike.

A friend of mine from Harrisburg, Pennsylvania, taught me another way of dealing with these persnickety fish. He likes to fish with two boats together. He has found that when most muskies follow and turn down a lure they dive down and lay underneath the boat. If boat A, for example, gets a follow, the folks in boat B will cast around boat A and try to tempt the fish up. He has caught an awful lot of large musky using this technique (see figure 4).

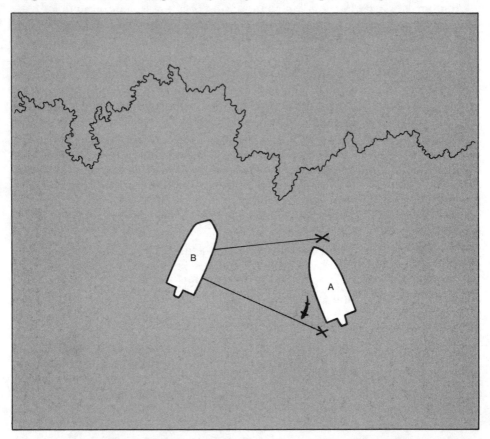

Figure 4. *An old trick to take some muskies is to fish with two boats together rather than splitting up. The reasoning behind this is when most muskies follow and turn down a lure they will dive down and lie beneath the boat. If boat A, for example, gets a follow, the folks in boat B will cast around boat A, giving the fish a new lure to look at. Many times this is all it takes to get them to strike.*

Probably the most proven method for spring muskies is fishing with a sucker. The colder it gets, the more a sucker will out-produce other presentations. You should carry a good selection of hooks so you can handle different sized sucker minnows. It is important to hook the sucker properly. Hook the minnow lightly through the upper lip in the whiteish cartilage portion of the mouth (see Figure 5). This way you get a good clean hook set. Many people hook the minnow farther back up through the head and they don't get enough of the hook exposed. It can be a terrible experience to have a trophy musky swallow your bait, set the hook, and reel back a raked minnow because the hook didn't catch. Use a hook that is large enough so that it isn't buried in the minnow. A 9/0 to 12/0 hook is not too big.

Suckers can be fished a number of different ways. They can be trolled using a "free lining" method, an excellent way to take early season fish. Hook the sucker once under the dorsal fin and let it go. The sucker will instinctively head for the bottom. Don't add any weight to the rig, but let the sucker do its own thing. Any musky nearby will know it is there. All you need to do is wait till the fish grabs on.

Trolling the rig can be accomplished by using the outboard, electric trolling motor, or by drifting with the wind. Whatever method you decide to use, remember that the faster you move, the more your sucker rig will plane up toward the surface. You have to add enough weight to keep the sucker in the fish zone. I usually experiment to see which boat control method will work best, often settling for a combination of drifting and trolling.

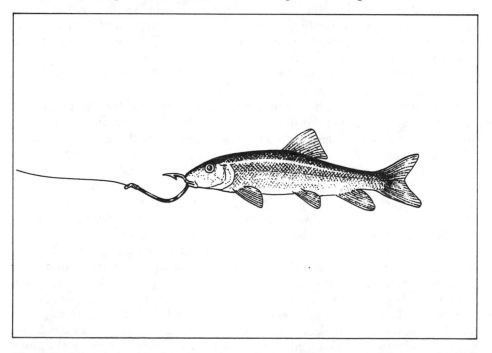

Figure 5. *A properly rigged sucker minnow has possibly accounted for more big fish than any other rig. But rigging them properly is vitally important.*

Sucker rigging is a versatile presentation that can be customized to fit certain conditions. With a weedless hook you can make your rig weedless. Some people doubt the hooking qualities of a weedless hook. However, in snag-infested waters it might be the only way to effectively get your sucker where the fish are. Just be sure to set the hook with a long, hard, fast sweep.

If the muskies are in a bad mood and won't quite take a sucker minnow all the way, I give them a sucker harness to chew on. There is nothing more frustrating than to have a monster musky take a sucker and just carry it around. When you set the hook, all you get is a shredded sucker. A harness will put the odds in your favor by increasing the number of hooks. There a number of good sucker harnesses on the market.

Finally, there is always the bobber rig. This works the best of all when you're fishing heavy, dense weeds, in brush or in snag-filled waters of uniform depth. Where other rigs will continually get hung up in the debris, a bobber rig will drift the minnow right over the mess.

It is hard to know when to set the hook after the musky takes your sucker. I've had big muskies and northerns carry my minnows around for as long as 45 minutes, only to drop them without ever taking the bait down enough so I could set the hook. However, if you know what the fish is doing after he takes the bait, it will help you know when to "give it to em." A musky will usually grab a sucker sideways in its mouth and carry it around like a dog with a bone. Eventually the fish will stop, turn the sucker around and swallow it head first.

The secret is to wait until the musky stops to eat the minnow before you set the hook. Many times a fish will stop several times before the "eating stop," but these are short and the fish will quickly move on. Wait until there is a definite, long stop before you lean on the rod. When you do set the hook, jam it home at least three times in order to make sure it it set. If not, the fish may come up to the surface, jump high into the air with a disdainful look in his eye and throw your sucker right back on your lap.

If the temperature continues to rise normally, the muskies will be in their summer haunts by the end of June. Those fish that head for deeper water on some of the big, deep lakes will be out chasing ciscoes by the end of June, too.

Muskies can be found in weeds anywhere from two feet to however deep the weeds will grow in a given lake. In a very eutrophicated lake such as Lake Wabigoon in Ontario, where the water is extremely dark, the muskies may be 2 to 6 feet deep. On the other hand you have Eagle Lake just down the road from Wabigoon, where the water is very clear. Here the muskies may be using weeds 15 to 25 feet deep. Water clarity can be very important.

Muskies may also hang around rocks on the ends of rocky points, rock shelves, rocky humps or islands. Usually if the fish are using rocks, there will be weeds not far away. They may roam back and forth. If you don't find fish in the weeds, they should be in the rocks.

Don't neglect to hit little unique spots like single boulders, tiny bays and stands of shallow lily pads. All fish like to relate to some kind of object, and the big, bad musky is no different. So try all those weird little spots, they may turn up something big.

Next to the sturgeon, the muskie is the largest freshwater fish. This giant caught by Joe Bucher is a good example of just how big they really get.

The weedbeds or rocks that will produce the most muskies are those that are connected with the best forage producing areas. Large, expansive flats, their edges, plus any connecting structures and edges are where you should concentrate for summer muskies.

Of course the big flats get thrashed by all the other musky fishermen, yet they still will have the largest fish relating to them. That is why the areas connected to the flats is where you should concentrate. Those small, flats-related areas can be the gold mines. Often fishing pressure will force big fish out of the major spots and into those less conspicuous structures and breaklines related to the major spots.

An example would be a visible, well known weedbed. More than one angler a day might stop by to throw a bucktail or jerk bait over the weed tops. Although this tactic has produced many muskies, keep in mind that most anglers only fish the bed in this manner. Because of that, I've often moved to the deep growing, shorter "fringe" weeds that grow just outside the major weedbed and done well when others who just fished the major bed got skunked. And, these spots just keep getting better as the more well-known spots gets worse.

A typical example of fringe weedline is illustrated in Figure 6. With a wind-aided controlled drift, two anglers can cover the major weedbed and fringe area. The angler covering the deeper weedline should throw an occasional cast out into deep water for any open water "roamers" that have suspended out there (see Figure 7). Use a crankbait for fishing the deeper water and open water. Lures such as Lindy's Musky Shad and Bombers are perfect. Or you can even use large bass crankbaits in crayfish or chartreuse. In the shallow weeds, try bucktails such as Bucher Tails, Lindy's Musky Hot Spots or Windels' Musky Harassers. Jerk baits such as Teddie's, the Bobbie Bait, the Suick, Bagley's B Flat Shiner, the Magnum Rapalas and great big jointed Creek Chubs will work as well as large musky tandems and musky buzz baits.

Figure 6. After the main weed beds have been "thrashed" by dozens of muskie hunters, the fish will often move out to small holding areas connected to the main weed bed. Examples of these are small weed fingers, little rock piles and fringe areas.

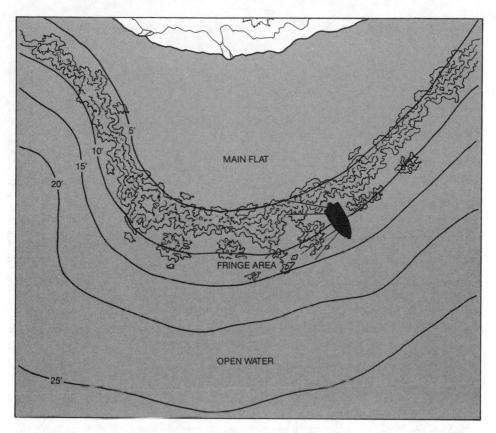

Figure 7. By using a buddy system you can cover the main weed bed and any connected "fringe" areas. With a wind aided, controlled drift you can slide down the weedline while one person works the weed bed and the other casts out deeper to cover any fringe areas and open water fish.

Another commonly overlooked type of summer structure is the fingers of weeds that extend out from a large, frequently fished weedbed or sunken island. These areas often get overlooked by anglers who are intent on working the main structure.

Normally the fish that are found in these fingers run larger than the ones that hang in the main weed area, which is probably a result of heavy fishing pressure. If the conditions are right, the big fish may move up onto the main structure, but during the summer they'll generally hold back and sit on these adjacent structures and edges, such as these weed fingers.

In a situation like that shown in Figure 8, I'd fish over and through the weeds with a bucktail or jerk bait. These lures will work especially well on windy days, overcast days, or other days with low light conditions. Under bright conditions I would use a deep running lure such as a crankbait that would run down and brush the deeper weed tops.

Or, I might use a jig and fish the deep water weed edge. Jigs can be your best choice at times for many reasons. First, when the muskies are holding

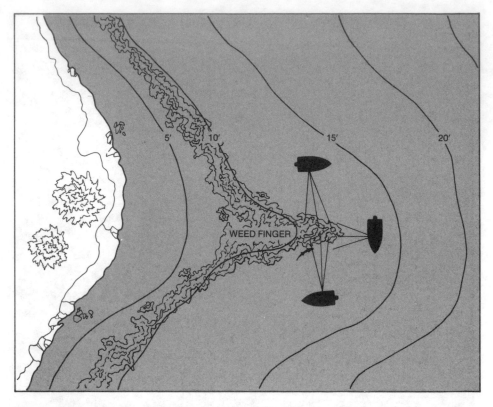

Figure 8. *Weed fingers that extend out from the main weed bed can hold some huge muskies. On bright days the fish will sit deeper so I would use deep running lures that would just brush the weed tops. Under windy, or cloudy conditions, the fish will be higher up so bucktails and jerkbaits are the ticket. Make sure you work the point from different angles to cover all spots.*

tight to the weed edge, multi-hooked lures will continually get hung up while a single-hooked jig will slide through the weeds with few hangups. Second, there might be bass, walleyes and pike on these weedlines. Usually these fish won't look at a conventional musky lure, while they will strike a jig. Moreover, jigs are much more manageable in tight inside corners and turns of the weedline. Most lures won't get deep fast enough to hit the bottom when you're working super tight, inside turns.

I generally stick with jigs such as Dingo Jigs, Mr. Twister Pow-rr Heads or other lead heads dressed with artificial lizards, or Reapers in the five- and eight-inch sizes. For those deep muskies that lie on or near the bottom, you will want to use a jig head style that will get the lure down in a hurry. A jig with its head in a vertical plane cuts through the water and sinks to the bottom much faster than other shapes. Examples are the Burke's Wig Wag Minnow Heads and Mr. Twister Sassy Shad heads.

For "swimming" a jig through the weeds off the bottom or when a slower dropping jig is required, a flat head or swimming head works better. This type of jig has a head that is flat and horizontal to the bottom so it has plenty of water resistance on the drop. A productive one is the Grassl's Swim-Head jig. Or you can make your own swimming or stand up jig heads. I make my own with extra large hooks to get good solid hook sets.

Swimming head jigs should be moved through the water with three or four quick turns of the reel handle rather than moving the jig with the rod tip. After the quick burst with the reel handle the jig should be allowed to flutter to the bottom. Once the jig has settled on the bottom, move it again, repeating the process. But remember to hang on to your rod because the hits will come usually when the lure is settling down toward the bottom.

When you're working the weed bottoms with a fast-sinking jig head, use a hopping retrieve. After the jig has settled on the bottom, lift it up with a smart snap of the rod tip about 12 to 18 inches off the bottom. Then allow it to fall toward the bottom on a tight line, feeling for any subtle pick ups. After the lure has hit the bottom, repeat the process.

You can also add different hops and variations to your retrieve. For example, use a two-hop method by snapping your lure upwards, wait a fraction of a second, then snap it again. Little changes in action like this can trigger a moody musky into changing his mind real quick.

An excellent set up for this is to tip a stand-up jig head with a silver Reaper. When there are clumps of coontail, I let the Reaper settle into them and then snap it out with a sharp whip of the rod tip. The silver flecks in the Reaper will glitter and sparkle, catching the eye of any nearby muskies. Keep up the erratic, jerking retrieve as you bring the lure in to keep it flashing.

Seeing, and feeling, the raw power of a trophy muskie is perhaps the ultimate in freshwater fishing.

Another common structure in Canadian musky lakes is a "saddle" between two land masses, such as shoreline points, islands or peninsulas. Any large schools of baitfish in motion will be funneled through this necked down area…setting up a perfect ambush area for Mr. Musky. These areas can be especially good if there are weeds on both sides and an open cut running through the middle (see Figure 9). Crankbaits are the best for working the open cut, while jerk baits and bucktails are better for the shallow, weedier situations.

When you're working a weedline, the edge of a bar, or a breakline, keep an eye out for any inside turns. These little corners in the weedline have been well known places for walleyes and bass, but they also prove to be excellent musky hotspots, too. Concentrate on those turns that are especially tight. The sharper and more slot-like the turn, the better, and turns that have hard bottoms are consistently more productive than those with soft, mucky bottoms (see Figure 10). These inside turns are perhaps the most over-looked areas in the world of musky structure, but probably the hardest to fish properly. To do it, use one of the jigging methods.

Summer is also the time for using topwater techniques to take muskies. There are a variety of good lures to choose from, although some are better suited for certain conditions. For example, when working in shallow water with thick cover or very high weeds, I'll use a buzz bait. Large weedy bays, flats and bars as examples.

Basically the buzz bait is a sub-surface lure designed to be retrieved so that it will bulge or break the surface. When I come across an area with weed tops coming up near the surface, I'll cast the lure back into the weeds and briskly retrieve it over the weeds, breaking the surface. This is especially effective early in the morning. The muskies are sometimes right up on the flats or weed edges, hunting for some unfortunate critter. At times like this they are real suckers for a buzz bait.

When you hook a muskie in a thick weedbed, get to that fish as soon as you can or it will bury itself in the giant salad. Once a musky wraps up in the weeds it is almost as good as lost if you don't act quickly. This is where teamwork is important. While one partner keeps tension on the fish, the other needs to crank up the motor and move the boat over the fish. Then it is much easier to control the fish and pull it up.

Buzz baits really shine during those hot, muggy, foggy mornings that occur toward the end of summer. In the morning you should work very shallow next to shore around timber, rocks and weed clumps. Reeling a buzz bait next to these obstructions can produce some musky fishing at its finest.

Late evenings in August are also a good time to do some buzzing. Use black or very dark colored lures because the fish can pick up the dark silhouette of the lure against the night sky. Cast around timber, reed clumps, rocks, reefs and underwater points. This can produce some nice muskies, plus some surprise action from smallmouths and walleyes.

Jerk baits occupy a special place in the hearts of musky anglers. "Stick baits" will weigh three ounces and be as long as six or eight inches. These "heavyweights" are responsible for many 30 to 40 pound fish every year. Jerk

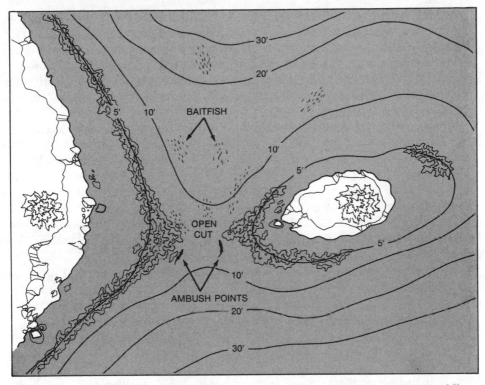

Figure 9 A common situation in many Canadian muskie lakes is when a saddle is formed between two land masses, such as shoreline points, islands or penisulas. Roaming schools of baitfish get funneled through this bottleneck making it a perfect spot for a hungry muskie.

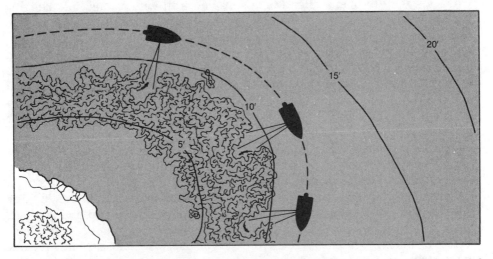

Figure 10. Inside turns in weedlines are great spots for walleyes, smallmouth bass and hungry muskies that feed on them. Look for the turns that are super tight. The sharper and more slot-like the better. And, turns that have hard bottoms are consistently better than those with a mucky or soft bottom.

175

baits are versatile. They can be retrieved at various depths down to eight feet. Just retrieve them with a snapping, jerking retrieve to give the lure a lot of action. With jerk baits, however, you need to remember to set the hook hard...as hard as you possibly can. Many times the long needle-sharp teeth of a musky will sink right into the soft wood and you won't be able to slide the lure through the fish's mouth to set the hook. So rear back hard on the fish, two or three times.

Diving plugs are another example of topwater lures. All divers have an enticing action that catches fish. They depend on flash and action to make them look alive, so their use is somewhat limited to calm and clearer conditions. However, don't let this discourage you from trying them. These lures will outproduce all other lures on clear lakes during calm, daylight conditions. With their high visibility, diving plugs are just right for these conditions, whereas noisy jerk baits may be too much for the fish. Diving plugs that I rely on are Magnum Rapalas, the Hi-Fin Splashtail, and Musky Shads in black or other dark colors.

If you haven't tried topwater fishing for summer muskies, you'll be pleasantly surprised with your results. Not only are these methods productive, but they provide the most exciting musky strike of all: the heart-stopping explosion of a musky hitting a topwater lure.

But what about those elusive muskies suspended out in the deeper water? Is there a way to catch them? You bet! The best method is trolling. One of the reasons that trolling is so effective on these fish is that it is necessary to cover a lot of water in as efficient a way as possible. When trolling you are always moving, and your lure is always working for you. But, in order to troll effectively, there are some things to keep in mind.

First of all, you can spook the muskies if you put a boat right over them when they are in open water. Make sure you troll with a long line, keeping your lure down where the fish are. Don't troll too slow, but you don't need to race along to trigger strikes, either. Just keep moving at a reasonable clip.

Remember you will have to troll over open water. This will be tough on those anglers who can't bear the thought of leaving the weeds. You'll just have to go "cold turkey" and get out in open water! But don't just hop in your boat and troll randomly around the lake. Try trolling tight to the weedline, then try a second pass out a little further. If you have no luck, move out and troll over the sunken islands and reefs (see Figure 11).

If trolling just isn't your cup of tea, or if it's illegal in your area, you can try the same thing by casting. Just work out from the weedline and cast out to deep water. It isn't as efficient as trolling, but it works.

For deep water it is necessary to use a lure that will get down quickly. For this reason I use crankbaits such as Lindy's Shads or other deep diving plugs. If the water is relatively shallow, you can use a bucktail such as Mepps Giant Killers or Musky Hot Spots. Whatever lure you use, just make sure it will work at the right depth.

Proper rods and reels are perhaps more important for muskie fishing than for any other kind of fishing. You need a strong rod that is light enough for

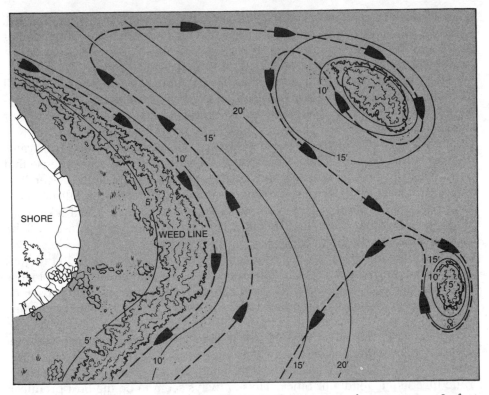

Figure 11. *Not all muskies are taken from weed areas or sunken structures. In fact, many muskies are taken every year by people trolling in open water. Now random trolling in a lake is not the answer. Try trolling tight to the weedline as shown here, then try a second pass out a little farther. If you have no luck, try moving out and trolling around sunken islands and around reefs. Some of these areas are practically virgin waters.*

nonstop 12-hour casting, yet with enough backbone to beat a 50-pound fish. Without a doubt, a Lew Childre SG6X-159 is the best musky rod I've used. It is a tremendously strong yet well-balanced rod that is perfect for all types of musky fishing. It is especially well suited for working jerk baits. If you put a BB2N reel with a wide spool on this rod you've got an outfit second to none.

Line is also important. Many excellent musky fishermen have personal theories about whether to use dacron or monofilament, but I almost always use dacron. These braided lines are much tougher, have less stretch and more abrasion resistance than mono. But when the water is very clear, I'll switch to mono. When I'm using a smaller jig and minnow or light baits in the spring I'll use mono. Early spring muskies are not so rambunctious, so I'd rather use a lighter, less visible line if I can get away with it. Whichever line you choose, make sure that it is adequately strong.

When trolling, use a line between 25- and 40-pound test. With line this heavy you can really set the hooks, an extremely important part of landing these hard-mouthed fish.

If you are interested in catching a lunker musky, there is no time like fall. Most musky guides agree that September and October are the best months for trophies. The water temperature drops down from the summer peak to the middle 60s, the temperature where muskies feed most actively.

Many musky fisherman don't slow down their retrieve enough for fall muskies. Since the water is getting colder, the fish are reluctant to chase anything moving very fast. Even their natural forage fishes move slower, so your bait should, too.

Live bait is one of the best ways to take muskies in the fall. The water temperature is similar to what it was in the spring, so it only makes sense that muskies will respond to spring tactics. Except, you should think bigger. The small minnows that were used in the spring can be deadly on fall muskies, however, you'll find that larger minnows from 8 to 16 inches will take more and bigger fish. Be careful that you don't retrieve the minnow too fast. And the deeper the water is, the slower you should retrieve or troll.

You'll find that the water begins to get clearer as it grows colder in fall. Jerk baits and diving plugs start to become more effective and bucktails start to lose their efficiency. Again, in artificials you should use bigger lures now. I switch to bigger Suicks, Bobbies, Teddies, Pikie Minnows, Ciscoe Kids and even bigger spoons.

The clearer the lakes are, the more erratic you should make your retrieve...except for bucktails. My best luck with bucktails has been with a straight retrieve. But, it's hard to beat the success that comes when using an erratic lure like a Teddie or Suick. These always seem to be the best producer. Sometimes when the muskies are actively feeding it seems that, no matter what you are using, you'll catch fish. On the other hand, there are days when muskies want one type of lure and nothing else. Sometimes they'll fall all over themselves going after a big spoon and ignore a big jerk bait. The next day it will be just the opposite. But, that's musky fishing.

In order to be prepared for the challenge of musky fishing, there are some tools that you should include in your gear. You should never go out without a quality pair of polaroid sunglasses. Many times a king sized musky will follow your lure close to the boat, but with the unaided eye you wouldn't see it. Often these fish will take a bait on the second cast, but only if you saw them and casted back to the same spot again. You will be amazed at how well you can see down in the water with a pair of polaroids, and that will help you hook more muskies.

Always include a fish billy club if you intend to keep a trophy musky. Never try to land a lively, trophy musky. I learned not to land a "green" muskie some time ago. I was participating in a musky tournament at the time. My partner and I were fishing near a father and son team who suddenly tied into a real nice fish. That musky was a real jumper, leaping several times before it dove for the bottom. It hung deep for several minutes when suddenly the boy's line went slack. I knew what was happening. That fish was heading for the surface and was going to leap. Sure enough, the fish erupted from the water and sailed right into their boat. Gear, buckets, spare rods and lures went flying in every direction. That fish tail-walked from one end of their boat to another and smashed their styrofoam bait pails and lure boxes. The frightening thing is how the fish was swinging the huge treble hooks on the lure that was hanging from its jaws. But in an instant the fish snagged the lure on a boat seat, tore loose and flopped overboard. I've often wondered what would have happened if the hooks had sunk into a hand or leg rather than the boat seat. So, whatever you do, don't try to bring a lively fish in the boat. Make sure you subdue it somehow first.

Though it may take a lot of hard work to connect with a legal muskie, most will agree it was more than worth it.

Musky fishing is becoming more popular all the time. More people are fishing them, so more muskies are being taken from our lakes all the time. This pressure is beginning to tell on the quality of musky fishing. In the last few years, the average weight of keeper sized muskies has dropped sharply. However, it should be known that some years before that, muskies were not as plentiful as they are now, thanks to advanced stocking programs and the efforts of conservation-oriented muskie organizations. For an example of improvement, we can look at the international tournament put on by Muskies Inc., a group dedicated to furthering musky research and providing quality fishing. In 1970 there were only 58 muskies caught during the tournament. In 1975 there were 632 muskies caught. Now of course there were probably more anglers using more advanced techniques. But, an increase in fish like that can only reflect an increase in the population.

Canada began musky programs as long ago as 1927, when Ontario started musky propagation programs. Up until then, "maskinonge" were commercially exploited until the original population dwindled and became restricted to isolated bodies of water. When the government of Ontario realized the value of the musky as a sport fish they prohibited commercial harvesting of muskies. Later they discontinued the sale of muskies during spawning and in 1927 artificial rearing began.

Today the muskie still needs all the support it can get, especially in some areas. For that reason, all anglers should practice modern catch-and-release fishing. A trophy musky is a fish over thirty pounds; anything smaller should be released. If we continue to keep smaller fish there will soon be no big ones at all. If you hook one you wish to release, do not try to land it. Lead the fish up to the boat, reach down and pop the hook out with a pliers. That way the fish is not even touched. This also means that you shouldn't fight a fish until it is totally exhausted. If you release a totally spent fish, its chances of survival are slim. Try to release them as soon as you can subdue the fish enough to release it.

If you wish to find out how big your fish is before you release it, tape a yard stick or tape measure to the side of your boat. You can buy decals marked off in inches, too. Most muskies will allow you to lead them along the side and get a good look at how long they are. Of course if the fish is badly hooked and chances of survival are slim, you should keep the fish and eat it.

Today, Canada boasts of some of the best musky fishing in the world. In her waters swim a tremendous population of this awesome gamefish. There is no better place to take a trophy. But, be careful. Once you get a taste of what a musky can do when hooked, or even have one follow your lure to your boat, you'll get the "fever." And the only cure for musky fever is a *lot* of time on the water...perferably in Canada.

MUSKY SEASONAL LURE SELECTION

Season	Bait or Lure Type	Size	Color	Remarks
Spring	Live bait rigs	Sucker sized hooks		Fish will be slow, give plenty of time before setting hook
	Minnow baits	Baitfish size	Perch, shad, silver	Smaller lures will outproduce big muskie-sized baits
	Bucktails	3″ to 4″	Black/orange, yellow	Work high/over shallow areas
Early Summer	Spoons	Medium	Various	Troll outside river mouths
	Jig & minnow	Heavy stand-up heads	Black, hot yellow, orange	Cast along weedlines and fringe areas
	Bucktails	Small musky size	Fluorescent colors	Work over newly forming weedbeds
	Crank baits	Small musky size	Various	Good on sunny days when fish lay deep
	Jerk baits	Small	Black and sucker finish	Best on cloudy days when fish are up
Late Summer	Jerk baits	Big Teddies	Cisco, black, sucker	Work fast covering lots of water
	Bucktails	Largest	Black, orange, red	Work over weed tops
	Jigs & artificials	Heavy; ¾ - 1 oz	Various	Tip with Reapers and Lizards
	Buzzing baits	Bass size	Yellow	Fast retrieve over weedbeds
	Crank baits	4″ to 6″	Various	Excellent on hot sunny days
	Bucktails	Small musky size	White, fluorescent colors	Best in early fall
Fall	Jerk baits	Smaller versions	Various	Better in late fall
	Sucker rigs	1 lb to 4 lbs		Use super big suckers around stream mouths

Chapter 9
Stream Trout:
Gems of the Rivers

Canoeing down a wilderness Canadian river can produce some amazing experiences. The trip I'm remembering had thus far been no different. The scenery was nothing short of heavenly; the fishing beyond that. Every bend in the river offered something new and exciting, including a bull moose that had let us drift so close that the rings from his splashing lapped on the bow of our canoe.

I was fishing with my friend, Jeff Howard, and we were having a ball! Walleyes and northern pike were almost everywhere. And even though we were more than happy to take advantage of the obliging fish, we were after the trophy brook trout that our host, Phil Robinson of Miminiska Lodge, had told us about.

After we wound our way through a vast meadow for some time, our guide stopped near the mouth of a marshy spring hole that flowed into the main river. Without a word we began to methodically work the hole with spoons, spinners and eventually jigs. The walleyes responded and we kept a few for our supper that evening.

Suddenly, the calm water up in the spring hole was shattered by a huge swirl that sent water splashing up against the grassy banks. My rod went double when the fish slammed the lure and I felt the throbbing that only a trophy brookie can give. Swapping ends, the fish turned and streaked by our boat, heading back for the main river. As the fish went by we could make out the unmistakable white-tipped fins that give the brookie a ghost-like appearance. The brute power of the trout surprised me. I had caught plenty of trout before, but none as powerful as this one.

A few moments later the fish was thrashing in the mesh and we lifted it in the canoe. The beauty of a freshly caught brook trout is hard to describe. Its dark green sides were speckled with blue, red and orange, its belly a deep copper. But the stunning thing about this fish was its size. I knew that it would easily go over four pounds, possibly five. This is what we had come for!

However, the spring hole had more surprises in store for us. Jeff's next cast resulted in another second strike, fight and landed fish that was a photo copy of the first. By the time we paddled out of the spring hole we landed over half a dozen trophy brookies, topped off by a gorgeous wall-hanger that weighed six pounds.

It is hard to comprehend fishing like that in this day and age. You'll hear that all the good brookie fishing is gone and as likely to come back as 29 cents-a-gallon gas. But, believe me, Canada still has some monster brook trout.

To fully appreciate how outstanding these brook trout are, you need to realize that to most trout fishermen a big brookie is any fish over 14 inches. Hard-core trout men will spend thousands of dollars, plus travel for many days just to get a shot at a brookie over four pounds. Yet we were able to get into unbelievable fishing like this in just a little more than one day's travel from central Minnesota.

Canada not only has giant brook trout, but other members of the trout family, such as rainbow, cutthroat, Dolly Varden and browns also swim in her waters. Each of these species is common somewhere in Canada.

In the Rocky Mountains, fly fishermen pursue the colorful cutthroat trout. This willing fish makes up a large portion of most angler's creels. On the west coast you'll find that the rainbow is king. Along the southern border, where many streams have become too warm and fertile for the brook trout, the brown trout finds suitable habitat. But probably the most common trout in Canada is the brookie. For the purpose of this chapter however, we will deal with only the brook, brown and the rainbow (see Figure 1).

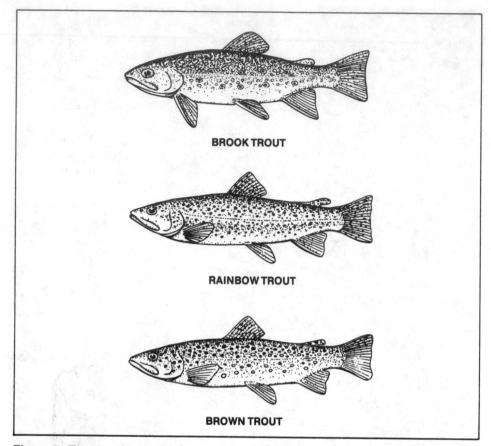

Figure 1. *Trout are amongst the most beautiful fish anywhere in the world. Their beauty, plus the reputation of being tenacious fighters, make them some of the most prized sportfish available.*

Brook Trout

These colorful fish are also known as brookies, speckled trout, specks or square-tails. Normally they average 10 to 12 inches long, but brookies up to eight pounds are caught every year in remote Canadian rivers. Actually the brook trout is not a trout at all, but is a member of the char family.

These fish sport an olive-green to dark brown back that lightens on the sides. The belly is usually silvery white, but may become orange-red, or coppery on the males as spawning season nears.

Light green or cream colored vermiculations cover the back and sides, giving the fish a marbled appearance. These worm-like markings are one of the things that separate the members of the char family from the trouts. The sides are profusely covered with spots that range from pale orange to ruby red surrounded by a blue halo. Sea run brook trout of the east coast become silvery after living in the saltwater for a while. They also have a purple iridescence that makes them strikingly beautiful.

In Canada, the brook trout is widely distributed throughout the Maritime Provinces on the east coast, including the offshore islands. Their range then extends westward through Quebec and the Great Lake drainage of Ontario, then northward to James and Hudson Bay including the Belcher and Akimiski Islands.

Brook trout have been successfully introduced into various areas in western Canada where they intermingle with their western relatives, the rainbow and cutthroat trout.

Indeed, the appeal of the brookie has caused it to be stocked much farther away than that. Many Canadian brook trout have been stocked in exotic corners of the world, including Europe, Asia, New Zealand, and even the Falkland Islands.

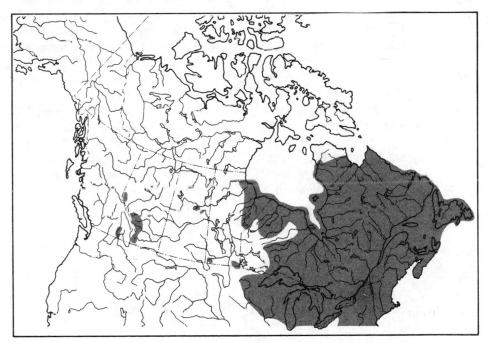

The Home Range of the Brook Trout

Rainbow Trout

The rainbow trout, like other members of the trout and char family, is a "plastic" species that differs in appearance considerably over its extended range. For some time these populations in different watersheds were believed to be separate species of fish. However, recently biologists have concluded that they are all different strains of the same fish.

Rainbows are found in many varying types of water, including lakes, rivers, trickling streams and the vast Great Lakes. Those found in inland rivers and streams are usually the Kamloops rainbow trout, while those that roam the Great Lakes and tributary streams are known as steelhead.

The Kamloops rainbow usually exhibit a stockier body than the steelhead and it's coloration is darker. The back, top of head and upper sides are olive-green, steel-blue or yellow-green. The sides are silvery, and the underparts are silvery-white. The cheeks and sides of the fish are marked with a rose, red or pink stripe that runs laterally from the cheek to the tail. This vivid stripe is what gives the rainbow its name. The sides, back upper fins and tail are marked with scattered black spots, mostly restricted to above the lateral line.

The steel-blue head and back of the steelhead rainbow give it its name. This bullet-shaped speedstar of the Great Lakes is usually more streamlined than the chunky Kamloops. In the Great Lakes, the steelhead has a grey, grey-blue, to black colored back with brilliant silvery sides that are covered with black spots. As with its inland cousin, these spots are mainly located above the lateral line.

What mostly sets the steelhead apart from the Kamloops is its greater size. While the Kamloops averages 12 to 28 inches in length, steelhead will run between 20 to 30 inches long. Those who have been thrilled to catch 12-inch rainbows in streams find it hard to imagine one running up to or even over 20 pounds. But they do exist, and giants like this are caught every year.

The native range of the rainbow trout, and all its' varieties, was from the rugged Canadian Rockies and westward to the Pacific Ocean. Around the turn of the century, however, the rainbow trout was introduced in southeastern Saskatchewan, southern Manitoba and Ontario. Then the steelhead was introduced along the northern shores of the Great Lakes, and today makes yearly runs up the tributaries in ever-increasing numbers.

From this range description it should be understandable that the rainbow trout is an important gamefish to many visiting anglers.

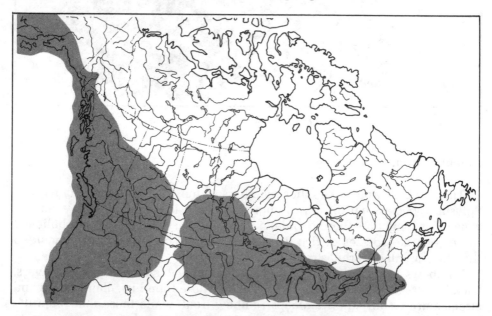

The Home Range of the Rainbow Trout

Brown Trout

Like most trouts, the brown is a strikingly beautiful fish. It has a typical trout-like body and averages about 16 inches in length.

As with the steelhead, there are brown trout that migrate to the Great Lakes where they spend most of their lives living in the big lakes. These browns may get as big as 20 pounds or more.

The brown have an overall tawny or light brown coloration, a darker brown on the back that becomes silvery on the sides. The sides and back have black spots in addition to rusty-red spots that may be surrounded by lighter colored halos. In the Great Lakes, the overall coloration is silvery, almost masking the spotting on the body.

The brown trout is native to Europe and Asia. But in the late 1800s and early 1900s it was introduced to many parts of eastern Canada and eventually western Canada. Today the brown trout is found in isolated spots throughout southern Canada, but is an important gamefish only in the provinces north of the Great Lakes, the southern Maritime Provinces and the rugged mountains in Alberta.

One of the reasons the brown trout has earned such a high regard in fishing circles is that it can survive in waters that are too polluted and warm for the native brook trout and rainbow trout to survive. So, today the brown trout thrives in the warm, fertile waters around large metropolitan areas in the east and Great Lakes region.

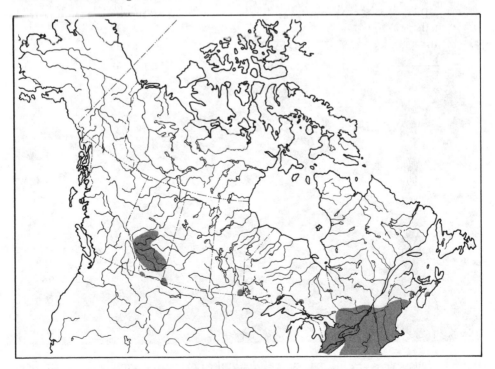

The Home Range of the Brown Trout

Wild, rushing rivers are just one of the plentiful resources in Canada. Many of them are called home by the most beautiful fishes of all, the trouts.

Whether brook, brown or rainbow, the trouts flourish in cold, clear water, one of Canada's plentiful resources. Even though these different species live side by side in many rivers, there are distinct differences at times that will separate them. The biggest difference is the preferred temperature range. The ideal feeding temperature for brook trout is when the water temperature is between 55 and 62 degrees F. Above 70 degrees F. the brookies become lethargic and lose all interest in food. On the other hand, browns and rainbows are most active when the water is between 60 and 66 degrees. They will survive in water that is 80 degrees F. for a limited time, but they will feed so little that successful angling is out of the question.

A typical trout stream is illustrated in Figure 2. The cold, spring-fed headwaters of many Canadian rivers will only support the brook trout because of the cold water temperatures. As the river begins to build in volume, gets wider and slower, rainbows and brown trout will begin to take the place of brookies. As the river nears its final stages you may only find the warm water resistant brown trout.

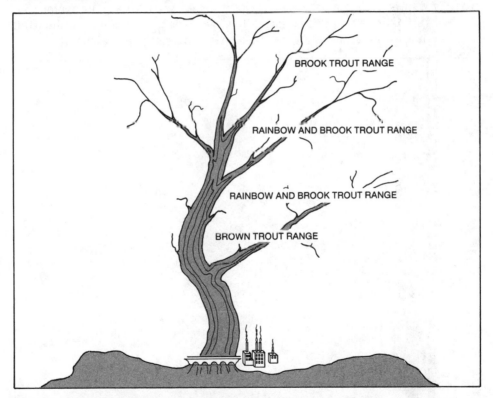

Figure 2. *Many streams and rivers will have brook, rainbow and brown trout in them, but they won't always inhabit the same areas. The cold, spring-fed headwaters of many Canadian rivers will support only the brook trout because of it's preference for very cold water. As the river builds in volume, gets wider and current slows, you'll begin to find more rainbow and brown trout. As the river nears it's final stages and industrialization tends to alter the river, the warm water resistant brown trout may be the only trout able to exist.*

Though this is a capsulized example, it is an important concept to grasp in order to understand trout and their preferred habitat. An example such as this may cover many hundreds of miles, but this transition takes place in many trout streams.

Stream trout under normal conditions do not usually go through major seasonal movements like many of the other gamefish that we have talked about. Many trout are born and die within a single stretch of river. However, this is not the case all the time. In some northern rivers that are fed by good-sized tributaries there may be extensive annual migratory movements. Or, in rivers that run in or out of lakes there may be movements between the lake and river.

One example in particular that comes to mind is the Albany River in north central Ontario. The Albany is a good sized river that holds a super population of king-sized brook trout. Along its route there are many tributary streams that flow into it (see Figure 3).

During the spring and early summer when the ice leaves the main river, the trout will already begin seeking out optimum temperatures. The water that flows in from the tributaries is normally several degrees colder and the trout will begin to gather at the mouths of these tributaries soon after ice-out.

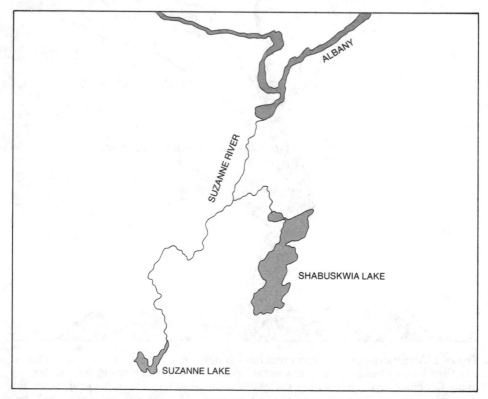

Figure 3. *A typical, Canadian wilderness river will often have several, cool, spring-fed tributaries. When the water in the main river becomes too warm, the brookies will move up the tributary arms toward the springs.*

In the early season, fishing can be outstanding at these tributary mouths. However, as the main river gets warmer, the trout will move up the tributary streams many miles. During this time they will stop in deep holes above and below rapids or in deep cuts in the river bends. As the water temperature rises even further the trout will actually move in large numbers to the mouths of spring holes that flow into the tributaries (see Figure 4). The number of trophy trout that can be stacked in one of these spring holes is mind-boggling. It is not out of the ordinary to catch up to eight trout weighing two to six pounds out of a single spring hole. If you were to take a temperature reading in one of these spring holes you would find that the water is several degrees cooler than the main tributary. Those few degrees are all it takes to pull trout in like a magnet.

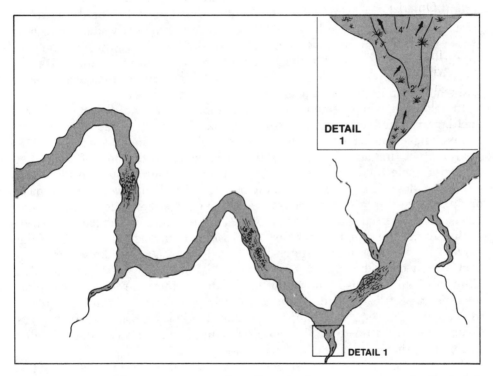

Figure 4. *Later in the summer, even the tributaries become too warm for the brook trout. In this case they will move right into the spring mouths as shown in Detail 1.*

With the approach of fall, the waters will start to cool. Now the trout will reverse their movements and move downstream to winter in the main river. This cycle has been repeated for many years and will continue to do so. It is the way the trout have adapted to survive.

Basically, trout spend much of their lives seeking out water temperatures where they can find comfort. If they can find cool water in springs or deep holes only a few yards away they will only move a few yards. If it takes swimming 20 miles to find the right temperatures, they may go 20 miles. Even though this may be an extreme case, it happens.

Years ago, when I was just getting my feet wet as a trout fisherman (pardon the pun), an older friend took me under his wing and taught me a timeless lesson. He said, "You've got to learn to read a trout stream. After all, a trout is just like you, he wants something to eat, a comfortable place to rest and something to protect him."

Since then I've learned that a fisherman who learns the conditions that create these essentials should be able to catch trout from any stream in the world.

This lesson was driven home to me on a small trout stream that was a typical example of the streams that course through Canada. In a section of the river was a log jam that funneled most of the stream flow into a small pool. Many was the night that I would sneak down to that spot, shoot a number 16 caddis imitation into the current and let it drift down into the pool. Soon there would be a splash and a tug as a sleek trout took to the air with my fly stuck in his jaw. It was rare when there wasn't a trout waiting in the pool waiting for the current to wash some morsel to them. Some nights I'd find two or three trout in there. Why would these trout wait in line to fall for a dry fly? Because this spot had what the trout was looking for. Food, cover and comfort.

In a sense, a trout stream is like a book: some parts are dull and others are exciting. Experienced fishermen can recognize the sections that have promise for excitement and save valuable time by skipping over the dull parts.

One of the first clues to trout location is current. It is the flow of water that sucks food into feeding lanes, gouges deep holes where trout can hide, and creates eddies and cushions where the trout can rest. Wherever a rock or a log or an upturned tree stump breaks the flow of the stream there are current breaks, and where there are current breaks there should be fish (see Figure 5).

But, sometimes it is not that easy. Occassionally the fish will lie out of the current for one reason or another. In the early season when the water is uncomfortably cold, the fish may move into still shallow water along the edge where the sun has raised the water temperature a few degrees. In a situation like this, comfort is more important to the fish than cover or finding a plentiful food source. Consequently later in the season, when the water temperatures become too warm for trout, the same fish will poke their noses into a feeder stream or spring hole and lie in its cool flow.

So at any time of day or year, one of the trout's three basic needs may become more important than another. For example, if the water is high and the current strong, comfort may be the trout's immediate need. So I look for the fish in backwaters and eddies, outside the brunt of the main current. This is especially important in some remote streams where big brookies are found (see Figure 6).

Is the water low and clear? Then cover becomes the dominant need. Trout will move beneath undercut banks, dark holes under rocks and boulders, or areas of broken water like riffles and rapids.

Some of these holding spots are so obvious that a beginner can find them. Others show only faintly at the surface as gentle boils and creases that form when the current hits a submerged rock or other obstacle. These are more dif-

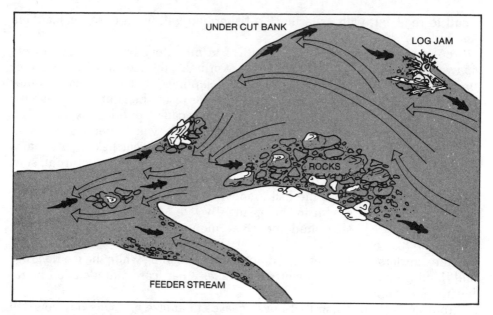

Figure 5. Trout are much like any living creature in that they are continually trying to fulfill their needs for food, protection and comfort. If you find a spot in a river that provides these, you will find fish.

Normally the first clue to these fish holding areas is current. It is the flow of water that sucks food into feeding lanes, gouges deep holes where trout can hide, creates eddies and cushions where the trout can rest. Wherever a rock, log or upturned tree stump breaks the flow of the stream there are currents, and where there are currents there should be fish.

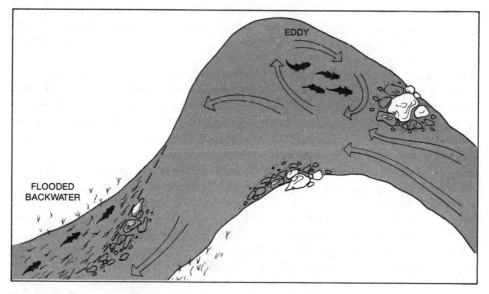

Figure 6. When spring runoffs or heavy rains cause the streams to swell and over-run their banks, trout will move to places out of the brunt of the heavy current. Ideal places to look for trout under these conditions are eddies and back water areas.

ficult to read, but with experience a fisherman will learn to recognize them and put more trout in his creel.

You can apply these same principles to migratory trout that move into spawning streams from the Great Lakes. Normally, the schools of steelhead or browns will move up stream in stages, stopping in deep holes or other protected places such as log jams, boulder piles or washed out trees that have fallen in the river. Just like other trout, these fish can be predictably located.

Seasonal movements are very important when you're dealing with migratory trout that move in from lakes, such as the Great Lakes, to streams where they will spawn. Fall spawners, like the brook and brown trout, start into the rivers anywhere from October through November. Of course, early signs of winter will cause the fish to move more quickly. On the other hand, most rainbow trout spawn in the spring. By late March, or early April, the steelhead will school around the river mouths, preparing to ascend the streams to spawn.

Many anglers have experienced phenomenal fishing while the ice floes are still floating in the rivers. Of course this takes a hardcore attitude and several layers of long underwear.

Trout are a unique fish that never ceases to amaze me. One day you will carefully work a feeding fish by using long casts, 12-foot leaders and tiny #22 flies, only to have the fish totally refuse them. Thirty minutes later you can toss out a huge nightcrawler threaded on a #8 hook and the same trout might go head over fins to gulp down the crude offering. Is there a lesson in this? You bet there is! Like the Boy Scouts say, "Be Prepared!"

On a drizzly, dark day, some time ago, I learned this lesson. We had planned a trout fishing trip, and my anticipation was great as the day approached. On the night before it literally poured and everything was saturated. But by the time I readied my gear the next morning the rain had stopped. Out of a whim, I grabbed my spinning rod along with my fly fishing gear. Just why I did I'll never know, but I'm glad of it.

Upon arriving at the river, I was shocked at how my pretty, little babbling brook had turned into a raging torrent the color of chocolate milkshake. But, undaunted, I tied on a colorful streamer and began to fish. However, after 45 minutes of getting casting practice with no results, I was getting concerned. And after another 45 minutes I decided to head for more accommodating water.

As I rounded one of the last bends on the way back to camp, I encountered another soggy fellow who was patiently drifting worms into a deep hole.

"How's it going?" I asked. "Not too good," was the reply.

"I see you're using worms," I ventured again. "Yup" was his reply. By then I got the feeling that our conversation was not going well.

As I stood there trying to excuse myself and still maintain my pleasant attitude, I noticed he had a canvas creel hanging by a strap from his shoulder. It was all wet and had a bulging look to it. At that point his eyes caught mine and was what I was looking at. He suddenly looked like a kid caught with his hand in the cookie jar. Just as he turned away, the canvas creel began flopping, giving away its hidden contents. With that the fellow turned and confessed to me

194

about how he had been killing the trout with nightcrawlers all morning. I guess he was trying to make up for his fibbing. In fact, he insisted that I take half his worms and join him. Then I remembered that I did have my spinning rod, some split shot and small hooks with me.

With worms and rod in hand, I returned to one of the trout holes that had just recently disappointed me that morning. I picked out one of the biggest worms and hooked it once underneath the collar. Then I lobbed the outfit out into the upstream side of the hole where it landed with a "plop." I could feel the worm tapping along the bottom when suddenly it stopped. I slowly tightened up on the line to feel if it was a submerged rock I had snagged, or if it was a hungry trout. A slight jerking at the end of the line told me it was not a rock, and I set the hook. Out from the water shot a brilliantly colored brown trout, with gills flaring red and sides gleaming. After several more jumps and splashing acrobatics, I gently slipped my hands under the gill cover and lifted it out of the water. I took a moment to admire his dark brown back with flaming ruby spots and his brilliantly colored fins. What a prize it was! Later, I weighed the fish and it dropped the needle to over six pounds, not bad for a heavily fished river where smaller fish are the rule.

Within an hour later I walked back to camp carrying a limit of chunky brown trout. I waved to my new friend, who was still working the deep hole and he waved back, acknowledging the string of fish I hoisted up to show him.

Since then it is second nature for me to include spinning gear along with my fly fishing tackle when I leave on a trout fishing trip. Of course there have been times when the trout have rejected worms, yet took dry flies readily. Sometimes the fish fall for spinners spoons or crankbaits over anything else. So, if room permits, take along whatever tackle is necessary to meet each situation.

While fishing in Canada, I have caught trout on fly fishing tackle, spoons, spinners, crankbaits, jigs and live bait rigs. One type of tackle may be better at certain times, or all of them may work under the same conditions. However, certain stream conditions may make one technique easier to use than another. For example, a tiny brook with a low ceiling of trees would make fly casting very difficult, so drifting a worm might be the best here. Or if you encounter a wide-open section of river, it may be more effective to cast streamers with a fly rod, or cast spoons with spinning gear.

Another factor you must take into consideration is the predator/prey relationship. If you're fishing a stream that has abundant insect life such as mayflies or caddis flies but few minnows, flyfishing with nymphs or dry flies will probably be your best bet. If you see trout rising to take insects off the surface, take notice of what they are feeding on and try to match it with your selection of flies.

In many Canadian rivers, the big trout feed on sculpins, a small minnowsized fish that hides under rocks, boulders and other debris. Streamers such as the Muddler minnow imitate the sculpin, and many deep-bodied wild trout have been taken on it.

Bit trout get big by eating big. Trout that have grown to trophy proportions often do so thanks to an unpleasant feeding habit, namely cannibalism. These lunkers do not get the necessary energy from eating insects, so they eat the available forage fish, which many times are young trout. Sculpins, walleye fry and minnows also fall prey to these monsters. To hook these big fish you need a large lure or bait. Spoons are a very popular big trout lure along with spinners, crankbaits and jigs.

The thing to ask yourself before you choose your tackle is, what am I trying to imitate? What do the fish eat here? What conditions am I faced with? These considerations will make the decision for you (see Figure 7).

MATCHING PREDATOR/PREY RELATIONSHIPS

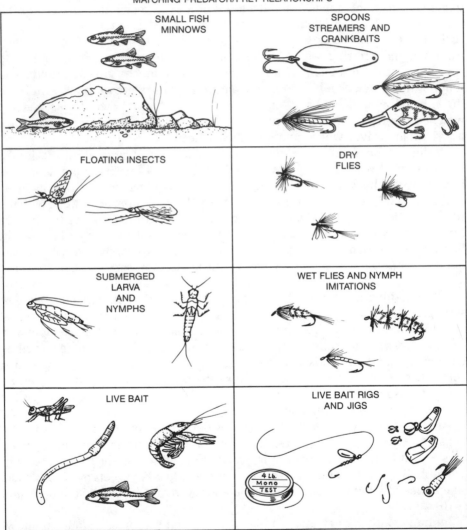

Figure 7. *A good rule of thumb to go by when selecting lures is to consider the predator/prey relationship. If the trout are surface feeding on insects, use dry flies. If they are feeding on minnows, use minnow imitating streamers or lures and so on. It's all very simple to grasp, but you always need to be prepared to give the fish what they want.*

Many young trout fishermen cut their teeth on trout with a can of worms in their hand. Live bait has always been a deadly way of taking these wary, spotted fish.

The list of necessary tackle is not a long one: hooks, sinkers, Lindy trout snells and some sort of bait should about do it. I use a thin wire hook, such as an Aberdeen style, because they penetrate easily, yet they bend easily under a steady pull if snagged. A size 8 or 10 will work well, depending on your choice of bait. Carry an assortment of various size split shot because you'll need to experiment to come up with a combination that will give you the proper drift. Add enough weight so that your bait will bump along the bottom slightly slower that the current flow. If you put on too much weight it will anchor your bait to the bottom, which tends to frighten away even the dumbest trout. Too little weight will not keep your bait near the bottom where the fish are. To select the right amount of weight you need to consider the type of spot you are fishing and the current.

I suggest you use spinning gear for this type of fishing. A spinning rod will let you carefully drift a worm into a trout's hiding spot or fire a spinner out across a wild foaming river. Either a pack rod or a telescopic rod such as Lew's graphic ETUL-5S will allow you to easily carry your fishing outfit to remote places.

Your choice of line can be very important. Six-pound test will work fine during low light periods or when the water is cloudy during runoffs. But, when the water is clear, or very low, don't hesitate to switch to four-pound or even two-pound test. A high quality, clear line, such as Stren Clear will really make a difference. Your line will get cuts and nicks from rocks, logs or other stream debris. Occassionally cut off the last two feet so that you always have strong, fresh line when you have to pull a big rainbow out of a log pile.

Trout can be taken on a variety of live baits including worms, crickets, grasshoppers, minnows, nightcrawlers, leeches, salmon eggs or spawn. The most effective baits tend to be those that naturally occur in the surrounding environment. During the late summer, grasshoppers are a prime bait in streams that run along meadows and fields. Trout will hang in the currents that run along overhanging banks, waiting for an unfortunate hopper to fall in. During rains or runoffs, your best bet may be worms or nightcrawlers. These wriggling morsels often get washed into the rivers, and the trout know it. Leeches are found in many Canadian rivers and can be a dynamite bait for trout. In fact, some of the biggest brook trout I've caught have been on leeches. These critters can seduce a big trout out from the heaviest cover.

Remember, don't thread your bait on the hook, but hook it lightly once. The bait needs to look natural. Threading a worm or nightcrawler on a hook takes away much of the advantage of live bait. Let the bait move and work for you.

Other popular live baits are small crayfish, grubs and nymphs. Checking the stomach contents of your catch will help you determine just what the fish have been feeding on.

Fly fishing and trout have been synonymous for centuries. A good number of Canadian streams have an abundance of aquatic insects, mayflies, caddis flies, and terrestrial insects, and most trout depend on them for survival. The only way to imitate these minute insects effectively is with flyfishing gear.

To be properly prepared for the myriad of insects that the trout can be feeding on, you should have an assortment of dry flies, wet flies, nymphs, bucktails and streamers. Once you've concluded what the trout are feeding on you can match the hatch.

A proven assortment of flies, nymphs, bucktails and streamers are:

Dry Flies
Sizes 12, 14, 16

Quill Gordon	Adams	Renegade
Hendrickson	March Brown	Various Wulff patterns
Light Cahill	Hairwing Royal Coachman	Elk Hair Caddis
Ginger Quill	Various cream colored patterns	Grasshopper patterns

Wet Flies
Sizes 12, 14

Brown Wooly Worm	March Brown	Montreal
Black Wooly Worm	Coachman	Parmachene Belle

Nymphs
Sizes 10, 12, 14

Tellico	Breadcrust	All-purpose light pattern
Zug Bug	Hare's Ear	All-purpose dark pattern

Bucktails & Streamers
Sizes 2, 4, 6, 8

Muddler Minnow (weighted and unweighted)	Mickey Finn	White Marabou Muddler
Muddler/leech	Black Leech	Platinum Blonde
Black Nose Dace	Brown Leech	Tri-color Bucktail

Fly fishing and trout fishing are nearly synonymous, and in Canada it is no different. Most of the world record brook trout have been taken on flies or streamers. But spinning rods with small hardware work just as well most of the time.

In order to cut down on weight and confusion, I like to use a rod that will handle wet flies and dry flies and streamers. An eight foot graphite rod that will handle seven weight line is just the ticket. A rod like this can delicately cast a dry fly, or punch out a weighted streamer into the teeth of a strong wind. Top this off with a reel with interchangeable spools and you are all set. Load one spool with a double tapered floating line and a spare spool with a weight forward sinking line and you'll be ready for anything.

One classic pattern of trout movement that takes place in mid-summer is when the trophy brook trout move into the spring holes. One of the best ways to take them, and by far the most enjoyable, is using a fly rod and casting Muddler Minnows to them. I guarantee that when one of those big brutes smacks your streamer and roars by you you'll be so excited that you may squeeze your rod grip into cork dust.

Perhaps the easiest, and many times the most effective, method for trout is using lures. Using crankbaits and jigs may sound odd to many trout purists, but they can turn some really big trout.

If there is one rule referring to lures and stream trout that is cut in stone it is "always cast upstream...usually." I add "usually" because there are times when retrieving your lure against the current may catch fish. But, the vast majority of the time a lure swimming against the current will scare the spots off a wary trout.

The reason upstream fishing pays off is that the lure or bait comes to the fish in a more natural manner. The lures will sink naturally and wash through the feeding lanes along with the other food. It's tricky, because of the difficulty of keeping the lure near the bottom where it belongs without getting snagged all the time. The trick is to cast upriver from an angle, hold the rod high, and retrieve the lure just a touch faster than the current speed (see Figure 8).

Figure 8. Trout are accustomed to having their dinner washed down to them by the current and anything that behaves unnaturally, or seems to be doing something out of the ordinary, may scare the spots off a wary trout. Always make sure you allow your lure or bait to wash down with the current in a natural manner.

Small lures work the best because they require very little water resistance to keep them fluttering.

Of course, it isn't always possible to work a trout looking hole by casting upstream. For an example, some of the best spots are pockets surrounded by frothing, foaming water. In these situations, you cast your lure to the spot any way you can. But, whenever possible, try to work your lure in a natural manner, flowing downstream. It'll show up in the number of trout lining your creel at the end of the day.

The stream condition, depth and current speed will determine what type of lure can be used. Keep in mind that you first must try to imitate whatever the fish may be feeding on. In shallow water, a minnow bait such as a Lindy Baitfish, Rapala, Rebel or Hellcat will work well. These lures can be retrieved over submerged rocks and logs without hanging up.

For intermediate depths you can use crankbaits or the ever-popular spoons and spinners. Lindy Shadlings, Snipes, Fat Raps and Bagley's Small Fry Shads are all proven crankers that drive trout crazy. Some spoons that you will want to include are small Daredevles, Little Cleos, Swedish Pimples, and Al's Goldfish. Spinners such as Lindy's Crazy Spin, Mepps, Rooster Tails and Panther Martins work well too.

To most people, all of these trout are once in a life time trophies, but to Phil Robinson and crew, they are just another day's catch.

During the early summer, when the water hasn't gotten too warm yet, the trout will often move into deep holes and runs. You can usually find these deep spots above and below rapids. Also, where the river makes a tight turn the current will erode a deep channel. It takes a deep-running lure to get down to the bottom in the feeding range of the trout. In conditions like this my first choice is a jig. With a Lindy Fuzz-E-Grub, Quiver jigs, Crappie Queens, Mr. Twister or Dingo Jigs, you can scour the depths and turn the fish on when other lures just can't cut it.

Tipping a jig with a crawler or leech can really make a difference. At times I have worked a deep hole with a variety of spoons, and the trout wouldn't even give them a look. But when I threw out a chartreuse Fuzz-E-Grub tipped with a leech I got jumbo brookies one after another.

It pays to experiment and try different lures. Don't discount a lure or bait until you've tried it. These wild trout are by no means dumb, even though they haven't been subjected to much fishing pressure. They still have the legendary trout wariness and sharp vision. Just remember to use simple and effective techniques.

One little trick that I use when I'm fishing with lures is to have two rods rigged with different lures. Normally one has a spoon and the other a jig. If I have a fish swirl at but miss the lure I'm using, I'll immediately grab the other rod and cast the other lure to the same fish. More often than not, the fish will hit the second lure without hesitation.

Nobody enjoys fishing for the variety of fish that Canada offers more than I do. However, taking trophy trout from these wilderness rivers has to be one of the greatest experiences of all. The beauty of these fish, matched with the splendor of Canadian wilderness where they are found, makes for wonderful experiences.

I'll never forget the evening some of my friends and I slipped down to the edge of a small stream north of Lake Superior in Ontario. The stream was well known for its excellent trout fishing and we were anticipating an exciting evening.

The sun was just starting to settle over the horizon and the trout were beginning to feed in earnest. We could see dimples on the surface as the trout gobbled floating insects. I tied on a small dark fly that a streamside friend had given me on our last trip. He said it was dynamite fly for evening rainbow trout, and I was going to give it a try.

I had chosen to work upstream toward a set of rapids where I'd enjoyed good luck before. And sure enough, soon I could hear a trout swatting at swirls of small black insects that were buzzing near the water. With a long cast, I dropped the small dry fly just upstream from the circles left by the rising fish. The current plucked gently at the fly and it began to drift over the fish. *Splash!* The acrobatic rainbow came right out of the water with the small fly clenched between its jaws, and I reacted instantly. My rod bent double and throbbed at the racing fish. It was nip and tuck for a moment as the fish got under a log jam, but I worked it out and soon slid the net under it. Even in the waning light, the crimson sides of the fish gleamed. "What a beauty," I said out loud to

Some people will go to any length to catch fish. Babe will agree that balancing in this precarious position is worth it when you can catch a trophy like this.

myself. But after a moment of admiration of the fish's beauty, I slid it back into the current and watched it slowly fin itself down under the logs.

By now the sun had slipped down the sky behind the tree line. In the excitement I hadn't realized how dark it had become. But the fish didn't care. Up ahead the riffle below the rapids was alive with feeding fish. The surface was continuously broken by leaping, slashing trout. I slowly crept along the shore and positioned myself so I could safely cast without getting hung up.

On my first cast, the fly had scarcely settled on the surface when a trout smashed it. I brought it in quickly so it wouldn't spook any of the other fish. Like my first fish, this one was a chunky, rainbow trout. I laid out another cast as quickly as I could and was onto another trout before I could get ready. What a night it was! I don't even remember how many trout I landed from that stretch of river.

As I headed back to my friends in the dark, I could still hear the feeding trout rippling the surface. A marvelous night. And that spot, and many more just like it, are waiting in Canada for some lucky angler to enjoy.

STREAM TROUT SEASONAL LURE SELECTION

Season	Bait or Lure Type	Size	Color	Remarks
Spring	Live bait systems	#8 - #12 hook small split shot		Drift into deep holes, work very slow. Worms or crawlers are best
	Small spoons	1" to 2"	Metallic or fluorescent	Fish slowly with current
	Streamers	#8 - #12	Various baitfish colors	Use weighted streamers to get deep and slow
	Weighted nymphs	#10 - #16	Dark brown or black	Use weighted nymphs
Early Summer	Live bait systems	#8 - #12 hook small split shot		Try other baits, minnows, crayfish, Hellgramites, and nymphs
	Spoons	1" - 3"	Metallic or fluorescent	Excellent around tributary mouths
	Nymphs	#10 - #16	Match local insect larva	Best around midday and afternoon
	Dry flies	#12 - #18	Match hatching insects with blacks, browns, and cream colored flies	Best in evenings
Late Summer	Spoons	1" - 3"	Metallic or fluorescent	Fish faster and experiment various retrieves
	Spinners	Small to medium sizes	Brass, silver, and black blades	Fish with current, letting spinner slowly turn
	Live bait	#8 - #12 hook small split shot		Try grasshoppers and minnows
	Jigs	1/16 oz	Hot yellow	Tip with leech or minnow
	Crank baits and minnow baits	Small sizes	Gold, silver, and natural finishes	Work big fish areas
	Streamers	#8 - #12	Big, bushy and dark	Try night fishing, especially for browns
	Dry flies	#8 -#18	Match color of local insects	Use terrestrials such as grasshoppers, beetles, and ants
Fall	Streamers	#8 - #12	Various natural and attractor colors	Fish slower as water cools
	Live bait systems	#8 - #12 hooks		Use any local bait, fish slower, try spawn and salmon eggs
	Spoons and other artificials	1" -3"	Metallic, fluorescent, and natural finishes	Work streams near lakes or tributary mouths

Chapter 10
Miscellaneous Fish

Canada's waters offer a marvellous smorgasbord of fish species. So far we've discussed in detail some of the major species sought after by anglers in Canada, but within the countless lakes and rivers swim some exotic species as well that are not found any other place on the continent. Fish such as the brilliant Arctic char, native only to the northern most waters, and the delicate grayling, an unbelievably beautiful fish prized by fly anglers as one of the ultimate trophies. Or the elusive inconnu, a king-sized member of the whitefish family that's rarely caught by sport anglers. Trophies? To be sure. And they're found only in the Canadian wilderness.

But there are other species as well. A frying pan favorite, the yellow perch, is a highly sought after gamefish in some regions. Other areas offer fantastic largemouth bass fishing. Even the crappie and bluegill play an important role in the Canadian fishing scene in some waters.

While many of these fish are found only in certain regions of the country, they comprise a segment of Canadian fishing that we certainly don't want to overlook if we want to understand the total spectrum of the Canadian fishing frontier.

Arctic Grayling

Perhaps no other fish is more reminiscent of the grandeur of the Canadian northwest than this small, delicately colored gamefish. Many anglers have been thrilled by its acrobatic leaps, unique appearance, and willingness to bite.

The arctic grayling is not a large fish, only getting up to 18 or 20 inches long. Though there was one caught on the Katyseyedie River in Northwest Territories that was almost 30 inches long and weighed 5 pounds, 15 ounces. But the grayling makes up for its relatively small size with its spunk and fighting ability.

It's hard to describe the beauty of the grayling. The body is an irridescent purplish gray and silver, sprinkled with small, dark spots. The most unique characteristic of this fish is it's sail-like dorsal fin. This overly large fin is dark gray with rows of violet or blue spots set off by light borders. The upper edge of the fin is bright red. All in all, a strikingly beautiful fish.

Perhaps no other fish is more reminiscent of the Canadian Northwest than the delicate grayling. It's fighting acrobatics, unique appearance, and willingness to bite make it a favorite amongst anglers.

The favored habitat of the grayling is the cold, clear waters found in the northwest portion of Canada. The range specifically covers the Northwest Territories and Yukon east of Alaska, to Hudson Bay and south to central British Columbia, Alberta and northwestern Manitoba.

Grayling will be found in lakes, rocky rivers and streams. But, they will avoid extremely turbulent water found in some of the bigger rivers. The grayling are definitely not a deep water fish. In fact, in Great Slave Lake they have never been netted any deeper than 10 feet.

These fish are almost completely insect feeders. Stomach samples show they feed heavily on mayflies, caddisflies and midges, in all insect stages. They also feed on terrestrial insects such as grasshoppers, ants, beetles and wasps. Ciscoes and small grayling will occasionally be taken by grayling, but they depend on bugs for most of their nutrition.

Grayling will feed especially heavily on hot, still days when the water is like glass. On one occasion I was fishing a small lake out from Chummy Plummer's camp in northern Canada. The conditions were perfect, and I was anticipating great fishing. When I walked up to the shore to start fishing I was greeted with an unforgettable sight. There in the ultra-clear water were vast schools of grayling moving in toward the shallows. Even though I could hardly restrain my casting hand, I took a moment to watch the beautiful fish swirl and chase as they fed.

My first cast landed just behind the largest fish I could see. The fish turned to grab the spinner. That grayling put on a showy fight, leaping and throwing

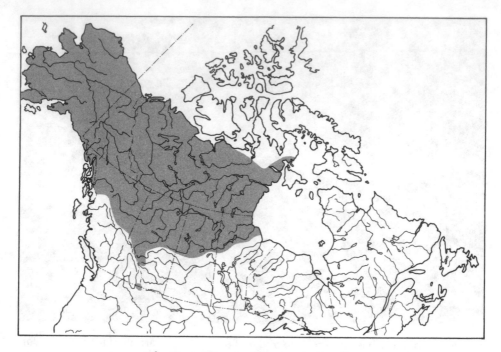

The Home Range of the Arctic Grayling

water everywhere. In a few moments I was unhooking it and sliding it back into the water, looking for the next one. It was a day to remember, as fish after fish tore into spinners, jigs, flies—anything I put on. Before I returned to the main camp, I caught and released over 70 grayling up to 3½ pounds. Outstanding, but typical of grayling fishing.

Grayling have a definite weakness for wet and dry flies, particularly in the late summer. During this time they will feed most actively in the late afternoon and early evening. Grayling will take most flies readily, but I've had my best success using dark flies such as Black Gnats and some of the darker mayfly patterns. I also include some caddis patterns, black McMurray Ants, McMurray Grasshoppers and Black Midges in sizes #18 to #14. In wet flies, I have used Black Wooly Worms and Coachmans with success, as well as other miscellaneous patterns in sizes #10 to #12.

Grayling are particularly fun for flyfishermen. At times, anglers throwing hardware on spinning rods will go fishless for hours while the flyrodder is constantly into fish. While nymphs or wet flies take their share of fish, often the best fly is one that rides the surface. And that just adds to the fun. Because a grayling's mouth is low and almost under its head, it takes a surface fly with a distinctive, aggressive strike. The best fly for catching a bunch of grayling in an actively moving river is one of the parachute-style patterns. These have hackle swirled in a circle around a high-standing, easily seen white wing. Parachute flies will float even after catching 50 fish, and they make it much easier to keep track of your fly as it rides the currents. Usually it is not necessary to match the hatch.

208

Having a good fly rod will help you present the flies in a more natural manner. This is very important when even these wilderness grayling decide to become finicky about what they take. So I use a Lew Childre's GF-28, an 8-foot graphite rod that will handle versatile 5 and 6 weight lines. This rod also features aluminum oxide guides for smoother casting. It isn't necessary to have an expensive multiplying reel. A good quality single action reel such as a Plueger Medalist or Berkley Specialist works perfectly well.

Many grayling are taken on hardware, too. Never fail to include some small straight-shaft spinners, jigs and small spoons in your tackle box. Small spinners such as Mepps OO and similarly small Rooster Tails work extremely well. Little Cleos, Daredevils, Aqua Spoons, Als Goldfish and other small spoons also take their share of grayling. But, even though it may surprise some, I've taken most of my grayling on small jigs. Small ⅟₁₆ ounce Fuzz-E-Grubs and Quiver Jigs in brown, black and black/orange are all dynamite.

For an array of lures like this, a spinning rod is the most efficient outfit. If you plan on traveling, or backpacking into an area, a telescopic rod or pack rod works great. Use a light reel like a Speed Spin 1 and fill it with light 4- or 6-pound test mono. Avoid using heavier line as it will cut down on your casting distance and might spook any line-shy fish.

Grayling are an exciting fish to catch and really reflect the fragile environment they live in. Their habit of tasting everything on the surface of the water make them an attractive sport fish. This, plus their need for clear, cold, unpolluted water and their slow growth rate endanger them today as populated areas close in on them. Anybody who is lucky enough to travel to the Canadian Northwest should get in on the action. But please release your fish. Your unselfish fishing practices will ensure fantastic grayling fishing for years to come.

Arctic Char

This strikingly beautiful fish is the most northernly located freshwater fish of all. But that hasn't stopped anglers from pursuing them to the far regions of the north.

Chars are closely related to the trouts, but there are subtle differences such as smaller scales and different tooth arrangements. However, the char is most well known for the vivid colors they develop during their spawning runs. Their sides will turn brilliant red or scarlet. When the fish aren't spawning, they'll usually be silver colored. But their colors may vary between bright red and silver.

The flesh of the char is usually red orange in color but may be pinkish or white. But, whatever the color, the flesh of these arctic fish is highly esteemed in the finest restaurants in the world.

Char are a good-sized gamefish, running between 2 to 10 pounds normally. Right now the largest recorded char was one weighing 32 pounds, 9 ounces, caught by Jeff Ward out of the Chummy Plummer Camp on the Tree River, in Northwest Territories.

The Arctic char is the most northernly located freshwater fish there is. But this hasn't stopped anglers like Nick Adams of Lindy-Little Joe from going after them.

The range of the arctic char is roughly circumpolar, that is, it circles the arctic polar region. This includes the islands of the Northwest Territories, all the way down to southeastern Quebec in the east.

Char are normally found in the estuaries near the mouths of large rivers flowing into the ocean. Then during the spawning runs they will move upriver and spawn in quiet pools. At times char can be found in huge numbers below barrier falls where their upstream movement is stopped. The runs take place in September and October in the northern part of the range. In the south along the eastern seaboard they may run as late as November and December.

It is during these fall runs that the char is most susceptible to angling methods. Each year anglers hike up rivers such as the Matamek or George River in Quebec. Most famous of all is the Tree River in the Northwest Territories, where many record char have been caught. Most of these rivers cover many miles, so it might require some long distance hiking in order to find the fish. Char are not great leapers like some of the trouts and salmons, so they will not usually get past any good sized waterfalls. Thus one of the best places to find concentrations of char is below a barrier falls. When the runs are heavy, the water will look almost blood red because there are so many fish.

The most common food of the char are small fishes, including small codfish, sand lances and capelin. And, these forage fish are best imitated with spoons, spinners, plugs and jigs. Bring plenty of lures with orange, chrome and brass colors. When it comes to jigs, I've done well with ¼-ounce Fuzz-E-Grubs and Quiver Jigs in shad, black and hot pink with white.

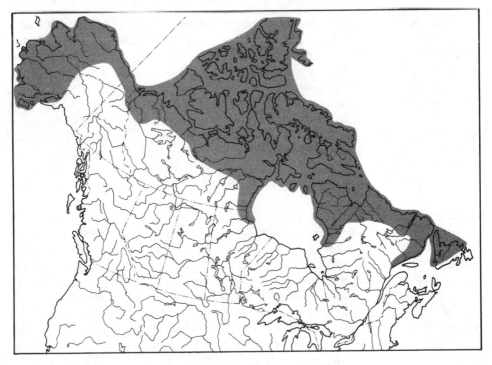

The Home Range of the Arctic Char

Either spinning or baitcasting gear will work well for char. But these fish are tough customers, so bring a sturdy 6-foot spinning rod such as Lew's SG4-16S or a G056X casting rod with a BB 2N reel filled with 8- to 12-pound high quality mono.

Fly fishermen also take their share of char. Because char feed on minnows, not insects, stick with streamers. Minnow-imitating streamers such as the Black Nosed Dace, Silver Doctor, White Muddler with a rabbit fur wing, and the Tri-Color Bucktail.

Because you might be facing big rivers, you should use a hefty rod that can punch out a streamer across a 70-foot pool. I use a 9-foot graphite rod that can handle 8 weight sinking line. In some cases it pays to switch to a shooting taper such as Cortland's 444 or the Scientific Anglers Wet Cel Hi-D in order to get the streamer down to the fish.

In the past few years I have witnessed an increased angling interest in the arctic char. The beauty, delectable eating, and feisty nature of the char has made it a most sought-after fish in the world. These qualities plus the wild, exotic land they are found in, make char fishing one of the world's most exciting wilderness fishing trips.

Largemouth Bass

This highly regarded sport fish is quite common in parts of southern Canada. In fact, some lakes have such a high population of bass that they rival the fabled largemouth fishery of the southern United States. The Ten Thousand Island Regions of the St. Lawrence River plays host to some very prestigious largemouth bass tournaments.

However, there is nothing like experiencing it for yourself, and last spring I had the chance. On the opening of bass season I decided to try fishing the Sioux Narrows area on the Lake of the Woods. Now I've been in some pretty hot bass fishing tournaments and have caught my share of bass, but that day was something I'll never forget. In a little over one day of fishing, I caught over 75 bass from the reed banks. It was almost like they had never seen a hook before.

The range of the largemouth in Canada includes the St. Lawrence River system and its tributaries from Lac St. Pierre north through the Ottawa system to Temiskaming. Then the range runs west across the region north of Lake Superior to Southeastern British Columbia that support largemouth bass. The overall range of the largemouth bass is very similar to that of the smallmouth bass, but largemouth are only very common in a smaller southern area.

The largemouth bass may vary in color from one area to the next due to environmental differences. Usually, the bass will be dark green or olive on the back and upper sides. The lower sides are lighter green and the belly is white. Most bass exhibit a bold black band that runs along the lateral line from the · cheek to the tail.

Even though Canada is not well known for it's largemouth bass fishing, it has some fantastic largemouth fishing. Not only are they plentiful in areas, but get very big too.

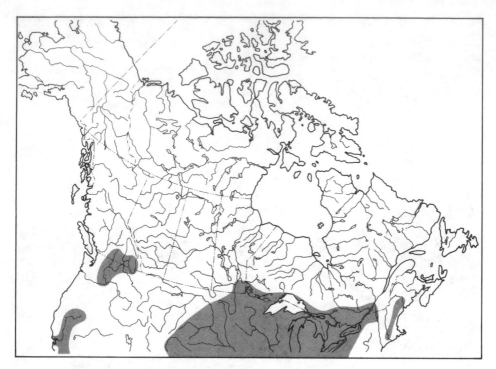

The Home Range of the Largemouth Bass

At times the largemouth may be difficult to differentiate from its near relative the smallmouth bass. But there are two sure ways to tell the two bass apart: the largemouth bass's jaw will extend beyond the middle of the eye, and the spiny dorsal fin is separated from the soft rear dorsal fin by a notch.

Largemouth bass are found in a variety of lakes and rivers. They require some vegetation for shelter and some sort of forage fish. In the spring the male bass will move to the shallows to fan out a nest in the bottoms of sand, marl, or soft clay with reeds, bulrushes or lily pads growing. After the female arrives and the eggs are laid and fertilized, the male will protect the nest and young fry until they are able to fend for themselves.

The usual habitat of summer largemouth is the warmer, shallow levels of water. Typical examples include areas such as reed banks, submerged timber, vegetation, shallow bays of large lakes and sunken islands. In some cases lily pads are the only cover for the bass to use. During times of low light such as morning, evening and cloudy weather, the bass will move into the shallows to feed. Their diet will consist of minnows, small fishes such as panfish and perch, frogs and even small mammals. During the day the bass tend to move deeper to sunken structures and deep water weedlines.

As the water cools with the coming fall the bass will pretty much stick to deep water weedlines all the time. This is a good time to go out after that trophy bass because all the fish are on the move to fatten up before the coming winter locks in the lake. The key to locating fall bass is to find any living, green weeds. Most of the weeds along the deep water weedlines will be dead. But, if you find any green, live ones you may have found bass heaven. Concentrate on the inside turns and bends in the weedlines and you should find the bass. In fact, the tighter the turn in the weedline the better.

A wide array of lures and baits will catch largemouth bass. This predatory fish has been known to smash just about anything that swims through its domain. Alas, however, that isn't always the case. There usually is one type of lure or color that will outproduce any other choice.

When the bass are shallow during the low light periods mentioned earlier, I like to use shallow running lures such as spinnerbaits, buzz baits, floating minnow baits and small crankbaits. It may take some experiencing before you come up with the right lure or color, but if you know the bass are there, be assured the bass will turn on to one of these lures.

Work the lure around any submerged timber, emerged vegetation, or pockets in the weeds. These are the places big old bucketmouths will usually haunt. Once you tie into one of these bruisers you'll know why they are one of the most sought-after sport fishes in North America.

When the bass abandon the shallows and head for the deep water weedlines and structures, it's time to switch your tactics. To get down deeper you need to use deep lures like plastic worms, deep running crankbaits and jigs tipped with live bait.

The key areas to fish will be the sunken weedlines and islands. Locate these with the use of a sonar depth finder and key in on the tight inside turns and points. Either retrieve a crankbait so that it dives down to the fish holding areas, or drop down a plastic worm rigged Texas style. Probably the most effective technique is to use a jig with a stand-up head tipped with a minnow. Just work the tipped jig along the deep weedline, concentrating on the inside turns and corners. This technique is my "ace in the hole" in the fall. If there is one method that will take them on tough days, this is it.

If driving north to catch largemouth bass seems a little strange to you, I guess I understand, but in this land of the lake trout, walleye, and smallmouth bass, the largemouth bass is alive and well. In fact, sometimes 6- to 8-pound fish turn up. Now that's enough to get any red-blooded fisherman going!

Panfish

These spunky little saucer-shaped fish are the delight of many anglers, young and old alike. Even in this land of exotic fishes, the sunfish is still a popular fish in southeastern Canada.

Sunfish are small sized fish that have an extremely flattened body, which puts them in the group dubbed "panfish." They exhibit a spiny dorsal fin which contributes to their flattened out appearance. Sunfish are very colorful, at times having blue, green, red, orange and yellow markings on their normally greenish-yellow body.

This group includes the pumpkinseed, bluegill, longear sunfish, green sunfish and rock bass. Depending on the species, they can reach lengths of up to 12 inches and weigh well over a pound.

Though many people consider sunfish a "kid's fish", the big, slab-sided adults are very sporty and challenging.

In Canada, the range of sunfish is fairly limited. They are specifically found along the extreme southern border in New Brunswick and Quebec, in the vicinity around the Lake of the Woods and in isolated pockets in southern Alberta and British Columbia.

They prefer clear fresh waters found in lakes, rivers, back waters, reservoirs and farm ponds. However, these species are hardy and can be found in fertile, weed-choked lakes that suffer from the encroachment of population centers.

Sunfish are spring spawners. They move into the shallows when the waters reach about 68 degrees F., which is usually in the late spring. They will seek out areas that have a sand, clay, or gravel bottom with some vegetation. Prime areas will be in water that is about three to six feet deep.

Many times you can see spawning grounds from a distance away because of the beds that sunfish make. These beds, or nests, are shallow depressions in the lake bottom that the adult fish will fan out. Once you find any new nests in an area, you know the large adult fish are not too far away.

After spawning is completed the adult fish will move toward deeper water along weedlines, weedbeds, vegetated bays or other deep water areas. These summer haunts of sunfish can be anywhere from 8 to 30 feet deep, even deeper in some cases. They will cruise through the weeds, sometimes in large schools, feeding on small invertebrates and small minnows. They will also feed on emerging nymphs, flying adults and terrestrial insects on the surface.

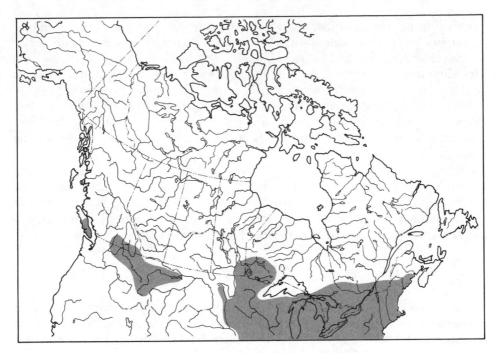

The Home Range of the Sunfish

You can catch sunfish on a wide range of baits, lures and rigs. However, some ways are easier and more efficient than others.

Probably the most effective way to take these slab-sided adults is an old fashioned cane pole, or telescopic pole such as Lew's Bream Busters. These neat rods all retract to one third of their extended length for easy transportation. Just rig up a slip bobber, split shot, and #8 hook, and you're all set for some fun. Some of the better baits to try are worms, pieces of nightcrawlers, grubs, grasshoppers, and crickets. Just dunk these in along the bulrushes or other vegetation near where you've found spawning beds.

If you like things a little bit more sporty and advanced, try ultralight spinning gear for these bedding bluegills. I place a few light split shot about 18 inches above a #8 or #10 hook and bait up with a small leech. Big bluegills and pumpkinseeds gobble these little leeches like they were candy. Once rigged up, you cruise the shallows looking for signs of bluegills. A good qualilty pair of polarized sunglasses will help you spot beds and cruising schools of fish. Then just cast the leech where the sunfish will see it and get ready for some of the most fun fishing you'll find everywhere. I've been able to fish all over North America and have caught plenty of trophy fish, but give me an ultralight rod and some big bluegills and I'll be in seventh heaven. If you don't believe me, try it yourself and I think you'll change your mind.

When the fish head for deeper water as summer progresses, you'll have to get down to them with some different methods. An effective way is to use a Lindy rig tipped with a small minnow, leech or piece of crawler. Work this along weedlines and cabbage beds. Once you catch one, throw out a marker.

Sunfish are a schooling fish and where you find one you'll probably find others. Once you locate a school anchor your boat and cast the Lindy rig to them.

Another super method is to use a small jig tipped with some sort of live bait. Try slow trolling along the weedlines or beds and work the jig in a tantalizing manner. Again, once you locate the fish, stop and cast before you move on.

Some of the best jigs are ⅟₃₂ and ⅟₁₆ ounce Quiver jigs, Fuzz-E-Grubs, Doll Flys and Mr. Twisters. But when you're using jigs, you'll need to use a rod that can cast these light baits. That pretty much limits you to ultralight spinning gear and 2- or 4-pound test line.

Whatever method you use, you'll find that these scrappy panfish are wonderfully fun. They bite well, they travel in big schools, you can keep lots of them to eat and they are a great treat for the taste buds. On top of that, they are feisty fighters for their size. They might not be very big sometimes, but can you imagine what a six-pound sunfish would do to your tackle?

Crappies

Crappies are another member of the sunfish family and exhibit the usual flattened body and spiny dorsal fin. There are two types of crappies, the black crappie and white crappie. Both have dark backs with silvery sides. Their sides are covered with dark speckled markings, which gives them their nickname "specks." Even though they are very similar, the white crappie is much lighter colored than the black crappie.

These silvery panfish average 8 to 10 inches in length, but can get up to 14 inches and bigger. A "slab" crappie is one that weighs two pounds or more. They are the biggest member of the sunfish family except for the basses.

Crappies are a prized gamefish along the extreme southern border in parts of Canada. Their schooling habits and active feeding frenzies can make even a seasoned angler's heart race.

218

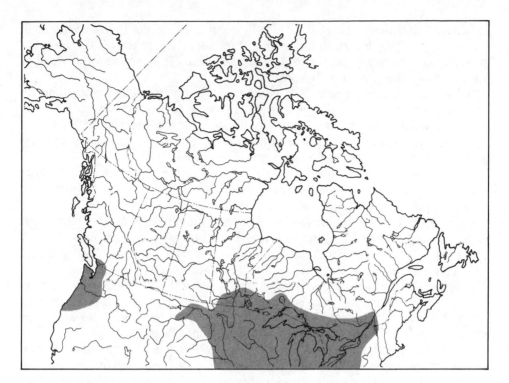

The Home Range of the Crappie

Crappies live in clear fresh water lakes, rivers, reservoirs, and other bodies of water. In Canada their range is the extreme southern border along the Great Lakes and in southern British Columbia.

Regardless of what type of water you find crappies, they will always be near some sort of submerged cover such as weeds, bulrushes, timber, brush, diving rafts or docks. Finding sunken cover is the first step to locating schools of crappies.

Crappies are attracted to underwater cover because that's where the food is. Small fishes, minnows and minute invertebrates all flourish around these underwater sanctuaries. Crappies will feed on surprisingly small—almost microscopic—creatures because they are equipped with many, ultra-fine gill rakers. With these they can sift out even the smallest water fleas.

At ice-out, crappies move to shallow water. They will seek out warmer water and the minnows that come into feed on newly emerging plankton that appears here. These early season crappies feed heavily on the minnows after the slim pickings of winter. This pre-spawn movement is when crappie fishermen really cash in on the crappies.

The place to begin your search for pre-spawn crappies is on the northwest side of the lake, since that is the side that is warmed first by the sun. At times the fish will be found in huge schools, cruising through the dead weeds looking for minnows to feed on.

Many fishermen don't realize that the crappies are not in the shallows to spawn, but simply to eat. In fact, when the deeper water warms up the crappies move back to the depths for a period of time. They are more difficult to find during this period, but they are there.

When the shallows reach 66 to 68 degrees F., the fish return once more to spawn. As with all sunfish, the males will come in first to fan out the nest. Soon after, the females come in and lay the eggs for the males to fertilize. This spawning routine will take place in areas with a sand, clay or gravel bottom. There must be some vegetation present if the crappies spawn here.

Once the crappies move back to the deep water, they suspend in large schools over sunken islands, weedbeds or reefs where they can feed on minnows. At times they will even go down to water 35 feet deep or deeper.

A powerful sonar depth finder is a real asset when hunting for these suspended crappies. Many times when I've gone over a big school with my Lowrance 2360, the face of the dial lit up like a Christmas tree. When you find this, you may be in for wild time, pulling crappies in one after another.

Whatever time of year it is, whether the fish are shallow or deep, a minnow is the best bait for crappies. You can present that bait in a great variety of ways, but the bait itself will almost always be a minnow, not a big shiner or sucker, but a small minnow about one to two inches long.

For shallow water crappies, I'll use a slip bobber system to dangle the minnow right in front of their noses. If you are not sure how deep the fish are, set the bobber so the minnow is about half way between the surface and the bottom. That's the best place to begin.

Hook the minnow under the dorsal fin with a #8 hook. Or you can add a little flash by tying on a small ⅓₂ or ⅟₁₆ ounce jig instead of the bare hook. Hook the minnow through the eyes rather than under the dorsal fin. Now you can jerk and pop the bobber, giving the jig some action.

Colors can be very important. I have seen times when the crappies will utterly ignore one color but go head over tail to gulp down another colored jig. I always start with white, yellow, or black; then I'll change if the fish don't like those.

As with the other shallow water conditions, I'll use a light spinning rod or telescoping Bream Buster for these shallow water fish. But, once they move out and suspend you'll need to switch to spinning gear. Lew Childre's make the model SGUL-156S spinning rod, which is just perfect for jigging for suspended crappies. It's light and has a soft action so you won't tear the hook out of the crappies' tender mouth.

Once you've located a school of fish, cast out a jig tipped with a minnow and let it free fall down into the school. The fish will take a slowly falling jig much better than a jig falling at a fast rate. For this reason I prefer light quiver jigs, small bucktails jigs, and Grassl's Flu Flu jigs.

Even though crappies are not Canada's foremost gamefish, they're fun to catch and good to eat. A great combination! Many a trip has been saved when the walleyes or northerns wouldn't bite. So keep crappies in mind if you want lots of action and good eating.

Yellow Perch

Many times people overlook the small things in life. But, not in Canada. Every year, anglers by the thousands pursue the yellow perch. These small fish are extremely delicious and easy to catch, making them especially popular with ice fishermen. However, spring and summer anglers love them too.

The color of perch will vary with size and habitat. Normally they have a dark green or olive back with greenish or yellow sides. The sides will have about seven vertical dark colored bars.

These smallish fish will usually range from 4 to 10 inches in length, however, they can get bigger. These "jumbo" perch will get up to 12 inches or better.

The normal food of the perch is largely made up of insects, larger invertebrates and baitfish. They move about in schools looking for feed mostly in the mornings and evenings. So, these are the most popular and productive times to fish.

Perch inhabit weedy bays, shallow flats with some weed cover and submerged structures such as islands, bars and reefs. These areas offer plenty of small prey for themselves and provide cover for their own protection. Perch are not only the predator, but also are the favored prey of walleyes, northern pike and muskies.

A bunch of jumbo perch probably make for better eating than any other freshwater fish, at least according to many Canadians. Anglers pursue them throughout the year, especially during the winter when thousands of hearty ice fishermen fish them through the ice.

221

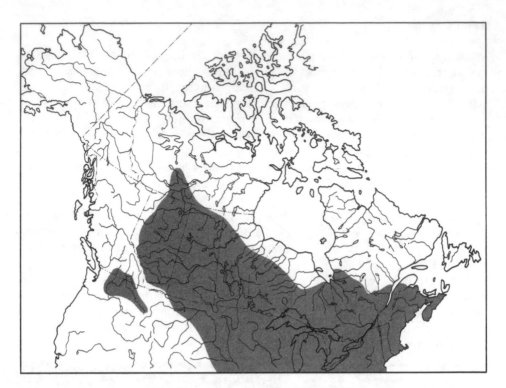

The Home Range of the Yellow Perch

Once you find perch, it is usually easy to catch plenty of them. One of the most effective methods is bobber fishing with worms, grubs or small minnows. Remember that perch are notorious bait stealers, so use a small #8 or #10 hook. Put on a small bobber, set so the bait is suspended from one to three feet off the bottom.

You may also want to try small jigs, tipped with a minnow or pieces of worm. Working these over deeper structures with a swimming retrieve can fill up a cooler quite quickly. Other productive bait rigs and lures are small spinners, tiny spoons and Lindy rigs.

Yearly, ice houses and ice fishermen dot lakes such as Lake Simcoe, Erie and Nipissing in southern Ontario. These hardy folks take excellent catches of perch, plus other fish, through the ice. In fact, anglers often speak of catching over 100 jumbo perch in a single outing.

The most popular outfit is a simple tip up with some light monofilament, a split shot and a #8 hook. Just hook on a minnow such as an emerald lake shiner, lower it down and relax. But be ready; perch fishing can be fast and furious. You may have to wait till you're cleaning your catch before you can do any relaxing.

The list of various gamefish in Canada can go on and on. In many of the deep, trout lakes you can catch whitefish, tullibees and ciscoes. Or in the Mackenzie River in the Northwest Territories you can pursue the inconnu, a large predatory whitefish. These big "connies" have been known to get up to thirty inches in length. If trophy fishing for rare fish is your bag, there is nothing like fishing the inconnu.

Of course if you've got trophies on the mind, by all means you should check out the Pacific salmons on the west coast, or the Atlantic salmon on the east coast. The king salmon, found along the western coast, can reach sizes in excess of 70 pounds. Now, that is trophy in anyone's book! However, getting into these fish and the methods that take them will fill another entire book.

After all has been said about the vast fishing opportunities and the grandeur of this country, the bottom line is this: there is probably no other place on earth where you can find the variety of sport fish and catch them in such great numbers as you can in Canada. This, along with the splendid scenery and variety of geography, make it a sportsman's paradise. With a little planning and preparation, anyone can enjoy a trip here and realize for themselves why Canada is a final frontier of fishing.

Chapter 11
A Shore Lunch
Fit for a King

After a successful morning of fishing in Canada, there is only one right way to top it all off. And that is feasting on those delicious fillets on a picturesque shoreline or pine-studded island. Shore lunches, as these marvelous meals are called, are a tradition in the Canadian wilderness. There is certainly no better way to truly savor the wilderness and a bunch of fresh-caught trout or walleye. Not only that, but it gives you a chance to stretch your legs and do a little exploring.

Most Canadian guides are shoreside gourmet cooks, and preparing shore lunches is part of their service. But if you aren't using a guide, there is no reason not to enjoy this treat. Even if you are all thumbs when it comes to cooking at home, you'll find shore lunches are quite easy to prepare. With a little bit of camp savvy, some fresh fish, a frying pan and some other simple side dishes, you can whip up a meal fit for a king...or, better yet, a hungry fisherman.

Of course, one of the key ingredients in a shore lunch are the fish. In Canada that is usually no problem. Walleyes, bass, lake trout, and northern pike are all delicious. It makes no difference what fish you're fishing for, they'll all nicely fit on the menu.

If a shore lunch is on your agenda for the day, there are a few things you should include in your "grub box." A complete list would include a couple of large cast iron fry pans, coffee pot, cooking pot, eating utensils, salt and pepper shakers, a plastic bag partly filled with flour and cornmeal, cooking oil or lard, a couple of cans of baked beans, matches, a pot holder, fillet knife, a jar of coffee, potatoes and some type of bread. There are also pre-mixed fish batters and flours, such as Shore Lunch made by Pillsbury, that are very convenient. You may also want to toss in some aluminum foil if you want to bake your fish rather than fry them. This list includes just about everything you will need, but personal tastes vary and you might want to add something or cut down on the list.

When your stomach tells you it's time to come in for a bite to eat, take time to pick a convenient and practical site. The spot you pick for your shore lunch can make or break it. While sandy beaches look inviting they are not a good choice. Sand tends to get in the food and a gust of wind can blow it all over everything. Also make sure that suitable wood for the fire is nearby. A good choice is a point of land that comes out in the lake with a nice breeze to ward off insects and maybe some large rocks to use as tables or something to lean against.

The secret to cooking fish out-of-doors is actually your fire. You should start your fire as soon as you arrive at your site. That way it will have burned down to red-hot coals by the time you are ready to start cooking. A flaming, smoking fire that keeps spitting out hot sparks is no fun to cook over. Let it burn to a nice bed of coals before you begin to cook. But remember to keep a backup pile of wood ready to throw on the fire. In the middle of cooking a meal is no time to be frantically looking for firewood.

While the fire is burning down to coals you should be preparing the rest of the meal, slicing potatoes and onions and cleaning your fish. If you are going to fry the fish, you should fillet the meat off the fish with a sharp knife. Or, if you are going to bake the fish you might want to just scale the fish and remove the insides.

Once the fire is ready, put on the pans and start heating the grease. It is very important to make sure the grease is boiling hot so that the fish will turn out crisp and golden brown on the outside, yet nice and flaky on the inside.

You can test your grease to make sure that it is hot enough by dipping just the tip of a fillet in the grease. If the grease is right it will bubble and sizzle as the fillet begins to cook. If it doesn't, let the grease heat up more.

Once it's ready add your potatoes and fish. Let them cook to a golden brown and then flip only once so the fish will cook evenly. If you have brought baked beans, punch a hole in the top of the can so the pressure can escape and then put it close to the fire to warm up. If you are going to have coffee, tea, or another hot drink, you should get these going now, too.

If you have planned well, everything will be done at the same time. Then it's just a simple matter of dishing it up and enjoying a delicious shore lunch meal. If done right, you'll wonder if you enjoy the eating more than the catching.

Once you try your hand at frying up a mess of fillets, you'll probably want to try other recipes and methods of preparing fish. But another delicious and easy method is baking your fish. Take a three- to five-pound fish, scale it, remove the insides and wash it in cold water. Lay a large piece of tin foil flat on the ground and sprinkle it with cooking oil or grease. Prepare a stuffing for the fish by mixing a stick of margarine or butter with onions. Salt and pepper the fish inside and out, then add the stuffing. Then roll the fish up tightly in the tin foil. If you have started your fire in advance it should now have begun to burn down to coals and be all ready to accept the fish. Place the foil-wrapped fish in the hot coals and cover with more coals. It may be necessary to keep the fire going by adding more wood.

In about 30 minutes the fish will be ready to be removed from the fire. After you have removed it from the fire, remove the foil carefully. If the fish is done, the scaled skin will peel off with the tin foil leaving the delicious, flaky, white meat for you to eat. Add to this some heated vegetables or canned fruit and you'll have a meal you won't soon forget.

Some fish, such as lake trout, brook trout or salmon, have very high fat content and the meat is very rich. One fun and tasty way to prepare them is to "plank" them. This method broils them and removes much of the fat from the meat. After you have started your fire, find a nice dry slab of wood or a log

How you clean your fish depends on how you plan to prepare it. If you like to fry them, filleting will be the best way. But, if you prefer to bake the fish, you might just want to scale the fish and remove the insides.

227

split in half. Then prepare your fish by cleaning it and rinsing it in cold water. Split the fish open so it will lie flat when laid on its back.

Put the split fish on the slab of wood and attach it with small sharp pegs or with a roll of thin wire. By propping the planked fish near the coals, you can broil it to perfection. You may want to baste occasionally with melted butter or lemon juice to give it that little extra flavor.

To set your planked fish so that it will broil nicely, test the heat by holding your hand next to the fire. If you can hold it there only a couple of seconds before having to take it away, it's right for broiling.

The ways of preparing fish for shore lunch are limited only by your imagination. You can bake them, fry them, broil them or even boil the fish just to name a few. I would suggest reading some of the excellent books printed on outdoor cooking if you have ideas of becoming an outdoor gourmet. Some of my favorite ways of preparing fish are listed near the end of this chapter.

Once you've finished your meal and have taken a little afternoon break, you'll want to head out and give the fish another chance to do battle. However, before you do, make sure that you have completely cleaned up your shore site. Burn all of the flammable garbage and take any cans, tin foil, paper scraps or other garbage with you. Make sure that your fire is completely out by dousing it with plenty of water from the lake. Leave the area *better-looking* than you found it. If someone else has left litter, clean up after the slob.

Most Canadian guides are experienced shore side gourmets. It seems that within minutes they can have several dishes cooking at the same time, all fit for a king.

Beggars in the remote wilderness? That's right. Bears are a common, yet sometimes unwelcome visitor to many shore lunches.

RECIPES

Fish Patties

Ingredients:
1 cup cooked fish
½ teaspoon onion salt
1 egg
½ teaspoon celery salt
salt & pepper to taste
¼ cup cracker crumbs

Boil the fillets of a medium sized fish until you can easily flake the meat away from the backbone and rib cage. Do this before you leave on your trip. Take the boneless meat (1 cup cooked fish) and combine all ingredients into small round patties. Wrap these in waxed paper or aluminum foil until you are ready to eat them. Fry the patties in butter in a pan over the medium heat of the edges of your campfire. Once they are brown on one side, turn them.

Simple Boiled Fish

Ingredients:
2 pounds of fish fillets
½ cup celery, including leaves
1 sliced onion
1 teaspoon salt

Place fillets in a pot with enough water to cover fish. Once you are certain you have enough water, remove the fish. Bring the water to a boil and add the other ingredients. Place the fish back in the pot and cover it. Reduce the heat until the water just simmers. If you boil the fish, it will ruin the flavor and texture of the fish. When the fish becomes tender, drain and place on platter and serve with a garnish.

Poor Man's Lobster

Ingredients:
3 qts of water
1 chopped onion
salt
4 pounds of northern pike fillets cut into 2-inch chunks
¾ pound butter
½ cup lemon juice
paprika
3 pieces celery
1 cup wine

230

Boil water, onion, celery, salt, lemon juice and wine in pan or pot. Add fish and boil for five minutes, drain and place fish on aluminum foil sheet. Brush with melted butter and sprinkle with paprika. Broil over open fire on foil for two minutes. Turn, brush with melted butter, sprinkle with paprika and broil another two minutes. Eat and enjoy.

Jeff Howard

Catching fish has always been one of Jeff Howard's main loves of life. However, once he gets his hand on a camera he feels that capturing a fish on film can be just as exciting and rewarding. After earning a B.S. Degree in Fisheries and Wildlife Research and Public Relations at the University of Minnesota, Jeff worked for Minnesota Department of Natural Resources. Following that, he taught a popular fresh water fishing program for the Minneapolis Public Education Program. Now as the Production Manager at Babe Winkelman Productions his writing and photography have been used in their popular television series, articles, seminar and outdoor productions.